Theo. Frelinghuysen

NEW YORK HARPER & BROTHERS

MEMOIR

OF

THE LIFE AND CHARACTER OF

THE LATE

HON. THEO. FRELINGHUYSEN, LL.D.

BY TALBOT W. CHAMBERS,

A MINISTER OF THE COLLEGIATE CHURCH, NEW YORK.

NEW YORK:

HARPER & BROTHERS, PUBLISHERS,

FRANKLIN SQUARE.

1863.

INTRODUCTION.

SOON after the death of Mr. Frelinghuysen, a desire was expressed, in many and various quarters, for some permanent memorial of his life. His long course of private worth and public usefulness, the eminent positions he had occupied, his ability, his eloquence, his stainless probity, his consistent piety, his catholic spirit, his recognized leadership among evangelical Christians of every name, and his relations to all the great Christian enterprises of the age, seemed to call for a volume which should trace his career from its origin, and indicate the sources of the rare and rounded character which he maintained even to the last.

Circumstances, which it is needless to mention, turned the author's attention to the subject. Having a connection by marriage with some of Mr. Frelinghuysen's relatives, he had for more than twenty years enjoyed a considerable degree of intimacy with him, and was enabled therefore, on many points, to speak from personal observation. From the living representatives of Mr. Frelinghuysen he met the heartiest sympathy and co-operation. It was, indeed, at their suggestion and by their aid that the present volume has been prepared. It does not pretend, therefore, to have the coolness of judicial impartiality. The remembrance of Mr. Frelinghuysen's genial goodness is still too fresh to allow those who knew him familiarly to speak of his character with stoic calmness. *Hic liber * * * professione pietatis aut laudatus erit, aut excusatus.* Yet the reader will look in vain for indiscriminate eulogy. It is believed that the delineation given does not transgress the bounds of truth, in letter, in spirit, or in the impression it is calculated to produce. The great aim has been to give, in moderate compass, as just and accurate an account of the growth and development of this remarkable man as could be obtained by patient and diligent inquiry. One reason of the insertion of so many statements and letters from different persons, as will be found interspersed through the volume, is to show how similar, or, rather, identical was the impression made by his virtues on all the classes of men, lay and clerical, with whom he came in contact. If any still deem the character described to be one of impossible perfection, it only remains to assure them that nothing is stated except what is believed on the amplest and most satisfactory evidence—nothing which would not be accepted by any of his numerous neighbors and townsmen as either true of their own knowledge, or as what their acquaintance with him would naturally lead them to believe and expect. Close and prolonged inspection is a severe test of character, but it is precisely those who saw Mr. Frelinghuysen at nearest hand and for the longest time who cherish the deepest reverence for his memory, and the strongest conviction of his unexampled excellence.

The author begs leave here to offer his grateful acknowledgments to the kind friends, too numerous to specify in detail, who have aided him by the communication of useful papers or statements. He has spared no pains to gather such information as bore upon the subject, but has reason to lament that, in several instances, it was found impossible to obtain details sufficiently authentic and definite to be inserted in this biography.

Still, he trusts that his work will not be found wholly unworthy of its subject, and he commits it to the press with the prayer that the blessed Savior, who was pleased to make Mr. Frelinghuysen so useful in his life, will vouchsafe to honor with a portion of the same blessing this imperfect record of his course and character.

New York, June, 1863.

CONTENTS.

CHAPTER V.

CHANCELLOR OF THE UNIVERSITY OF THE CITY OF NEW YORK.

1839—1850.

CHAPTER VI.

PRESIDENT OF RUTGERS COLLEGE.

1850—1862.

CHAPTER VII.

PERSONAL TRAITS AND HABITS.

CHAPTER VIII.

ORIGIN AND CHARACTER OF HIS PIETY.

CHAPTER IX.

HIS RELIGIOUS LIFE.

CHAPTER X.

PERSONAL EFFORTS FOR THE SALVATION OF MEN.

CHAPTER XI.

EXTRACTS FROM HIS CORRESPONDENCE.

CHAPTER XII.

CONNECTION WITH BENEVOLENT INSTITUTIONS.

CHAPTER XIII.

THE CLOSING SCENE.

CHAPTER XIV.

CONCLUSION.

THE LIFE AND CHARACTER OF

THE LATE

HON. THEO. FRELINGHUYSEN, LL.D.

LIFE OF FRELINGHUYSEN.

CHAPTER I.

HIS ANCESTRY.

I. The Rev. Theo. Jac. Frelinghuysen.—II. The Rev. John Frelinghuysen.—The Jufvrouw Hardenbergh.—III. Major Gen. Fred. Frelinghuysen.

"THE glory of children are their fathers," nor is any reasonable man insensible to the value of an honorable descent, especially if to earthly distinction there is added the blessed memory of the just. The subject of this volume was not accustomed to boast of any thing, but he is known to have had pleasure in contemplating the virtues of those who went before him, and to have derived a healthful stimulus from their example.

I. The first of the name who came to this country was the Rev. Theodorus Jacobus Frelinghuysen, or, as he sometimes wrote his signature, Freylinghausen. He was born in East Friesland, now a part of the kingdom of Hanover, about the year 1691, and was ordained to the pastoral office in 1717. The circumstances which led to his coming to this country were strikingly providential. The Dutch churches in America were at that early day chiefly supplied with ministers from Holland. It happened that a request had been received by the Classis of Amsterdam, asking them to send a pious minister to America, and one of the pastors, named Sicco Tjadde, interested himself to procure a proper person. While Tjadde was pursuing his inquiries, Mr. Frelinghuysen passed through the town where this pastor lived, being on his way to Embden to assume the rectorship of the academy at that place. He spent the night at the house of an elder of the Church, who invited him to conduct the evening devotions. He readily consented, and, after reading a chapter in the Bible, gave a short exposition, and concluded with prayer. The elder was so much pleased with the service, and with the whole spirit and conversation of the young minister, that on his departure in the morning he made Mr. Frelinghuysen promise to stay at his house on his return, and then hastening to his pastor, cried out, "I have found a man to go to America." In due time the promise was fulfilled by Mr. Frelinghuysen, and, after consultation, he agreed to accept the call and emigrate to America.

He arrived in this country in the first month of the year 1720, and at once entered upon his labors, which extended over a wide field upon the banks of the Raritan and its affluents. His place of residence was about three miles west of New Brunswick, from which, as a centre, he made excursions as the wants of his people demanded, preaching alternately in Raritan, New Brunswick, Six-Mile Run, and North Branch, and was constantly active in catechising and instructing the youth. He encountered many difficulties, owing in part to the scattered population, dense forests, unbridged streams, and ill-marked roads incident to a newly-settled country, but still more to the state of the people, among whom formalism abounded, leading, as it always does in the end, to a great relaxation of morals. But the man was equal to the occasion. The times required a ministry prosecuted "in the spirit and power of Elias," and such he aimed at. He not only presented the great doctrines of the Gospel with fidelity and energy, but applied them with a fearless pungency, which often gave great offense. And although bitterly opposed and cruelly slandered, he never yielded, but maintained to the last the spirit exhibited in the declaration of one of his early discourses: "I would sooner die a thousand deaths than not preach the truth." His prevailing temper of mind seems to be indicated by the concluding words of the preface to a small collection of sermons first printed in 1733, "*Laudem non quæro; culpam non timeo*"—I seek not praise; I fear not blame. All accounts agree in reference to him, that he was a great blessing to the Dutch Church in America. The Rev. Gilbert Tennent said of him: "The labors of Mr. Frelinghuysen, a Dutch minister, were much blessed to the people of New Brunswick and places adjacent, about the time of his coming among them. When I came there, which was about seven years after, I had the pleasure of seeing much of the fruits of his ministry. Divers of his hearers, with whom I had the opportunity of conversing, appeared to be converted persons by their soundness in principle, Christian experience, and pious practice; and these persons declared that his ministrations were the means thereof. This, together with a kind letter which he wrote me respecting the necessity of dividing the Word aright, and giving to every one his portion in due season, through the Divine blessing, excited me to greater earnestness in ministerial labors." Similar testimony is borne by Whitfield, who, in his journal of 1739, speaks of an extensive work of grace as the fruit of Frelinghuysen's ministry in New Brunswick and that vicinity. So, also, does President Edwards, in his Narrative of Surprising Conversions, first published in 1736. There were added at this time to the Church of Raritan alone forty-four persons, a number which, in the judgment of the Rev. Dr. Messler, the present pastor of the church, must have been nearly, if not quite, equal to one from each family in the congregation.

His printed sermons, which a few years since were collected and translated by the Rev. WILLIAM DEMAREST, show him to have been an evangelical and pungent preacher. His labors continued for more than a quarter of a century; and although he was often attacked in the civil courts, before the colonial authorities, through the press, and by complaint to the Classis of Amsterdam, he never succumbed. Amid all his trials, he was sustained by the countenance of his ecclesiastical superiors, by the consolations of grace in his own heart, by the Divine blessing upon his "weak ministrations," as he called them, and by the fulfillment of the covenant to his household. All his children were believers. His five sons were ordained to the ministry, and his two daughters were married to ministers.

The eldest son, THEODORE, was sent to Holland for his education, and, after being ordained to the ministry, came to this country in 1745. The next year he was settled over the Church in Albany, New York.

Mrs. Grant, of Laggan, in her "Memoirs of an American Lady," speaks of him as "the apostolic and much-beloved Freylinghausen." According to the same authority, he was ardent in his disposition, and frank and popular in his manners. His preaching was earnest and eloquent, his life spotless, and his concern for his people warm and tender. He was very much endeared to the Church and the whole community; but, toward the end of his career, a regiment of royal troops stationed at Albany introduced customs and manners which led to a serious deterioration of religion and morals, despite all the influence and authority he could exert. Deeply wounded by the failure of his efforts to stay the torrent of fashionable innovation, he withdrew from the contest, and sailed to Holland, whither, according to some accounts, he went for the purpose of obtaining funds to establish a literary and theological institution; but he was lost at sea. The people of Albany long mourned his departure, and cherished his memory with the deepest affection.

The third and fourth sons, JACOBUS and FERDINANDUS, were sent to Holland, where they passed through the usual course of study, and were ordained to the ministry. They embarked for home, with the intention of taking charge, the one of the Church of Wawwarsing or Marbletown, the other of that of Kinderhook; but both, while at sea, fell victims to the smallpox in the year 1753.

The youngest son, HENRICUS, pursued his studies in this country, and was licensed to preach the Gospel by the direction of what was called the Coetus. In the year 1756 he took charge of the churches of Wawwarsing and Rochester, in Ulster County, New York. The next year he was regularly ordained and inducted into office. Very soon afterward he was attacked by smallpox, and died at Naponoch.

Of his daughters, one, ANNA, became the wife of the Rev. William Jackson, who, having begun his studies under John Frelinghuysen, at Raritan, finished them in Holland, where he was ordained. Returning home in 1757, he was settled over the churches of Staten Island and Bergen, where he prosecuted a faithful and successful ministry for thirty years, when he was laid aside by grievous afflictions. His life, however, was prolonged until July, 1813. His wife died in May, 1810, aged 72 years. The other, MARGARET, was married to the Rev. Thomas Romeyn, then settled on Long Island. She died early, but left one son, Theodore Frelinghuysen Romeyn, who became a minister, and succeeded Dr. Hardenbergh in the same charge at Raritan to which his grandfather and his uncle had successively ministered. He was a young man of fine promise, but was suddenly removed by death within less than eighteen months from the date of his installation.

II. The Rev. Theo. Jac. Frelinghuysen was succeeded in his charge on the Raritan by his second son, JOHN, who, having been educated and ordained in Holland, commenced his labors in August, 1750. He seems to have been a man of greater suavity than his father, but was equally firm in upholding the claims of spiritual Christianity. He was distinguished for his gifts in the pulpit, for his assiduity in the religious training of the young, and for his zealous endeavors to raise up worthy candidates for the sacred office. There is still standing in Somerville a house built of bricks brought by him from Holland, where he resided, and where Hardenbergh, Jackson, Leydt, and others attended a nascent theological seminary under his direction. Although the old troubles between the parties known respectively as Coetus and Conferentie* still continued, yet a more than ordinary blessing rested upon his ministry, and much was expected from him in the future; but these hopes were blasted by his early death in September, 1754. His ministerial life being so short, very little is known in detail of his character, but his death was very generally and deeply lamented. Much more is known of his wife, who survived him more than fifty years, and was as eminent in her day for intelligent piety as any of the female saints of the Old Testament or the New.

DINAH VAN BERG was the daughter of a wealthy and distinguished East India merchant who resided in Amsterdam. While yet young she was overtaken

* The "Coetus" consisted of an assembly of ministers of the Dutch Church (organized in 1738, but not put in operation until 1747), who proposed to administer discipline, and license and ordain candidates for the ministry, without requiring them to visit Holland to be educated and approved there. The "Conferentie" was a rival association (organized in 1755), who insisted that in every such case the express authority of the Classis of Amsterdam should be obtained. A lamentable schism thus originated, which, in some cases, scarcely stopped short of actual violence, and did immense damage to the interests of religion and morals. The difficulties were finally composed by a convention brought together through the agency of the late Rev. Dr. Livingston in the year 1771, and in the end all the ministers and churches of Hollandish descent were united under the title of the Reformed Protestant Dutch Church in North America.

by Divine grace, and at once became a firm and decided Christian. Although in a very unfavorable atmosphere, and surrounded by gay and worldly persons, she maintained an eminent consistency of character. This fidelity to principle subjected her to considerable and prolonged opposition, which, with other causes, at length affected her health. Her sickness increased to such a degree that her life was despaired of. She, however, insisted that, in answer to her prayers, she would be restored, and even went so far as to indicate the day when her recovery would commence. The prediction was laughed at by her attending physician, who considered her case altogether hopeless. When the day arrived, her condition remained unchanged until toward sunset, when she arose from the bed which she had not left for weeks, and walked across the room; and from that time her recovery was steady and rapid. The circumstance excited much interest in the city; and when Dr. Livingston visited Amsterdam many years afterward, he was inquired of by great numbers of persons respecting this extraordinary woman.

During her sickness, John Frelinghuysen, who was then pursuing his theological studies in the mother country, frequently called upon her, and the acquaintance ripened into a mutual attachment. Her parents were decidedly opposed to the connection, partly because of the profession of her suitor, and partly because of the hardships which must necessarily be incurred by those living in a newly-settled country. Finding their opposition invincible, Mr. Frelinghuysen set off on his return home alone, but, after being one day out at sea, a contrary wind drove the vessel in which he had embarked directly back to port. He seized the occasion as a providential opening for the renewal of his suit, and this time was successful. Re-embarking with his wife, he had a prosperous voyage, and, reaching home, commenced the ministry which, as has been said, was so acceptable, and yet so soon terminated by his death when only twenty-five years of age. His widow, who had greatly endeared herself to the community by her piety, energy, and usefulness, determined to return to Holland. Her preparations were all made, a passage engaged, and the day fixed for her departure, when she was surprised by a proposal of marriage from one of the young men who had been studying theology under the direction of her husband, to which, in her astonishment, she answered, "My child, what are you thinking about?" He had contemplated this step for some time, and had consulted their common friends, but, out of respect for her grief for her recent bereavement, had refrained from declaring himself until the last moment. This young man was JACOBUS RUTSEN HARDENBERGH, afterward widely known as a divine, a scholar, and patriot, a personal friend of Washington, and the first President of the college at New Brunswick, N. J., of which he was, to a large extent, the founder. He succeeded in persuading the widow to countermand the preparations for her departure and to accept his hand in marriage, all other considerations to this end being greatly aided in their influence by the wide prospect of usefulness to the Master's cause which opened itself before her in case she should remain in America. She continued the faithful companion of Dr. Hardenbergh's labors and trials in Raritan, in Mombacus, N. Y., and finally in New Brunswick, where, after having survived him for seventeen years, she terminated her useful career by a triumphant death, at the advanced age of eighty-one years, on the 26th day of March, 1807. The following stanza, engraved upon her tombstone in the grave-yard of the First Reformed Protestant Dutch Church in New Brunswick, indicates the degree in which her high attainments in grace were regarded by those who survived her.

> "Tell how she climbed the everlasting hills,
> Surveying all the realms above;
> Borne on a strong-winged faith, and on
> The fiery wheels of an immortal love."

The children of the first marriage, the Jufvrouw Hardenbergh, as she was usually styled by her neighbors, were a son and a daughter. The latter, named EVA, was married to Mr. Caspar Van Nostrand, who at an early day removed to Ulster County, N. Y., where numerous descendants of the family are still remaining. The former, who was the father of the subject of this memoir, was named Frederick.

III. FREDERICK FRELINGHUYSEN was born on the 13th of April, 1753. Dedicated in his infancy to the Lord, he was carefully trained in the knowledge and practice of the truth. It was his mother's constant and anxious desire that he should become, like his father and grandfather, a minister of the Gospel, and in this she was cordially seconded by her husband. But it was in vain. The young man did not feel himself fitted or called to the sacred office; and although he yielded to importunity so far as to study theology for six months, yet at the end of that time his disinclination still continued, and he turned his face in another direction. Tradition intimates that there was something in the rigidity and strictness of his stepfather, especially in the matter of Sunday observance, which somewhat repelled young people, and hindered them from seeing the natural attractiveness of that wisdom whose ways are ways of pleasantness, and all whose paths are peace. General Frelinghuysen, so far from becoming a minister of the Gospel, did not enter into the full communion of the Church; but it was the opinion of his last pastor, the late Rev. Dr. Cannon, who afterward became Professor in the Theological Seminary at New Brunswick, N. J., that at the end of life the pious lessons of his early years returned to his memory, and wrought a gracious result upon his heart.

He received his collegiate education at the College of New Jersey, Princeton, where the Rev. Dr. Samuel Stanhope Smith, Dr. Samuel Spring, and James Madison were among his fellow-students. After his graduation in 1770, he entered upon the study of the law, and when he was of age was admitted to the bar. Here he soon displayed the possession of rare gifts and attainments. Such was his reputation, that in 1775, when only twenty-two years old, he was chosen a member of the Provincial Congress of New Jersey, where he was placed on the important Committee of Public Safety. The next year he was chosen to the same body, which adopted a Constitution, and changed its title from "Provincial Congress" to the "Convention of the STATE of New Jersey." In 1778 he was elected, on joint ballot of the Legislature, to represent New Jersey in the Continental Congress; but in the following year he resigned his seat, not, however, from any failure of patriotism, or any desire to escape his share of the public burdens, as appears by the following extract from his letter of resignation, addressed to the Speaker of the House of Assembly of his native state:

"It is needless for me to remind the honorable Legislature that I did with great reluctance accept the appointment of a delegate for this state in Congress. I was then sufficiently sensible that the trust was too important for *my years* and *abilities.* I am now fully convinced that I should do injustice to my country did I not decline that service.

"In doing this I am conscious to myself that I am merely actuated by motives for the public good, well knowing that, whatever be my abilities, they will be useless to the state in the supreme council of the nation, and that the other appointment with which the Legislature of New Jersey have been pleased to honor me in the county of Somerset is more than sufficient to employ my whole attention."

It appears, however, that at a later period of the Revolutionary struggle he returned to the civil service of the country, for his name is found on the rolls of the Continental Congress for the years 1782 and 1783, as a representative from New Jersey.

While holding his seat in Provincial Congress in the first years of the Revolution, he had also been acting as captain of a corps of artillery, a volunteer company of Continental troops, and in this capacity took part in the bloody battle of Trenton. There still remains in the family of his oldest son a serviceable sword, which in that conflict was surrendered to him by a British officer. A tradition, the accuracy of which it is now impossible to determine, states that it was by a shot from his pistol that Colonel Rahl, the commander of the Hessian forces, was mortally wounded. He afterward was made a colonel in the militia of his native county, Somerset, and was actively engaged in the war. He was present in the skirmishes at Springfield and Elizabeth, and also at the battle of Monmouth Court-house, in June, 1778. After the conclusion of the war, he received repeated testimonials of public confidence in the shape of appointments to various offices in the county and in the state, and in 1793 was chosen to a seat in the Senate of the United States. This position domestic bereavements and the claims of his family compelled him to resign in the year 1796. During the administration of Washington, a formidable sedition arose in Western Pennsylvania, known as the Whisky Insurrection. A very large array of forces was summoned from the militia of Virginia, Maryland, Pennsylvania, and New Jersey, to put down the insurgents. The President gave Mr. Frelinghuysen a major general's command among the troops from the two latter states. Fortunately, the overwhelming number of men sent into the field made resistance hopeless, and the insurrection was quelled with little or no bloodshed.

On the 22d of February, 1800, he was called to deliver an oration in New Brunswick on the death of the Father of his Country. This oration, copies of which are still extant, glows with the ardor to be expected in one who shared in the toils and sacrifices of the Revolution. He continued actively engaged in various public and private duties until his death, which occurred in 1804, on the same day of the same month on which he was born. It is a curious but indubitable fact, that at the commencement of what proved to be his last illness, and when it was by no means of an alarming character, he foretold its fatal issue, and named the day on which he should die. And that day he did die.

Mortuary inscriptions are not always the most trustworthy evidences of character, yet it is believed that the following extracts from the lines engraved on the monument erected over his remains in the cemetery near Millstone are strictly correct:

"He died greatly beloved and lamented. Endowed by nature with superior talents, he was from his youth intrusted by his country with her most important concerns, and never did he disappoint her expectations. At the bar he was eloquent, in the Senate he was wise, in the field he was brave. Candid, generous, and just, he was constant and ardent in his friendships. Ever the patron and protector of merit, he gave his hand to the young, his counsel to the middle-aged, his support to declining years. He left to his children the rich legacy of a life unsullied by a stain, and adorned with numerous expressions of public usefulness and private beneficence."

General Frelinghuysen was twice married. His first wife was GERTRUDE SCHENCK, who died in March, 1794, and whose children were five in number: three sons, named John, Theodore, and Frederick; and two daughters—Maria, who was married to the Rev. John Cornell, and of whom some notice will be found in the Appendix, and Catharine, who became the wife of the late Rev. Gideon F. Judd, D.D., of Catskill. The general's second marriage was to Miss ANN YARD, a lady of great force of character and refinement of mind, who survived her husband for many years. Her children were two: Elizabeth, the wife of the late James B. Elmendorf, M.D., of Millstone, and Sarah, who died in her youth. Of all these children, the only one now surviving is the widow of the Rev. Dr. Judd.

Note.—The foregoing account has been compiled mainly from various publications of the Rev. Dr. Messler, of Somerville, New Jersey, especially the two entitled "A brief History of the Reformed Dutch Church of Raritan, from its organization to the year 1834;" and "The Hollanders in New Jersey, with Notices of some of their Descendants;" read before the New Jersey Historical Society, September 12, 1820; by Rev. Abraham Messler, D.D. Other details have been derived from traditions still existing in the family, and believed to be entirely authentic.

CHAPTER II.

HIS YOUTH AND EDUCATION.

1787—1808.

Birthplace.—School at New Brunswick.—Basking Ridge.—Princeton.—Letter of the Hon. Mr. Ingersoll.—Student at Law in Millstone.—Letter of the Rev. Dr. I. N. Wyckoff.—In the Office of the Hon. Richard Stockton.—Admission to the Bar.

THEODORE FRELINGHUYSEN was born in Franklin Township, Somerset County, N. J., on the 28th of March, 1787. The family homestead at Millstone, where he was brought up, and which he subsequently purchased from the estate of his younger brother, continued in his possession until the year 1840, when it passed into other hands, and shortly afterward was entirely destroyed by fire. The engraving on the opposite page presents a correct view of the spacious and convenient mansion as it appeared twenty-five years ago. Here he spent his early years, receiving such rudiments of learning as were afforded at a small neighborhood school on the banks of the Millstone. Afterward, about the year 1798, he, in company with his brother Frederick, was sent to New Brunswick for the purpose of attending the grammar-school in connection with Queen's College, at that time under the direction of the Rev. Jno. Lindsley, a clergyman of the Protestant Episcopal Church. The school was held in the old College building, erected on the ground where the Second Presbyterian Church now stands. Dr. Ephraim Smith, the late Col. James Neilson, and

THE FRELINGHUYSEN HOMESTEAD.

other gentlemen of social distinction, were at this time fellow-students of the Frelinghuysens, although in a more advanced class. In 1800 Mr. Lindsley relinquished his rectorship of the grammar-school, and the boys returned to their father's house at Millstone.

At this time an event occurred which Mr. Frelinghuysen considered one of the most important and decisive in his whole life. Being rather indisposed to close mental application, he requested his father to forego his purpose of giving him a liberal education, and allow him to remain upon the homestead and become a farmer. His father yielded to his earnest wish, and the point seemed settled. But some time afterward, when the general was called away to the seat of government on public business, his wife took the matter in hand, packed Theodore's trunk, and sent him off to a classical school. He was greatly vexed at this step, which seemed to him to be only an instance of the harshness and oppression usually attributed to stepmothers. But in after years he changed his view entirely. He declared that to her decisive action he owed all his subsequent success in life; nor was he ever weary of recounting his obligations in this and other matters to his father's second wife. That lady was a signal blessing to Theodore and Frederick. She took particular pains in forming their principles, and in inculcating the graceful and high-bred courtesy for which they were distinguished.

The school to which, by the wise foresight of Mrs. Frelinghuysen, Theodore was sent in order to be prepared for college, was the classical academy at Basking Ridge, a village at the northern extremity of the county. This institution had been founded the previous year by the Rev. ROBERT FINLEY, D.D., whose name has attained a widespread and enduring celebrity as the founder of the American Colonization Society. From the interesting and instructive memoir of his life prepared by the late Rev. Isaac V. Brown (2d edition, Philad., 1857), it appears that this institution was really worthy of the high reputation which it enjoyed for twenty years under the care of Dr. Finley, and afterward, for a shorter period, while conducted by his successor in the pastoral office at the Ridge, the late Rev. WILLIAM CRAIG BROWNLEE, D.D. Dr. Finley was an accomplished scholar, a thorough disciplinarian, a skillful teacher, and particularly distinguished for his ability to awaken the interest of his pupils in what they were studying. He had a natural fondness for teaching, and gave his whole mind to the work. His influence with the scholars was increased by his sacred profession, and the uncommon power and unction which marked his efforts in the pulpit. The academy soon obtained an honorable name, and attracted more applicants for admission than he was willing to receive. Such families as the Bayards, Lindsleys, Southards, Kirkpatricks, and others, were glad to secure its advantages for their children.

The Rev. Dr. Kirkpatrick, of Ringoes, N. J., states, in a letter to the author, that he and the late Hon. Saml. L. Southard (afterward Mr. F.'s colleague in the Senate) commenced the study of Latin with Dr. Finley in August, 1799. In the spring of the next year they were joined by Philip Lindsley (afterward President of the University of Nashville, Tenn.), and by Theo.

Frelinghuysen. They constituted the first class of the academy. Dr. Kirkpatrick says that Mr. F. was a moral and amiable youth, beloved by his classmates.

All these were admitted in September, 1802, to the Junior Class of the College of New Jersey at Princeton. Among the other members of that class were the Hon. George Chambers, of Chambersburg, Pa., and the Hon. Jos. R. Ingersoll, late Minister of the United States to the Court of St. James. Mr. Ingersoll has been kind enough to furnish the author with the following interesting reminiscences of his early friend and classmate.

"Nassau Hall, the now venerable College of New Jersey, has been naturally regarded as the becoming nursery of the sons of that patriotic state. Many of them have received the crowning portion of their education there, and not a few of them have carried away with them high and distinguished honors.

"The class of 1804 gave to the country more than one of these, who fulfilled their early promise by becoming legislators, orators, and statesmen in the councils of the nation. It was usual for the natives of New Jersey to enter college in the Junior year. They thus enjoyed advantages from comparatively mature cultivation in good preliminary schools; and they escaped some of the dangers incident to the college career of extreme youth, when surrounded by examples and temptations more attractive than meritorious, from different and distant places.

"Theodore Frelinghuysen and others came at the same time, prepared for the opening of the Junior class. He soon took a station of high merit, and he maintained his position to the close of his allotted time. In his studies he was faithfully diligent, and for his recitations he was always prepared. It was observed of him by one of his classmates that he never made a mistake in them. With excellent abilities, great industry, suitable ambition, and never-failing attention, it could scarcely be otherwise. The studies were susceptible of being mastered, and he took care to conquer them.

"In the observance of college duty his conduct was exemplary. He appeared to have no tendency to neglect, and no inclination or capacity for mischief. He met the routine of exercises with uniform punctuality, and appeared to have no wish except within the college rules. As a speaker, he gave full indication of the excellence which was manifested in a brilliant senatorial life. When a 'Senior,' he represented the Cliosophic Society on the morning of the 4th of July, in the exercises performed only by two persons, one being from each society. His discourse was patriotic in its theme. The order of speaking was determined by lot, and he chose to speak last. The classmate who preceded him selected a literary subject, and referred to his associate by saying to the audience that the wide and extended interests of the country he left on the occasion to his friend and brother, whose merits with them he would not envy, but would endeavor to emulate.

"The conduct and conversation of our eminent fellow-citizen were not only free from reproach, but amiable and delicate. Although a precisely devotional character may not have been observed at this early day, yet seeds of religious habit and exercise must have been planted which were afterward, in due season, developed into the ripe exhibition of a pious life.

"His merits and station in the class, at the final examination for degrees, were fully recognized by the proper authorities. In the distribution of honors among forty-two graduates, the valedictory oration was assigned to him. It was a testimonial of uniform and exemplary past good conduct, a reward for industry and excellence in his various studies, and a merited compliment to his talents as a speaker. This is always considered a touching farewell to companions, many of whom become separated for time and eternity, and was rendered peculiarly affecting in this instance. Mr. Frelinghuysen had recently lost his father, who had long been eminent in public, and highly esteemed in private life. The parting address of the son alluded, with great tenderness and delicacy of feeling, to this event, and it did not fail to convey a motive for earnest sympathy in the speaker's distress and the general sorrow.

"The valedictory, while it was a proof of past and existing merit, was a pledge for the future course of the youthful orator which has been nobly redeemed. His early professional efforts confirmed the promise of distinguished usefulness and stirring abilities. The entire development before the country and before the world has not only conferred lasting fame upon the individual, but has contributed eminently to verify the position long since taken, that the *alma mater* with which he was honorably identified in youth was *lux et gloria Novœ Cœsariœ*.

"Philadelphia, May 28, 1862."

It may add to the interest of the foregoing communication to state a fact which the modesty of its distinguished author induced him to withhold, but which the Rev. Dr. Kirkpatrick has preserved, viz., that Mr. Ingersoll and Mr. Frelinghuysen were competitors for academic distinction, and were pronounced by the Faculty to be equal, so that the first honor of the class was divided between them. Mr. Ingersoll pronounced the Latin salutatory at the commencement. A letter to the author from the Hon. Mr. Chambers confirms all the statements of Mr. Ingersoll, speaks of Mr. Frelinghuysen as a *model student*, and adds the farther fact, which will be interesting to some readers, that the thoroughness of his academic preparation at Basking Ridge contributed largely to the high stand he took in his class at college.

After his graduation Mr. Frelinghuysen returned to the homestead at Millstone, which was then occupied by his brother JOHN, who had removed his residence thither from the Raritan, in order, as the oldest son, to take charge of his father's household. In his office Theodore commenced the study of the law. Of John Frelinghuysen's character and course, some notice will be found in the Appendix. It is enough to say here that his influence upon his younger brothers was of the happiest kind in every respect. Nor were they slow to acknowledge it. Theodore, writing to his brother's widow immediately after the death of her husband, in April, 1833, said: "To my own heart this is a sore bereavement. It has taken my only brother, who watched over my youth, and was as a father to counsel and comfort me; one whose kindness never remitted, and who delighted to aid me, and contribute in all circumstances to my happiness."

Of Mr. Frelinghuysen's character and course at this period of his life, the author has had the pleasure of receiving some authentic statements from the Rev. Isaac N. Wyckoff, D.D., of Albany, N. Y., some of which are here given. Dr. Wyckoff says: "He had already graduated at Princeton when my fortunate acquaintance with him commenced. But this I well remember, that when a student of law in his brother's office, he was much engaged in promoting the mental advancement of the young men in his neighborhood. For this purpose he originated a debating society, and invited the young men several miles around to attend. He encouraged their efforts in composition and oratory, and by his unaffected simplicity of manners and condescending kindness endeared himself to every member of the association. I might mention an anecdote illustrating the attachment of the young men to him. On occasion of some earnest discussion in the neighboring hotel, a lively fellow took exception to some statement Mr. Frelinghuysen made, and threatened personal chastisement. A stout young farmer immediately interposed, and shouted, 'Touch him if you dare;' and the belligerent youth, finding that he must encounter, not a fair-handed collegian, but a brawny yeoman, slunk away and threatened no more.

"You will pardon me if I am egotistical in this communication. To myself, more than any one else, he showed great kindness. Having permitted me, though only a boy of fourteen summers, to enter the debating society, and observed my desire of improvement, he invited me to his office, furnished me with books, directed my reading, and ultimately became my classical teacher, and devoted his daily attention to me till I was nearly ready to enter the Junior class, when his brother Frederick—*par nobile fratrum*—took up the benevolent task till I entered college. The close of this disinterested kindness ought to be mentioned. When my father requested to know how he might reward Mr. F. for his care and tuition, he entirely refused compensation. But my father begged that he would accept some token of respectful acknowledgment for his laborious kindness. 'Well,' said he, 'if I must take something, please send me a box of Spanish cigars;' which was accordingly done. Although I do not use cigars myself, no one will expect me to join in King James's Counterblast against Tobacco, for its fragrant smoke was the visible price of my academic education. I have nothing farther to add but the testimony, which is abundant in our old neighborhood of Millstone, that Mr. Frelinghuysen was a youth of noble heart and benevolent impulses. None knew him that did not love him; none spoke of him but to praise him. For myself, my heart kindles with warmth when I think of him. I am inclined to be extravagant when I speak of him. He was my early patron, my unwearied benefactor, my friend till death. I invoke a thousand blessings upon all who were dear to him, and who belong to his lineage and partake in his spirit."

Mr. Frelinghuysen continued for somewhat more than a year in his brother's office at Millstone, pursuing his legal studies, and employing his leisure in the useful and praiseworthy manner set forth by Dr. Wyckoff. He then, at the suggestion of his brother, repaired to Princeton, and entered his name in the office of the Hon. RICHARD STOCKTON, who had at different times represented New Jersey in the Senate and House of Representatives of the United States, and who was for a quarter of a century the acknowledged leader of the bar in his native state. Under this distinguished man he prosecuted his legal studies with great assiduity until November, 1808, when he was admitted to practice, being then twenty-one years of age.

CHAPTER III.

PROFESSIONAL CAREER AT THE BAR.

1808—1838.

Settlement at Newark.—Marriage.—Studious Habits.—First Striking Success.—Patriotic Exertions in 1812.—Same in 1861.—Attorney General of the State.—Legal Characteristics.—Cases.—The Quaker Case.—Proprietary Case.—Leaving the Bar.

THE place which Mr. Frelinghuysen selected to establish himself in life was Newark, at that time a village which contained about four thousand inhabitants, and gave little promise of the growth of business which has converted it into one of the most prosperous inland cities in the whole country. One of the attractions which brought him to Newark, doubtless, was the fact that it was the residence of the lady whom he married the next year after his removal there. This was Charlotte Mercer, the daughter of Archibald Mercer, Esq., a gentleman of remarkable enterprise and business tact. Miss Mercer was a lady of great intelligence, amiable disposition, and numerous graces of person and manner; and the union formed with her by Mr. Frelinghuysen continued in unbroken affection for more than forty years, when she was removed by death to a heavenly home. Providence having denied them children, they were inseparable companions at home and abroad. Her cheerful spirits and buoyant temperament were a signal blessing to her husband, whose fatigues and vexations she was always able to soothe, while her winning courtesy gave an additional charm to the abundant and cordial hospitalities of his house and table.

The same habits of studiousness, sobriety, and attention which had marked Mr. Frelinghuysen's previous course, still attended him while awaiting the call of clients. He revised and perfected his legal studies. He was diligent in his attendance upon the courts. He gave considerable time to the pursuits of literature, especially to those histories which lay open the fountains of law. His evenings were in general spent in the society of Mrs. Frelinghuysen, to whom he was in the habit of reading aloud some favorite English classic. None of his faculties were allowed to rust through disuse, but, while in comparative obscurity, he labored as if with some prophetic foresight of the demands he would be called to meet in coming years. When, therefore, the cares of a full practice came rushing upon him, he was not unprepared.

The commencement of Mr. Frelinghuysen's professional life and reputation are well described in a pamphlet published in 1844, understood to be from the pen of Courtlandt Parker, Esq., a distinguished member of the New Jersey bar, who had studied in Mr. Frelinghuysen's office, and who was both familiar with his character and well able to describe it. "Retiring and studious in his habits, unassuming, modest, and finding the bar already occupied by men of ability and standing, he was for two or three years very little known, and contented himself with silently laying the foundation of his subsequently brilliant career. The bar of Essex County was then very distinguished.

Among the seniors of the profession were Aaron Ogden,* Matthias Williamson, Isaac H. Williamson,* Wm. S. Pennington,* Elias Van Arsdale, Jos. C. Hornblower,† Wm. Halsey, and Wm. Chetwood,‡ and other men of great distinction in the state, besides Richard Stockton,‡ George Wood, and others of great ability from other counties. Such were Mr. Frelinghuysen's competitors, and for some time he remained little known; but about the year 1812 his abilities were called into public notice, and he rushed at once into an extensive and lucrative practice.

"His professional success took its rise from his able conduct of an important cause which occurred about the year above named. It was a case of murder, alleged to have been committed by a colored man. The killing was admitted, but it was insisted by the defendant that he acted in self-defense. The prisoner was friendless and penniless, and the court, being obliged to assign him counsel, appointed as such Mr. Frelinghuysen, together with a senior member of the bar, the present Chief Justice Hornblower. In course of time the cause was tried, and the junior counsel was the first to present it to the jury; and so powerful was his appeal, that the jury, though the case is said to have been clearly one of manslaughter at least, immediately acquitted the prisoner. He dwelt with great pathos upon the situation of the defendant as one calling for the sympathies of the court and jury. Every thing was combined to darken his prospects: poverty, friendlessness, insignificance in public estima-

* Governors and Chancellors. † Chief Justice.
‡ Members of Congress.

tion on account of his color, and his being a stranger and without relatives, all contributed to swell the tide against him. The solemnity of his situation excited a morbid interest in the cause, but none for him. The lonely condemned cell, the scaffold and executioner, the fatal rope, and the awful moment of death, would rouse curiosity, but not sympathy: unthought of, unregretted, would his spirit, if their verdict was adverse, rise from the horrid scaffold to the bar of judgment. Ideas something like these, clothed in the purest diction, animated by his vivid imagination, and delivered with surpassing eloquence, completely overwhelmed court, jury, and auditors; the judge (the Hon. Saml. L. Southard), though by no means a man easily affected, was overcome by his feelings; and thus having enlisted popular sympathy for the forlorn state of his client, Mr. Frelinghuysen went on to argue the facts in so masterly a manner as quite to supersede the necessity of his colleague's address, and triumphantly acquit his client. A gentleman of another profession, present at the time, afterward said, in reference to it, 'I shall never forget the impression made upon me by the address of Mr. Frelinghuysen on that occasion. Though I was then but twelve or thirteen years of age, it has never left me, and ever since I have regarded him with intense interest from the feelings which his pathetic eloquence excited.'"

The same writer from whom we have just quoted proceeds to describe thus the elements of Mr. Frelinghuysen's professional ability and the grounds of his reputation: "The eloquence by which his forensic efforts were distinguished; his voice clear, mellow, and full; his manly appearance, brilliant imagination, vehement declamation, and fine flow of language, together with his acute knowledge of human nature, accurate legal acquirements, strong reasoning powers, and stern adherence to right, rendered him the most popular advocate at the bar of Eastern New Jersey."

In the outset of his career he exhibited the active love of country which he inherited from his father, and which characterized all his subsequent career. In the war of 1812 a draft of every seventh man was made upon the citizens of Essex County for the government service. He escaped the lot, but, with a number of others who were in the same situation, formed a volunteer company of riflemen, of which he took the command. Among the members of the company was the Rev. S. H. Cox, D.D., who acted as the captain's orderly, and who relates with great vivacity the thoroughness of the drill, the enthusiasm of the rank and file, and the fine appearance they presented when reviewed by the governor of the state on the national anniversary. They were never called into active service, but they lacked only the occasion, not the will. When the city of New York was supposed to be in danger from its defenseless situation, Mr. Frelinghuysen was among the most active in inducing the citizens of Newark to come to its aid with upward of nine hundred able-bodied men, who, with spade and pickaxe, rendered most efficient service in throwing up intrenchments on Brooklyn Heights and South Brooklyn. Fifty years afterward, when the country was threatened with the far greater danger of an internal foe, the voice of Theodore Frelinghuysen rang out in clarion tones, which showed that age had not chilled the patriotic fires of youth, nor the peaceful pursuits of education and literature deadened his sensibilities to the honor of his country and the maintenance of her government. With his own hand he raised the national banner on the College grounds, and accompanied the act with a speech, in the course of which he said: "Our forefathers felt the defects springing from the independence of single states, and saw that there could be neither glory nor safety in thirteen little independent factions. Hence the framers of the Constitution assembled for the purpose of forming a wise and permanent bond of union. The Union formed then is the Union of to-day; and under it our prosperity has been so great that we are all willing to sacrifice the last drop of our blood to see it maintained against traitors. The forbearance of the North was simply the calmness of conscious strength. The first cannon-shot, however, against Sumter struck the great heart of the American people, and that heart will never cease beating until this wrong is avenged. Despising the remedies offered by the Constitution itself for redressing their supposed grievances, they, just as wicked men always do, have gathered their forces, have stolen forts and arsenals, have plundered our public property, have murdered innocent citizens, and are now endeavoring to coil among the Stars and Stripes a serpent whose fangs shall strike out the emblems of seven states from its glorious folds. If a foreign foe had done this, the nation would have risen up as one man to hurl down the aggressor. How much worse is it when the foe came from within our own bosom! In fact, a more monstrous crime has not been perpetrated since the crucifixion of our Lord and Savior. We must fight: there is no alternative. Rebellion must be crushed, and then we shall once more become a happy and united people."

Nor were these stirring words the mere effervescence of a temporary excitement, but the expression of a deep and settled conviction, founded upon Mr. Frelinghuysen's origin, training, studies, and experience. And he never wavered. Even when lying upon the bed from which he knew that he was never to arise, and in full view of the solemn realities of the life to come, his interest in the national cause was unabated, and tidings of any success of the Union forces would call forth a prompt and hearty expression of joy and gratitude. Like his father before him, he was a patriot to the last, unconditionally and without reservation.

Mr. Frelinghuysen's practice, after 1812, became extensive and lucrative. He attended the courts in all the northern counties of New Jersey, every where acquiring a like reputation with that he had obtained at home. His legal and personal character daily raised him in public estimation, until, in 1817, he was appointed attorney general of the state—an office which, at that time, was one of immense care and responsibility. The holder of it was not only the legal adviser of the state, but in person or by deputy supervised the administration of the criminal statutes throughout the commonwealth. There were in this appointment some circumstances exceedingly complimentary to Mr. Frelinghuysen. The legislative majority by whom it was conferred were opposed to him in politics, and had able and prominent men of their own party before them for election. He was chosen, too, as indeed was the case with all the public honors and offices conferred upon him through life, without any solicitation on his part, and in the present instance without any expectation, as at the time he was engaged in his practice in a remote part of the state. He was afterward twice reappointed as his term of office expired; and when he resigned, did so in consequence of being elected, in 1829, a senator of the United States for the State of New Jersey.

No man ever filled the office of attorney general more to the satisfaction of the people than he. It was the field for the proper display of the lofty integrity, private and professional, which was always his peculiar distinction. Guilt, whenever it appeared, he prosecuted with every energy he could command, while in his dealings with the depraved he ever pursued so fair and just a course that even they who suffered from his efforts dared not blame them. He never sank the attorney general in the advocate of a side. Representing the majesty of the state, his endeavor was to ferret out the guilty and discover truth, not to gain his cause or to extend his fame. While he occupied this post, he was, in 1820, elected by the Legislature to a seat upon the bench of the Supreme Court of the state, a position usually deemed a fitting goal for the honorable ambition of a New Jersey lawyer. This, however, he declined, preferring to continue in the more active branch of the profession.

The reputation of Mr. Frelinghuysen attracted many

young men to his office as students of the law, and parents were always glad to place their sons under such a wholesome influence. He dealt faithfully and kindly with them all, and never failed to win their affectionate admiration and regard. They looked up to him as a friend and father, and throughout life cherished for him the highest esteem. From one of these, now eminent at the bar, the author has had the pleasure of receiving an authentic statement respecting Mr. Frelinghuysen's professional character and course, which is here reproduced almost in the writer's own words.

His moral influence upon his associates at the bar was very great and very salutary. No one ever questioned the sincerity of his religious professions. Hence his pure life was a constant power, felt and acknowledged by all. Probably no bar in this country ever presented a more uniform exhibition of moral integrity, high and honorable principle, and gentlemanly bearing than that of New Jersey during the first third of this century. This must have been due to some eminent examples in the profession, as well of an earlier as of a later day; and no individual example exerted a more benign and powerful influence than that of Mr. Frelinghuysen during the whole of his career. How many lines of influence go out, like the rays of the sun, in every direction, from a pure and lofty character!

The intellectual characteristics of Mr. Frelinghuysen as a lawyer partook of his general nature. His mind was strikingly rapid, correct, and comprehensive. His judgments seemed almost intuitive. He seized at once the strong points of a cause, never confused or embarrassed by immaterial facts or points, but always coming directly to that which was essential and decisive. An illustration of his correct and rapid judgment may be gained from the testimony of one who knew him intimately for many years. "Whenever I had a case of difficulty or perplexity, I was in the habit of going to my friend A., my senior at the bar, for advice. He had a very fertile and ingenious mind, and would soon suggest half a dozen explanations or expedients to obviate the difficulty, but would not decide positively on any one of them. I would then go to Mr. Frelinghuysen. He at once would tell me which of them all was the true solution, and I never knew him to make a mistake."

This sagacity in discriminating the essential from the non-essential gave him a complete mastery over forms and technicalities. He rose above them, and by the simplicity and directness of his legal diction, in documents as well as in discussions, he often evinced his power of making forms instead of being made by them. On one occasion, when dining with his professional associates at the hotel of a country town, while he was attorney general, a messenger from the grand jury came to him for the form of an indictment in some case which they had agreed to present. He immediately called for pen and ink, and in a few moments wrote out an indictment on the crown of his hat, dispatched it to the jury-room, and resumed his dinner. "I think," said one of his legal brethren present, "that you are now entitled to be called a *crown* lawyer, if never before." But all knew too well his accuracy, and his ability to defend his own work, to assail it with any technical objections afterward.

From the time when he took his first successful position at the bar of New Jersey in 1812, until he went to New York in 1838, he was engaged in almost every important cause which arose in the state. During this protracted period he acted as one of the pioneers of the law in establishing legal principles and settling precedents which, as they have stood in the past, will continue to stand for years to come. Yet very few traces of his forensic ability have been preserved in a permanent form. His speeches were never written out in full, and the movement of his eloquence was so *rapid, so brilliant,* so *like* a whirlwind in its sweep, that no ordinary reporter could catch the winged words as they flew from his gifted, almost inspired lips. The impression he produced was for the time being complete and overpowering. His speech in an important slander case, *Hall vs. Grant*, tried in Newark in 1821, was characterized by all the prominent peculiarities of his eloquence, and long afterward was referred to with admiration by those who heard it; yet the report which has been preserved of it gives to those who never knew the man no conception whatever of his extraordinary power.

The best report extant of any of his forensic efforts is that of the argument made by him in 1833 in what is commonly known as the great Quaker case. This cause convulsed the whole state with excitement, and even affected its political character in after years. It arose from a dispute between two parties into which the society of Friends had become divided, the Orthodox and the Hicksites, respecting the control of the public property of the body. The result of the suit was to establish the principle for which Mr. Frelinghuysen and his associate counsel contended, viz., that when a religious society is rent in twain, and the parties separate on account of differences of sentiment, that portion which adheres to the original principles of the society is entitled to the funds raised for the promotion of its religious and benevolent objects. The same doctrine has been held in other controversies of a similar character in this country and in Britain. This case was one exactly fitted for the display of Mr. Frelinghuysen's peculiar talents. Apart from the immense pecuniary interests at stake, it brought up great principles for investigation, and involved a discussion of the social value and relations of cardinal religious doctrines. The dry routine of technical law gave place to the consideration of those views which govern the course of the statesman and the philanthropist.

The argument in this celebrated case began in the Court of Appeals at Trenton on the 7th of July, and continued for about a month, the mere reading of the evidence consuming nine days. The counsel for the Hicksites were the Hon. Garret D. Wall and Samuel L. Southard; for the Orthodox, George Wood and Mr. Frelinghuysen. The case having been decided by the chancellor in favor of the Orthodox, the Hicksites had appealed, and consequently their counsel had the opening and reply. General Wall occupied four days in the discussion, Mr. Wood two and a half, Mr. Frelinghuysen three, and Mr. Southard four and a half. At the close of the argument on the 15th of August, the court immediately affirmed the chancellor's decision by a vote of seven to four. The great length of time consumed in the case was owing chiefly to the fact that the Society of Friends had no formal written creed or Confession of Faith; and hence their fundamental doctrines had to be elicited by a careful reference to the writings of the founders of the society, Penn, Barclay, Fox, and others, and to the prevailing tenor of its teaching and discipline during the intervening period of a century and a half. This wide range of investigation required much recondite study, and the exercise of sharp discrimination and solid judgment in the handling of the materials. Perhaps the salient excellencies of Mr. Frelinghuysen's mind were never more happily exhibited than in his masterly analysis of the evidence and the authorities relied upon in this case.

The opening counsel, apprehensive, probably, that his cause could not be supported on sound legal principles, insinuated that the court, being a court of last resort, and forming (as it did at that time) one branch of the Legislature, like the British House of Lords, were not bound by the rigid rules of established law, but might draw on their legislative authority, and decide according to their own notions of justice. It was a shrewd temptation to the judges to liberate themselves from the trammels of law, and seek to carve out some popular compromise to suit the prejudices of the hour. Mr. Frelinghuysen met the suggestion with a severe rebuke. "Your honors," said he, "have a high and sacred trust to administer. This forum is the last resort of truth. She casts her hopes on your threshold. I have no doubt that you will weigh well her claims. But even if truth can not stand without invading the functions of *legislative* authority, let her fall. Better that she should fall than that the great pillars of law and order should be overthrown. This doctrine, drawn from a volume of ecclesiastical reports, is a monstrous perversion of British law. It never furnished a pebble to the system which the American jurist delights to study. Why was it picked up here? Why was it brought forward at the opening of this case? What is it? It means that when the House of Lords find a defect of judicial power, they may draw upon their legislative department, and when there is no law, make a law to suit the case. * * * * It is a principle false in all its branches, as applied to the House of Lords sitting as a court of law or equity. That house has no legislative authority but in connection with the House of Commons and the king. Such a notion would destroy all certainty and security in our systems of jurisprudence, and subvert the very foundations of property and right."

The first part of his argument was directed to show that the Society of Friends had a real, substantive system of belief. They had, as has been stated, no formal confession or standard of faith. They generally expressed their views in the language of Scripture; but Mr. Frelinghuysen contended that, in the selection, and combination, and application of these passages from the Bible, it clearly appeared what their distinctive principles and doctrines were. The other side contended that they also believed in the Bible, and therefore held the views expressed in its language. To this he thus replied: "To say you believe in the Bible leaves the question unresolved. All but downright infidels say this. What does the Bible teach, what does it enforce, and what does it prohibit? These are the material distinguishing inquiries. There is not a Unitarian church in the country in which you will not find the Bible on the desk, in which they do not read from its pages, in which they do not speak of God and of virtue with reverence and admiration; yet, when questioned as to what they believe, you find that they believe in nothing essential to Christianity. When they reject the great doctrines of the divinity of the Savior, the atonement, and the inspiration of the Scriptures, what remains to be received or rejected? The Jews believed in the Bible. They read it in their synagogues every Sabbath day. They carried parts of it about with them on their persons; and yet they crucified the very Being to proclaim whose coming, and power, and work of redemption the Bible was given. Counsel tell us that the Society of Friends has no creed. The ancient members of that society were imprisoned on account of their faith. They have been brought before kings and magistrates, and compelled to give a statement of their belief. They have repeatedly put forth full and clear declarations of their views; and yet, in the nineteenth century, we are told that the Friends have no creed! The book of discipline makes it a duty to inquire periodically whether certain persons 'are sound in word and doctrine;' and yet we are told that they have no creed; that every man is to believe as he lists, without a leader, or guide, or system!"

On the use of the language of Scripture as a vehicle for the expression of doctrinal views, Mr. Frelinghuysen said: "The learned counsel, to show that the Friends have no creed, affirm that their declarations of faith have always been expressed in scriptural language. Granting this, does it prove no creed? In what better clothing could they exhibit their faith? I am not theologian enough to decide positively what is best upon a question like this; but it seems to me that the safest and clearest exhibition of a man's belief may be expressed in the words of the Bible * * * While we adhere to these words, we have the best truth in the best language. We know that, in literary excellence, the English Bible is the best composition in our language. Is it, then, matter of importance that the Friends should express their faith in its phrases? Let the Separatists, if they can, furnish us with a better lodgment for the truth."

Mr. Frelinghuysen then proceeded to show that the points before mentioned, the Deity of Christ, the Atonement, and the Inspiration of the Bible, were held by the society as fundamental articles of faith; and that Elias Hicks and his followers had rejected these articles, and therefore could not properly be said to belong to the society as it was originally constituted, and had been continued in successive generations.

It is well known that the Friends in New Jersey were nearly equally divided upon the opinions of Elias Hicks. The Court of Appeals, therefore, while they sustained the claim of the Orthodox party in point of law, recommended an amicable compromise in relation to the question in dispute. This advice was afterward sanctioned by a legislative enactment, and, being adopted by both parties, resulted in a general division of the property between them on equitable principles.

Mr. Frelinghuysen took part in another cause of great moment in relation to both the private and the public interests involved. This was the New Jersey Proprietary case, *Waddell vs. Martin.* It concerned the ownership of all the lands under water around the entire coast, and along all the tide-water streams of New Jersey. These lands are of immense value as oyster-beds and fisheries. Some of them, in the vicinity of New York and elsewhere, are of still greater value for the purposes of reclamation and improvement. The question at issue was, Whether they belonged to the state by virtue of its sovereignty, or to the Board of Proprietors, who originally owned the title to all the lands in the state, and had never made any grant of the title to these lands now in dispute? The Board of Proprietors claimed them as part of the private landed property of New Jersey; the state claimed them as belonging to the public domain. The former party retained Mr. Frelinghuysen, who supported their claim in a masterly argument before Judge Baldwin, of the Supreme Court of the United States, then holding circuit at Trenton. His effort was successful: Judge Baldwin decided in favor of the Proprietors; but on an appeal to the Supreme Court at Washington, which was argued by other counsel after Mr. Frelinghuysen had withdrawn from practice, the judgment was reversed, and the title of the state confirmed.

This was about the last case in which he was engaged. He left the bar in 1838 to take the charge of a literary institution; but his professional associates, and those who remember him as an advocate, uniformly contend that the bar was his proper sphere. It was in the forum that his peculiar gifts, his quick insight, his sharp discrimination, his impetuous eloquence, shone with greatest lustre. It is said that hardly a single Jersey lawyer of the last generation can be met, who will not, when reminded of Mr. Frelinghuysen's retirement to academic life, shake his head, and insist that that step was erroneously taken; that a man so admirably adapted in every respect to the bar should have remained there; and that to put him at the head of any university was like burying him in a marble mausoleum before his time had come. This statement does not lack some elements, or at least appearances of truth. Nor was Mr. Frelinghuysen insensible to considerations of this kind. His friends, his associations, his habits, his tastes, his pleasures, were all connected with the bar; his practice yielded him all the income he could ask or desire; and he was making a great sacrifice in many ways in becoming Chancellor of the University. But mere personal considerations never controlled his mind. Where duty beckoned, he had no hesitation in following. He believed that it was her voice which summoned him to New York; nor has any one a right now to say that this was a mistake. Doubtless it had been better for his professional reputation, his private fortune, and his personal comfort to have continued in the arena already thickly strewn with the trophies of his success. But no man liveth or ought to live only for himself.

And it may well be that the Omniscient eye sees a far larger harvest of usefulness gathered from the presence of Theodore Frelinghuysen in academic halls than could have been gained from the longest and most successful forensic career.

CHAPTER IV.

IN THE SENATE OF THE UNITED STATES.

1829—1835.

Composition of the Senate.—Great Questions agitated.—Mr. Frelinghuysen's Course.—The Indian Bill.—The Sunday-Mail Question.—Day of Fasting for the Cholera.—Encomiums of Clay and Webster.—Letter of the Hon. Edward Everett.

In the year 1829 Mr. Frelinghuysen took his seat in the Senate of the United States, where he continued until the expiration of the term for which he was elected. During the first four years his colleague from New Jersey was the Hon. Mahlon Dickerson, afterward Secretary of the Navy under Presidents Jackson and Van Buren; during the remaining two years, his old classmate, Samuel L. Southard, who had been Secretary of the Navy under Presidents Monroe and J. Q. Adams, was his associate.

It has generally been admitted that the Senate never contained a larger number of eminent men than it did at this period. The leading minds of every section of the country and of every political party were to be found on the floor of the upper house of Congress. Among these, three names stand out with a prominence not to be mistaken. Even now the person, character, policy, and influence of Daniel Webster, of Henry Clay, and of John C. Calhoun, are better known than those of more than one holder of that great prize, the presidential chair, after which they all unsuccessfully aspired, and will be freshly remembered long after the latter are buried in oblivion. These three differed widely in their origin, training, and cast of mind, but they were all men of strongly-marked character, of unusual natural gifts, and well adapted to lead great parties in the republic. Each was a well-read lawyer, an experienced legislator, a far-seeing statesman, and a practiced debater; and when they met in the Senate in opposition to the administration of General Jackson, it was in the maturity of their powers and fame. But besides these there were many others in the Senate inferior only to them in ability and influence. Such were Holmes of Maine, Woodbury of New Hampshire, Foot of Connecticut, Robbins of Rhode Island, Marcy and Wright of New York, Dallas and Wilkins of Pennsylvania, Clayton of Delaware, Rives, Tyler, and Tazewell of Virginia, Mangum of North Carolina, Hayne and Preston of South Carolina, Forsyth of Georgia, King of Alabama, Poindexter of Mississippi, Edward Livingston of Louisiana, Grundy and White of Tennessee, Bibb of Kentucky, Ewing of Ohio, and Benton of Missouri; every one of whom not only achieved distinction in his own state, but also had considerable national reputation.*

The period of Mr. Frelinghuysen's senatorial service was distinguished by the importance of the issues before the country, as well as by the greatness of the men who discussed and decided them. The bold and pronounced character of General Jackson did not al-

* One half of them either had been, or became cabinet officers or representatives of the country at foreign courts.

low him to follow tortuous courses or pursue an equivocal policy. On every question he took his position clearly, and was prepared to push his opponents to the wall. Debate was not confined to side issues or incidental points, but touched fundamental principles, and affected questions coeval with the formation of the government. The currency, the tariff, the autonomy of the Indian tribes, the scope of pension laws, the powers of the executive in relation to Congress, and the powers of the general government in relation to the states—these, and such as these, were the great themes which then occupied the time and thought of the statesmen of the country. On the last of these issues our generation has seen a decision practically reached by force of arms in resistance to a causeless and treacherous rebellion. But the principles underlying that subject have never been more thoroughly, ably, and eloquently discussed than they were in the years 1832 and 1833. The whole case was then exhausted; nor has any thing been added on either side, in the shape of argument, to what was then urged, although, of course, the appeal to force has forever settled the question, and shown that the proclamation of General Jackson in December, 1832, will henceforth be deemed a just exposition of the Federal Constitution.

In all these conflicts Mr. Frelinghuysen took a decided part, for he never affected a neutral position. Believing the principles of the party with which he acted to be correct and wise, he gave them a cordial and persistent support. But his fidelity to political associates never degenerated into mere partisanship.

He disliked a factious opposition to the administration, and rigidly confined his course to such measures as seemed clearly called for by the circumstances of the country. On one memorable occasion, when the Senate acted upon the nomination of the Hon. Martin Van Buren as minister to Great Britain, Mr. Frelinghuysen had great difficulty in concurring with his party in a vote of disapproval. He, however, yielded at last, and his name stands upon the record with the majority in opposition to the nomination. But he always declared that the measure, however justifiable, was an impolitic one, and predicted the very consequences which in a few years ensued from it. Indeed, his political sagacity was not often at fault. His coolness and fairness gave his mind fair play, and disembarrassed his judgment from the passions and prejudices which frequently mislead very able men.

At a time when party lines were very strictly drawn, and personal animosities added to the bitterness of political divisions, he still maintained an independent judgment; and although habitually acting with the opponents of the administration, he never hesitated to differ from them rather than violate his own sense of right.

His participation in the business of the Senate justified the hopes inspired by the success of his previous career. Although by no means the equal of any of the three great representatives of the East, West, and South, he yet held a prominent place in the committee-room and on the floor of the Senate, and maintained with signal ability the honor of the state he represented. Indeed, it may be doubted whether New Jersey ever had as much influence in the national councils as when Frelinghuysen and Southard were her senators at Washington. Whether in formal discussions on great topics, or in the current debates from day to day, they were uniformly found equal to the call made upon them, and even political opponents could not deny the ability with which they upheld the policy they had espoused.

Although there were seasons when the excitement of feeling reached a pitch almost unprecedented, Mr. Frelinghuysen throughout preserved the highest standard of senatorial dignity. He never descended to personalities, never engaged in unseemly altercations. His dignified bearing, his transparent candor, his unquestionable integrity, and his high sense of honor, secured him the cordial respect of all parties. They who attended to his course saw in him a coolness, discrimination, insight, shrewdness, and capacity which marked him out as a something more than a mere politician or debater. He was a statesman. He took large views of things. He looked beyond present emergencies, and acted for the future. Ardently attached to his own patriotic state, and ever sensitive to whatever touched her honor or welfare, he yet remembered that he was a senator of the United States, and legislated for the country as a whole. He was not a mere theorist, not "an impracticable." Firm and immovable where the everlasting principles of rectitude are concerned, well convinced that it is as true in history and experience as it is in Scripture that "righteousness exalteth a nation," he recognized the mixed elements with which every Legislature has to deal, the necessary limitations of all civil enactments, the wisdom of not governing too much, and the just claims of expediency in legislation. Notwithstanding the high conception of a free Christian commonwealth which lay at the basis of his public course, he was no Utopian. His ends were as rational as the means by which he pursued them. He may have erred in particular measures, but the general scope of his policy was large, comprehensive, enlightened, and judicious, yet eminently practical.

The Hon. George Chambers, of Pennsylvania, his classmate at Princeton, who was a member of the House of Representatives during two years of Mr. Frelinghuysen's senatorial term, says of him that "he was attentive, considerate, and judicious in his action, and ever faithful to his constituents, the Union, and the welfare of his country. He was not hasty or impulsive under any excitement, and seldom spoke in debate; but when he did, his remarks were appropriate, and commanded attention."

THE INDIAN QUESTION.

The first great topic on which Mr. Frelinghuysen addressed the Senate was the bill for the removal of the Indian tribes residing within states and organized territories of the Union, having particular reference to those within the limits of Georgia, Alabama, and Mississippi. The lands occupied by these aborigines, being admirably adapted to the growth of cotton, the culture of which had been greatly stimulated by the increasing price which the raw material obtained in the markets of the world, were looked upon by the white population with covetous eyes, and every inducement was offered to the original proprietors to sell their title and remove. But the territory was equally desirable to them, not only as having been the home of their forefathers and the place of their sepulchres, but also as being, by its natural features, just the country suited to their tastes and habits. Its mixture of hill and valley, forest and prairie, its numerous springs and streams, its abundance of fish and game, its fertile soil and equable climate, were exactly suited to the half nomad, half planting life pursued by the great body of the Indians. They therefore almost unanimously refused to sell. But their white neighbors were not to be foiled. They determined to make the Indians willing, and even eager to remove. This was accomplished by extending the state laws over them, with the abrogation of all their own "laws, ordinances, orders, and regulations of any kind whatever;" by making it a penal offense for any person to endeavor, by any means, to prevent any Indian from emigrating; and by disqualifying any Indian from being a competent witness in courts in any case to which a white person was a party, unless such white person resided among the Indians.

But, in order to give effect to these atrocious statutes, it was necessary to secure the assent of the federal government, or, rather, to prevent the continuance of the protection hitherto given by it to the aborigines against all intruders upon their lands. Accordingly, in conformity to the suggestions of President Jackson in his first annual message, a bill was introduced in Congress "providing for an exchange of lands with the Indians residing in any of the states or territories, and for their removal west of the Mississippi River." When this bill came up for consideration in the Senate, Mr. Frelinghuysen moved the following amendment:

"*Provided always*, That, until the said tribes or nations shall choose to remove, as by this act is contemplated, they shall be protected in their present possessions, and in the enjoyment of all their rights of territory and government, as heretofore exercised and enjoyed, from all interruptions and encroachments.

"*And provided also*, That before any removal shall take place of any of the said tribes or nations, and before any exchange or exchanges of land be made as aforesaid, that the right of any such tribes or nations in the premises shall be stipulated for, secured, and guarantied by treaty or treaties as heretofore made."

These provisos were sustained by him in a speech of very great power and eloquence. He showed that the principles they involved were not only founded in everlasting truth and right, but had been acted upon ever since the adoption of the Constitution by all branches of the government, beginning with the Father of his Country; that during the Revolution, and under the Confederation, they had been expressly recognized by the Continental Congress; and that, still earlier, the royal proclamations and ordinances from Great Britain had distinctly assumed the same ground. After reciting and explaining the various solemn treaties made by the national government with the Indian tribes, he riveted his argument by showing from the public records of the very states now engaged in this oppression of the Indians, that treaties with these tribes were recorded on their own statute-books as parts of their land titles, and that thus, by their own act, they were concluded on the point in question. The following is the peroration of this remarkable effort:

"Sir, our fears have been addressed in behalf of those states whose legislation we resist; and it is inquired with solicitude, would you urge us to arms with Georgia? No, sir. This tremendous alternative will not be necessary. Let the general government come out, as it should, with decided and temperate firmness, and officially announce to Georgia, and the other states, that if the Indian tribes choose to remain, they will be protected against all interference and encroachment; and such is my confidence in the sense of justice, in the respect for law, prevailing in that great body of this portion of our fellow-citizens, that I believe they would submit to the authority of the nation. I can expect no other issue. But if the general government be urged to the crisis, never to be anticipated, of appealing to the last resort of her powers; and when reason, argument, and persuasion fail, to raise her strong arm to repress the violations of the supreme law of the land, I ask, is it not in her bond, sir? Is her guaranty a rope of sand? This effective weapon has often been employed to chastise the poor Indians, sometimes with dreadful vengeance I fear, and shall not their protection avail to draw it from the scabbard? Permit me to refer the Senate to the views of Mr. Jefferson, directly connected with this delicate, yet sacred duty of protection. In 1791, when he was Secretary of State, there were some symptoms of collision on the Indian subject. This induced the letter from him to General Knox, then our Secretary of War, a part of which I will read: 'I am of opinion that government *should firmly* maintain this ground: that the Indians have a right to the *occupation of their lands*, *independent* of the states within whose *chartered limits* they happen to be; that until they cede them *by treaty*, or other transaction equivalent to a treaty, no act of a state can give a right to such lands; that neither under the present Constitution, nor the ancient Confederation, had any state or persons a right to treat with the Indians, without the consent of the general government; that the consent has never been given by any treaty for the cession of the lands in question; that the government is determined to exert all *its energy* for the patronage and protection of the rights of the Indians, and the preservation of peace between the United States and them; and that if any settlements are made on lands not *ceded by them*, without the previous consent of the United States, the government will think itself bound, not only to declare to the Indians that such settlements are without the authority or protection of the United States, but to *remove them also by public force*.'

"Mr. Jefferson seems to have been disturbed by no morbid sensibilities. He speaks out as became a determined statesman. We can trace in this document the same spirit which shed its influence on a more eventful paper—the declaration of our rights, and of our purpose to maintain and defend them. He looked right onward, in the broad path of public duty; and if, in his way, he met the terrors of state collision and conflict, he was in no degree intimidated. The faith of treaties was his guide; and he would not flinch in his purposes, nor surrender the Indians to state encroachments. Let such decided policy go forth in the majesty of our laws now, and, sir, Georgia will yield. She will never encounter the responsibilities or the horrors of a civil war. But if she should, no stains of blood will be on our skirts; on herself the guilt will abide forever.

"Mr. President, if we abandon these aboriginal proprietors of our soil—these early allies and adopted children of our forefathers, how shall we justify it to our country? to all the glory of the past, and the promise of the future? Her *good name* is worth all else besides that contributes to her greatness. And, as I regard this crisis in her history, the time has come when this unbought treasure shall be plucked from dishonor, or abandoned to reproach.

"How shall we justify this trespass to ourselves? Sir, we may deride it, and laugh it to scorn now; but the occasion *will* meet every man, when he *must* look inward, and make honest inquisition there. Let us beware how, by oppressive encroachments upon the sacred privileges of our Indian neighbors, we minister to the agonies of future remorse.

"I have, in my humble measure, attempted to discharge a public and most solemn duty toward an interesting portion of my fellow-men. Should it prove to be as fruitless as I know it to be below the weight of their claims, yet even then, sir, it will have its consolations. Defeat in such a cause is far above the triumphs of unrighteous power; and in the language of an eloquent writer, 'I had rather receive the blessing of one poor Cherokee, as he casts his last look back upon his country, for having, though in vain, attempted to prevent his banishment, than to sleep beneath the marble of all the Cæsars.'"

But all this display of argument, research, eloquence, whether by Mr. Frelinghuysen or others, was in vain. The question became mingled inextricably with the party divisions of the times; and the overwhelming popularity of General Jackson concurred with the pecuniary interests of the states immediately concerned to defeat the provisos, and the original bill was passed, although by inconsiderable majorities, numbering, indeed, in the lower house of Congress, only five votes. But Mr. Frelinghuysen's able advocacy of the cause of right, humanity, and Christian principle brought him prominently before the nation, secured him the title of the Christian Statesman, and made his name familiar as a household word to all the people of God throughout the land. The annexed stanzas, by one who has since attained an unhappy notoriety, may be taken as an expression of the feelings, not of the writer only, but of the great body of American Christians:

TO THE HON. THEODORE FRELINGHUYSEN, ON READING HIS ELOQUENT SPEECH IN DEFENSE OF INDIAN RIGHTS.

BY W. L. GARRISON.

If unto marble statues thou hadst spoken,
 Or icy hearts congealed by polar years,
The strength of thy pure eloquence had broken,
 Its generous heat had melted them to tears;
Which pearly drops had been a rainbow token,
 Bidding the red men soothe their gloomy fears.

If Honor, Justice, Truth had not forsaken
 The place long hallowed as their bright abode,
The faith of treaties never had been shaken,
 Our country would have kept the trust she owed;
Nor Violence nor Treachery had taken
 Away those rights which Nature's God bestowed.

Fruitless thy mighty efforts—vain appealing
 To grasping Avarice, that ne'er relents;
To party power, that shamelessly is stealing,
 Banditti-like, whatever spoil it scents;
To base Intrigue, his cloven foot revealing,
 That struts in Honesty's habiliments.

Our land, once green as Paradise, is hoary,
 E'en in its youth, with tyranny and crime;
Its soil with blood of Afric's sons is gory,
 Whose wrongs eternity can tell, not time.
The red man's woes shall swell the damning story,
 To be rehearsed in every age and clime.

Yet, Frelinghuysen, gratitude is due thee,
  And loftier praise than language can supply;
Guilt may denounce and Calumny pursue thee,
  And pensioned Impudence thy worth decry;
Brilliant and pure, posterity shall view thee
  As a fair planet in a troublous sky.

Be not dismayed. On God's own strength relying,
  Stand boldly up, meek soldier of the Cross;
For thee ten thousand prayers are heavenward flying;
  Thy soul is purged from earthly rust and dross.
Patriot and Christian, ardent, self-denying,
  How could we bear resignedly thy loss?

THE SUNDAY-MAIL QUESTION.

Prior to the year 1810 there was no law of Congress *requiring* the transportation of the mail and the delivery of its contents on the Lord's day. In that year, however, a statute was enacted, the 9th section of which made it "the duty of the postmaster, at all reasonable hours, on *every day of the week*, to deliver on demand any letter, paper," etc. Thus, what was before a matter of courtesy, became one of obligation. If the Postmaster General directed a mail to be carried on the first day of the week, the deputy was required to be in his office and receive it. Such an invasion of the sacredness of the day of rest did not pass without notice. Petitions and memorials requesting the repeal of the statute were presented in 1811, 1812, 1815, and 1817, without effect. In 1828 and 1829 a more formal and concerted effort was made, and memorials were sent in from all parts of the country. A report in opposition to the prayer of the petitioners was made to the Senate by the Hon. Richard M. Johnson, of Kentucky, on the 19th of January, 1829; and in the next year a similar, but much more elaborate report was made to the House of Representatives by the same gentleman, who had in the interval been transferred from the upper to the lower house of Congress. This second report of Colonel Johnson was made on the 4th of March, 1830. It aroused still more the feelings alike of the friends and the foes of the proposed reform. The question was extensively agitated in the pulpit and by the press, and the sentiment was very general among the Christian community that no pains should be spared to secure proper legislation on the point. Especially was it expected of Christian men in Congress that they would exert themselves in favor of the sanctity of the Sabbath.

On Tuesday, the 9th of March, 1830, Mr. Frelinghuysen offered the following paper in the Senate:

"The Sabbath is justly regarded as a divine institution, closely connected with individual and national prosperity. No Legislature can rightly resist its claims; and although the Congress of the United States, from the peculiar and limited constitution of the general government, can not by law enforce its observance, yet, as they should not, by positive legislation, encroach upon the sacredness of this day, or weaken its authority in the estimation of the people, therefore it is

"*Resolved*, That the Committee on the Post-office and Post-roads be instructed to report a bill repealing so much of the act on the regulation of post-offices as requires the delivery of letters, packets, and papers on the Sabbath; and, farther, to prohibit the transportation of the mail on that day."

This resolution did not come up for consideration until the 8th of May, when its author addressed the

Senate at length in its support. He was listened to with great attention by the House, and his argument was deemed cogent enough to require a reply from the celebrated Edward Livingston, of Louisiana.

A few extracts from this speech will indicate the course of his argument:

"The public recognition of the Sabbath is recorded in our federal Constitution. The President of the United States, in the discharge of the high functions of his legislative department, is expressly relieved from all embarrassment on Sunday. The business of the Supreme Court, the highest judicial tribunal of the country, is by law directed to be suspended on Sunday. Both houses of Congress, the offices of the State, Treasury, War, and Navy Departments, are all closed on Sunday, and all the states of the Union, I believe (twenty-three of them certainly), by explicit legislative enactments, acknowledge and declare the religious authority of the Sabbath. Sir, these state laws do not merely notice this day, but they in terms require its religious observance, and prohibit its profanation under proper penalties."

"The example of the Old World also pleads powerfully in behalf of this sacred institution. London, with all its wealth, business, and enterprise, regards the Sabbath. No mail is opened or closed on that day. And although there is probably five times as much commerce between London and Liverpool as between New York and Philadelphia, no mail leaves the metropolis for Liverpool between Saturday evening and Monday morning; and the mercantile classes of these communities make no complaint of this interruption. No, sir, they rejoice at the relief and refreshment from the toils of worldly business; that on one day in seven there may be a pause in the anxieties of eager speculation; and that even selfish cupidity is compelled to suspend its pursuits. Now, sir, in this review of the case, it must appear a most singular prejudice that is now excited and raised against all efforts to restore our national legislation to a consistency with its own principles, so often avowed. It is as absurd as it is unjust. Every state of the Union has, from its very origin, preserved just such a connection between Church and State as is now deprecated, and by means much more rigorous than the repeal of this oppressive section. They have fixed the day; they have enjoined its observance; they have specified and prohibited its profanation in particular details, and annexed the sanctions of legal penalties; and yet, after all this, when Congress is respectfully requested to be passive, and not to *command its violation*, but to leave the Sabbath alone, the note of alarm is sounded (and many good men are deluded by it) that a dangerous conspiracy is meditated against the freedom of conscience."

"Congress is not asked to legislate into existence the precepts of piety. No, these are enacted already; they can never be repealed, and it is a most dangerous and destructive delusion to suppose that while, as individuals and families, we are bound to respect the principles of religion, yet, when we assume the character of states and nations, these cease to exert any legitimate influence. Such was not the political faith of the Father of his Country. Washington loved to cherish that connection between Church and State which led to universal public and private virtue, and this result, he deeply realized, could flow alone from the prevalence of religious principles."

"Sir, this day is the ægis of a republican and free people. It is the poor man's friend. It elevates him and his family by promoting decency of manners, neatness, and order. It is the only time which the necessities of his condition and the constitution of society spare to him for rest and reflection; and hence every inroad upon its sacredness is a direct attack upon his best privileges. I believe, sir, that the adversary of our race, could he be permitted to select the single object, would strike the blow at this divine institution. He would say resign to me this great moral lever; let my votaries drive on the pursuits of business, the schemes of enterprise and ambition, without interruption; let there be no time for man to reflect, to gather in his thoughts, to renew his life, and to consider his origin and his destiny, and I desire no more. Mr. President, the Sabbath was made for man, not to be contemned and forgotten; the constitution of his nature requires just such a season. It is identified with his moral tendencies. God has ordained it in infinite benevolence. The reason for it, as recorded in his Word, was his own example. It began with creation. The first week of time was blessed with a Sabbath. The garden of Eden would not have smiled in all its loveliness had not the light of this day shone upon it. Blot it out, and the hope of the world is extinguished. When the whirlwind raged in France, how was it, sir? They could not carry their measures of ferocity and blood while this last palladium of virtue remained. Desolation seemed to pause in its course—its waves almost subsided—when the spirits of evil struck this hallowed day from the calendar, and enacted a decade to the goddess of Reason, after which the besom swept all before it.

"I firmly believe that the repeal of this single section and the suspension of the mail would exert the happiest influence. It would call up public attention. It would present the claims of the Sabbath with such weight of authority as would, I hope, establish and perpetuate it as an effective defense around our free insitutions. The mail arrested and the post-office closed on Sunday! by the solemn authority of Congress! who can fail to perceive the noble impulse that would be given? Sir, this would correct all false and degrading estimates of this sacred day; it would almost of itself form a public sentiment. The flood of vice and infidelity would be stayed in their course. Such high example would silence the cavils of the profane, and this, as I understand it, is the true old-fashioned way to popularity. It is not that sickly principle which flatters public vices and connives at national sins, but which, in the purity of its purposes, dares to rebuke them, and by wise and wholesome measures to correct them."

The following notices of this speech are found in the correspondence of Jeremiah Evarts. Under date of May 8, 1830, he writes, "This day Mr. Frelinghuysen called up his resolution in relation to Sabbath mails, and, I am sorry to say, I was absent. I have heard from a spectator that he spoke an hour and a half or more, and very much to the purpose. Mr. Livingston replied in a speech of three quarters of an hour, in which he gained no credit. It was a low piece of bar-room talk about Church and State, the Blue Laws of Connecticut, hanging witches in Salem, etc., etc. Mr. F., in a short reply, made Mr. L. rather ashamed of his tirade." Again, under date of May 16, "Mr. Frelinghuysen's discussion of the Sabbath-mail Question is spoken of with great approbation by those who heard it. His reply to Mr. Livingston was very happy. Mr. Hillhouse [himself a member of the Senate from 1796 to 1810] was delighted with Mr. Frelinghuysen's argument."*

The failure of this effort to guard the Sabbath from profanation under the forms of law was owing, doubtless, to the imperfect degree to which the Christian sentiment of the country was at that day developed.

* Tracy's Life of Evarts, pp. 369, 371.

This general cause was aided by the unwise measures adopted and the uncharitable spirit exhibited by some of the advocates of the Sabbath, and also by the artful manner in which the movement was represented as an interference with the rights of conscience and an insidious attempt to unite Church and State. There can be but little doubt, however, that the agitation of the subject in the halls of Congress awakened public attention to it, elicited the interest and zeal of Christians, and thus prepared the way for the movements in subsequent years, which, beginning at a different point, and operating in other forms, have caused a reduction of Sunday-mail service to an amount scarcely one fourth of what it was when the question was first mooted. The exact influence of public movements is not always correctly gauged by the measure of immediate success they gain. While for the time being the enemies of religion seemed to have achieved a victory in the matter of Sabbath observance, the earnest, and repeated, and thorough discussions of the subject through the press and on the platform consolidated Christian sentiment, and led, in the end, to a quiet but very great revolution in the tone and policy of the leaders of political opinion and action.

DAY OF FASTING FOR THE CHOLERA.

Early in the year 1832 the country was agitated by reports of the steady progress toward this country of a scourge which, originating in the farthest East, had swept over Europe, and every where spread destruction and dismay. At the present time, repeated visitations of the plague have made us familiar with its character and with the appropriate remedies. But thirty years ago the terror caused by its ravages was greatly increased by its novelty, and the seeming uselessness of all means to evade or resist it. Soon after its first appearance on American shores, Mr. Clay offered in the Senate a joint resolution, in which both houses of Congress recommended the President to appoint a day of fasting, humiliation, and prayer, when the nation should entreat the Most High to avert from our country the Asiatic scourge, or, if he allowed it to come, to mitigate its severity and shorten its duration.

In supporting this resolution Mr. Frelinghuysen said:

"As it is to be inferred from the call just made for the yeas and nays that this resolution is to be opposed, I beg leave to refer the attention of the Senate to the example of Congress in 1812. A day of humiliation, fasting, and prayer was then recommended by a joint resolution of the Senate and House of Representatives because of the war with Great Britain, in which the country was then involved. It was regarded as one of those seasons of public calamity in which it became a whole people to acknowledge their dependence and humble themselves before God. So far as I can learn from the journals of the day, the resolution was adopted without opposition. Now, sir, if a state of war, in which we had voluntarily engaged, was a fit occasion to call forth public expressions of humiliation for our sins and to invoke the merciful providence of God, how much more appropriately does it become us thus to feel and act on the approach of a pestilence that, in its ravages over the Old World, has swept many millions of our fellow-men into eternity, and which, in its character and progress through the earth, seems so emphatically to be the instrument of Divine Providence, beyond the influence of second causes, and especially selected to accomplish his purposes, and to come and go at his bidding.

"I hope, sir, that the present resolution will meet with no serious opposition. It surely becomes us to acknowledge our dependence, and to implore the interposition of God's mercy in this season of alarm. The Constitution can present no obstacle, for this is not an exercise of political power. It is far beyond the range of politics. It is an act of piety to God, becoming the whole nation, in which rulers and people are invited and advised to bow together before His throne of grace; and there, feeling ourselves to be in like need, to unite in our common supplication to Him who has the issues of life and death, that he would be pleased to spare us in the day of his righteous judgment. I trust, sir, that this motion will receive the same decided countenance which was accorded to a similar measure in the late war and on many occasions during the war of the Revolution."

The resolution was carried in the Senate by a large majority, but was defeated in the House. The policy implied in it has, however, been signally reaffirmed in later years. In the summer of 1861 the President was requested, by a unanimous vote in both houses of Congress, to appoint a day of national humiliation, in view of the perilous crisis of the country. He made such an appointment, and the cordiality and earnestness with which it was observed throughout the loyal states was without precedent in our previous history.

There were numerous other measures in the discussion of which Mr. Frelinghuysen took a prominent part, such as the Pension Bill, the President's Protest, the "Force Bill," the Removal of the Government Deposits from the Bank of the United States, the Compromise Tariff, etc.; but it would needlessly swell the size of the volume to enter into the details of these questions, or make extracts from the reported speeches of Mr. Frelinghuysen.

The general impression made by him on his senatorial colleagues is well expressed in the words of two of the most distinguished of their number, DANIEL WEBSTER and HENRY CLAY.

Mr. Webster, at a meeting held in Baltimore to ratify the Whig nominations in 1844, expressed himself thus:

> "With regard to the second great office in this country, it is only necessary to say that, from among several gentlemen, all of them my friends, and to scarcely one of them could a preference be given as respects their integrity and their talents—from among them a selection has been made than which a wiser and better could not have been made. There is not a man of purer character, of more sober temperament, of more accessible manners, and of more firm, unbending, uncompromising Whig principles, than Theodore Frelinghuysen; and not only is he all this, but such is the ease of his manners, such the spotless purity of his life, such the sterling attributes of his character, that he has the regard, the fervent attachment, and the enduring love of all who know him."

At the same time Mr. Clay gave his views in a private letter to the late John P. Jackson, Esq., of Newark, N. J., which was never printed until after Mr. Frelinghuysen's death. It is as follows:

"Ashland, June 4th, 1844.

"DEAR SIR,—I received your letter of the 28th ultimo, and am very happy to learn that the Whig nominations at Baltimore have been received with so much enthusiasm in New Jersey. While I share in the common regret, among Whigs, that so many good and true men, who had high and just pretensions for the office of Vice-President, were necessarily put aside, nothing could be more agreeable and gratifying to me than the association of Mr. Frelinghuysen's name with my own. I have long and intimately known that gentleman; and no man stands higher in my estimation as a pure, upright, and patriotic citizen. I served with him, with great pleasure, in the Senate of the United States, and shall never forget the memorable session of 1833–34. He always seemed self-poised, and bore himself uniformly with great ability and dignity. There was a vein of benignity and piety running through all his conduct and speeches which it was refreshing and delightful to contemplate.

"Such, my dear sir, is briefly my opinion of this most worthy and excellent man.

"I am, with great respect, your friend and obedient servant, H. CLAY.

"John P. Jackson, Esq."

Both of these eminent men were of the same party as the man whom they eulogize. But political opponents bore the same testimony. General Jackson, who could hardly conceive that there was any patriotism in those who opposed what he considered the true policy of the country, never questioned the integrity of Mr. Frelinghuysen. He said that the senator from New Jersey always meant well, but was misguided by the political leaders with whom he was associated.

When the Whig nominations were made in 1844, Messrs. Lumpkin, Dawson, and other leading men from

Georgia came to New York, and, visiting Mr. Frelinghuysen, expressed a very warm interest in the success of the ticket, on his personal account as well as on other grounds. He inquired how he was to reconcile this with the opposition he had incurred in their state by his course on the bill for the removal of the Indians. The answer was, that experience had satisfied them that he was right and they were wrong in that matter.

To these testimonials the author has much pleasure in being able to add that of a great living statesman, scholar, and patriot, the Hon. EDWARD EVERETT, as contained in the following letter:

"Boston, July 8, 1862.

"MY DEAR SIR,—I much regret that my personal recollections of Mr. Frelinghuysen are not such as to enable me to contribute any thing of importance to your proposed Memoir. He entered the Senate not long after I became a member of the House of Representatives; but, being without previous acquaintance, and both of us much occupied with our respective duties, I saw less of him than I could have wished. The distances are so great in Washington that there is little intercourse out of the committee-room, except among members who happen to live in the same part of the city. This remark does not, of course, apply to the active electioneering politicians, who, at Washington as elsewhere, possess a busy ubiquity; but neither Mr. Frelinghuysen nor myself were of that class.

"What I know of him is principally through public channels of information. He brought to Washington a brilliant reputation as a public speaker, with a character for unimpeachable personal integrity. His reputation and character were fully sustained in the Senate of the United States. He took but little part in the current daily business of the Senate; none in the fierce personalities sometimes exchanged between great political leaders; but upon a few prominent questions he spoke with great ability and effect. There was a classical finish in his language, and a certain sedate fervor, if I may so call it, in his language, which commanded the attention of his audience to a degree seldom surpassed. As he spoke but rarely, he was always listened to with deference, and soon took rank with the foremost members of the body, at a time when the Senate of the United States contained some of the brightest names in our political history.

"Mr. Frelinghuysen took an active part in opposition to that stupendous iniquity, the expulsion of the Indians from Georgia, and the division of their lands by lottery among the people of the state, in violation alike of the dictates of justice and humanity, and of the faith of seventeen treaties negotiated with them as an independent race. Having myself, to the best of my ability, opposed this scandalous measure in the other house of Congress, I took the greater interest in Mr. Frelinghuysen's efforts in the same cause.

"I have alluded to Mr. Frelinghuysen's unimpeached integrity. It was not, I fear, so great a distinction then, as now, to be above pecuniary corruption. The member of either house of Congress who, in those days, should have stipulated for a commission on a government contract, or had stooped to the mean brokerage of a cadetship at West Point or Annapolis, could never have held up his head among honest men again. Mr. Frelinghuysen would as soon have gone upon the highway as he would have been guilty of either of these infamies.

"Renewing the expressions of my regret that I can offer you nothing in greater detail, I remain, my dear sir, very truly and respectfully yours,

"EDWARD EVERETT."

CHAPTER V.

CHANCELLOR OF THE UNIVERSITY OF THE CITY OF NEW YORK.

1839—1850.

Return to his Profession at Newark.—Call to the University of the City of New York.—Installation as Chancellor.—Success.—Public Usefulness.—Nomination for Vice-President.—Letter of Acceptance.—The Canvass.—Letter to Louisville.—Result, and the disappointment it then caused.—Not now to be regretted.—Mr. Frelinghuysen retires from the University.—Letter of Dr. Tayler Lewis.

WHEN Mr. Frelinghuysen's senatorial term expired in March, 1835, a gentleman of opposite political opinions was elected to succeed him, and he retired to private life, from which he did not again emerge, with one notable exception presently to be noticed. He was received with open arms by his fellow-citizens in Newark, and returned with undiminished ardor to the practice of his profession in the various courts of the state.

While thus engaged, he was informed in March, 1839, that he had been unanimously chosen by the Council of the University of the City of New York to become the chancellor of that institution. The University, although it was then in its first decade of years, had achieved a high position, and gave promise of eminent usefulness, but was encumbered with heavy pecuniary embarrassments. Mr. Frelinghuysen felt that this appointment deserved very serious consideration, and such he gave to it. There were several circumstances which induced him to regard it with favor. His large and exhausting practice made a heavy drain upon his health, and sorely tried his nervous system; he felt a growing repugnance to the sharp antagonisms incident to the legal profession; he was assured that his accession to the chancellorship would be attended with such an increase of subscriptions to the funds of the University as would free it from the burden of debt; and he anticipated from his residence in New York as an academic executive a wider field of direct and immediate usefulness than he occupied at the New Jersey bar. After due consultation and reflection, he accepted the appointment tendered by the Council of the University. His accession to the post was hailed with general joy by the Christian public, and especially by that large class of influential persons interested in the prosperity of this important seat of learning.

He soon removed his residence to New York, and on the 5th day of June was formally installed with appropriate ceremonies, General James Talmage, the President of the Council, delivering an address on behalf of that body, and the chancellor-elect following with an inaugural speech, in which he indicated with great clearness and force his views upon the important subject of collegiate education. He at once entered upon his academic duties with great energy, and soon had the satisfaction of seeing the institution relieved of a large portion of the indebtedness by which it had, from the beginning, been embarrassed, while an increasing number of students came to avail themselves of its privileges. He gave to the University not only the prestige of his name and character as an eminent Christian statesman, but also the best efforts of his mind and heart, both in his professorial chair and in the general superintendence which devolved upon him as the head of the faculty. It was no perfunctory service which he rendered, but the conscientious devotion of all his powers to the interests of the institution and of the young men who thronged its marble halls. His influence upon the latter was of the happiest kind. His high character, his personal dignity, his indubitable integrity, his courtesy, his unaffected kindness and sympathy, gave to his instructions and counsels a force which was irresistible. The students revered and loved him. They could not doubt the sincerity of his desire for their welfare; they knew from his past career his competency to advise and direct, and they saw in his daily life a living illustration and exemplification of his own most cherished principles and oft-repeated inculcations.

But his usefulness while residing in New York was not confined to the walls of the University. The commercial metropolis of the nation was, as it still is, the chief seat and centre of the great religious and philanthropic associations, which reflect so much lustre upon our age. Of one or two of these Mr. Frelinghuysen was the president; of several he was a director or manager; of all he was a warm friend and advocate. And no small demands were made upon his time and thoughts in aiding the accomplishment of the designs for which they had been formed. Whether it was to contribute to funds, or to counsel in difficult matters, or to address a public meeting, he held himself in readiness to do what in him lay for the cause of God and of truth. Nor is there one of the national societies alluded to which can not recall signal services thus rendered by the Chancellor.

While thus engaged, he and many of his friends were surprised by his nomination as a candidate for the office of Vice-President of the United States, on the same ticket with Henry Clay, by the Whig National Convention assembled at Baltimore in May, 1844. There were some circumstances connected with this nomination which rendered it very complimentary and gratifying to Mr. Frelinghuysen. The Convention was held, it may be said, only for the purpose of selecting a candidate for this office, for no other name than Mr. Clay's was even thought of for the presidency; and when, as a matter of form, the resolution presenting him for the position was read in the Convention, it was scarcely found possible to proceed, the acclamations of the vast throng bursting forth with such enthusiasm and persistency at every mention of the great man's name that no formal vote could be taken. The entire proceedings in reference to Mr. Frelinghuysen's nomination were taken, from first to last, without the least solicitation or suggestion, direct or indirect, on his part. He had, indeed, withdrawn, as he supposed, finally from political life, nor had he any desire to re-enter upon that troubled arena. The balloting was of short duration, and the final result attained with unusual cordiality. He decidedly led the canvass from the first ballot; and although such eminent statesmen as John Davis, of

Massachusetts, Millard Fillmore, of New York, and John Sergeant, of Philadelphia, were proposed in competition, on the third ballot he received a majority of the whole number of votes, whereupon the friends of the other candidates withdrew their names, and gave a hearty adhesion to the choice thus indicated. The nomination, moreover, associated him with HENRY CLAY, whose views of public policy he had always approved, and with whom he had been on terms of intimate personal friendship for very many years.

He therefore, after thoughtful and prayerful consideration, accepted the position in a letter of which the following is the text:

"New York, May 6, 1844.

"HON. WILLIAM ELLSWORTH, Chairman, etc.:

"DEAR SIR,—I have duly received your favor informing me of my nomination to the office of Vice-President of the United States, by the Whig Convention of delegates, at Baltimore, on the 1st instant. To be thus distinguished by such a body of exalted and patriotic Whigs is an honor that I most sensibly feel. In accepting it, I can only promise the best efforts in some humble measure to justify the high confidence reposed in me. And I trust, in the goodness of Divine Providence, so to guide my steps that I may not disappoint the expectations of my friends or do harm to the interests of our country.

"Your obedient friend and servant,

"THEO. FRELINGHUYSEN."

The election was hotly contested, perhaps as much so as any which has ever been held, and very great excitement prevailed throughout the country. The Democratic party naturally wished to regain the power of which they had been deprived in 1840, and the

Whigs were anxious to secure anew a victory, the rightful fruits of which, when won at the preceding election, they deemed themselves to have lost through the early death of President Harrison. The tariff, the currency, the use of the public lands, and, above all, the annexation of Texas, were questions which entered into the contest and were very warmly discussed. Mr. Frelinghuysen, however, continued in the quiet discharge of his academic duties, and took a very small part in the canvass. On two occasions he made public addresses: one when the meeting assembled in New York to ratify the nominations adjourned to his residence and called him out; the other some months subsequently, when a meeting held in Somerville, while he was visiting his relatives in that village, made a similar call upon him, and, being composed mainly of his old friends and neighbors, could not be refused. The only letters which he wrote upon political matters were two, the first of which was addressed to the Whig State Convention at Trenton in May, and the second to a large mass meeting gathered at Millstone, near the spot where he was born. In the course of the summer two gentlemen of Louisville, Ky., propounded some inquiries, the tenor of which may be gathered from his answer here subjoined:

"New York, July 5, 1844.

"GENTLEMEN,—Your favor is duly received and its inquiries are cheerfully answered. Since my residence in this city as Chancellor of the University, I have felt it to be my duty to its interest to retire very much from party politics, excepting so far as the sacred right of suffrage was concerned. I have never spoken but in decided condemnation of the mob scenes of violence and blood in Philadelphia, and have had nothing to do with the matter of the division of the school funds between Catholics and Protestants in New York. Indeed, your inquiry is the first intimation I have had that such a subject has been agitated. Allow me to say, gentlemen, in the general, that I cherish the principles of our Constitution, which allow full freedom of conscience and forbid all religious tests and establishments, as sacred and fundamental.

"Yours very respectfully,

"THEO. FRELINGHUYSEN.

"Messrs. Henry Pirtle and Geo. D. Prentice."

It has always been customary among the more unscrupulous politicians of our country to subject the personal and private character of any candidate for high official position to a very thorough scrutiny, in the hope of finding some point of successful attack. Mr. Frelinghuysen did not escape the common lot, but he could defy the most unsparing ordeal. There was nothing in all his career, from the earliest period, which needed to be defended, apologized for, or even explained. Nothing unbecoming a man, a lawyer, a legislator, a Christian, was ever attributed to him. The most heated partisan, the bitterest opposers of the ticket, with one voice acknowledged the stainless probity of the Whig candidate for the vice-presidency, whatever objection they might feel to his political principles.

The election, as is well known, resulted in the success of Messrs. Polk and Dallas, the candidates of the Democratic party. Mr. Frelinghuysen was but little disappointed at the result. Thoroughly convinced of the correctness of his political views, he would have been glad to become an active agent in carrying them out, especially as a coadjutor of Henry Clay, in whose ability, integrity, and patriotism he cherished an unshaken confidence to the end of his days. At the same time, such was his soundness of judgment, and such his accurate perception of the surges of popular opinion, that he never was very sanguine of success, and was therefore, in a measure, prepared for the ultimate issue. Even the night before the day which brought the determining news as to the course of New York, which state was then justly considered as turning the scale of the election, when his Whig friends, having received some favorable tidings, gathered before the University to congratulate him and themselves on the auspicious issue, he reminded them that it was too soon to rejoice, and besought them to await the complete returns.

When those returns came in the revulsion of feeling was tremendous. The mass of the Whig party were animated not only by a deep conviction of the importance of the principles which they held to the welfare of the country, but also by a strong personal attachment to their recognized leaders, especially to Mr. Clay, who was remarkable above all the great men whom this country ever produced for the degree in which he concentrated upon himself as a man the affections of those who shared in his views of public policy. Remembering the brilliant victory they had achieved at the preceding presidential election, they cherished confident hopes of success in the present struggle, scarcely allowing themselves to think of failure as a possible thing. Nor did they spare any pains to secure the fulfillment of their hopes, but labored with enthusiasm unto the last. When the result was announced, it fell like a thunderbolt out of a cloudless sky. Stalwart men were moved even to tears, and multitudes mourned over the event as if it had been the loss of some dear relative. This was particularly true of many who desired Mr. Frelinghuysen's election, not only because of their personal esteem for him, but also and especially because they desired to see a high official station adorned by a man who, to all other qualifications, added that of an eminently consistent Christian character.

These regrets, however, have long since disappeared, not simply through the mellowing influence of time, but from a clearer apprehension of the connection of events. Painful and mysterious as was the defeat of Clay and Frelinghuysen to their friends at the time and for years afterward, subsequent events have lifted the veil, and enabled calm, practical observers to see the finger of Eternal Providence in that mortifying discomfiture. The question upon which the contest really turned was the annexation of Texas—whether this large province of Mexico, wrested by its inhabitants from the mother country, should be added to the United States at the risk of a war with Mexico, and of introducing under the protection of the federal Constitution an immense region to be filled with a slaveholding population. The question was decided in the affirmative, the North being doubtless led by the lust of territorial aggrandizement, which is always dominant in young and growing nations, and the South by the hope of securing additional strength for the domestic institution which they had come to consider the basis of their civilization. At first both seemed to be gratified. New Mexico and California, as well as Texas, contributed to swell the imperial dimensions of the American republic, and the South felt that the additional strength they had gained in the Senate was a new security for their cherished interest. But soon California knocked at the door of the Union for admission as a state, and the question at once arose whether she should be admitted with or without a provision against involuntary servitude. A fierce conflict was finally settled by compromise. But the fire still slumbered under the ashes, and a few years later the same question arose in reference to Kansas and all the other Territories. The issues became more clearly joined and more virulently contested, until at last ambitious leaders succeeded in inducing ten states of the Union to secede from the government and set up a new republic, the corner-stone of which was publicly declared by its vice-president to be the perpetuation of African slavery. The war which then ensued is still pending, and it is quite too early for the shrewdest observer to predict the final issue. But all unbiased men agree that one result is certain in any event, and that is the overthrow of African slavery. Its days on this continent are numbered. The mere friction of the war, if there were nothing else, must insure its disappearance. Its own friends have wrought its ruin. Had they been content to rely upon existing guarantees of safety, it might have continued indefinitely. But, dissatisfied with these, they insisted upon other measures, and hence has followed what we now see. The first one of these measures was the annexation of Texas; and they who once mourned that event as a great political disaster, may now admire the Providence of God, which, in his inscrutable wisdom, made that the initial step of a series by which the nation was to be gradually but surely led forever out of the land of Egypt, out of the house of bondage.

After the campaign, Mr. Frelinghuysen continued in the discharge of his academic duties, but not altogether with the same comfort as formerly. A severe attack of acute illness not only laid him wholly aside for several weeks, but left him in an enfeebled condition, with disordered nerves. Under these circumstances, the abundant hospitality which his situation, as well as his nature, prompted him to exercise, became somewhat of a trial. The finances of the University too, being hampered by the withdrawal, first of a part, then of the whole of the grant annually made by the state, imposed an embarrassing burden upon the head of the institution. Mr. Frelinghuysen began now to feel something of the weight of advancing years, and the thought more than once occurred to his mind that it would be better for him to seek some other position, where the duties would not be so arduous, and where he could escape the excitements and engagements of the metropolis. In the kind providence of God, such a relief was opened to him, without any effort on his part, by an invitation from a literary institution in a neighboring city, which, while withdrawing him from the noise and bustle of New York, yet offered a continuation of what he always felt to be the useful and congenial work of directing the studies and moulding the characters of young men in the course of a liberal education. He therefore resigned his position as Chancellor in the summer of the year 1850.

From one of the most distinguished of his associates in the literary faculty of the University, Professor Tayler Lewis, LL.D., the author has had the pleasure of receiving the following letter, containing some account of his career in this trying and responsible position:

"Union College, Schenectady, September 24, 1862.

"MY DEAR SIR,—I can best give you my thoughts of Mr. Frelinghuysen by relating three phases of my experience in respect to him. It is now more than thirty years since he first excited my admiration by his course in the Senate of the United States, especially his speeches on the important questions that then arose respecting the Cherokee Indians, and the obedience due to the decisions of the United States courts. It is now known that the party since so clamorous about the soundness of judicial decisions was then in a state of direct hostility to the decrees of Marshall and Story—not merely, while obeying them, seeking their reversal by constitutional means, which is the political right, and may be the duty of the most conservative citizen, but bidding them direct defiance, encouraging the President in his refusal to execute their issued process—in other words, nullifying them both in the letter and the spirit. In his speeches on these occasions, Mr. Frelinghuysen showed a knowledge of constitutional law equal to that of Webster; but that was the least part of their merit. The Democratic party had enlisted on its side the irreligious element in our land, and it was in rebuking this that the senator from New Jersey rose above all others in that deeply interesting debate. Here was something new in that Senate. Christianity had been often mentioned with approbation, but here was an exhibition of its very spirit and powers. There was something in the tone of those speeches, able as they were in other respects, which showed that religion was there in their midst—hearty, fervent, evangelical religion—religion as a higher law, first and before all things, instead of that mere political patronizing of Christianity which is so common among our public men. It is very easy to put forth the usual commonplaces about 'our holy religion,' and the value of Christian institutions, and the 'importance of morality and virtue as the foundation of all good government.' Men may say this, men have said it, and are fond of saying it, who are not religious, who are not even moral. It is always safe to talk in this way; it is sometimes a very popular course; it gains favor on the one side, while, by throwing in a word now and then about bigotry, and the 'preservation of our religious liberties' now so much imperiled, it is careful to lose no ground on the other. This patronizing style assumes too, at times, a profound and philosophical look; it affects to go below the surface of things; there seems presented a statesmanlike, senatorial view of religion, with which we are wonderfully pleased as coming from such a source; and yet, after all, there is no heart in it, and even the knowledge it displays, though magnified from its position, is often less than many a teacher imparts, and many a child acquires, in the Sabbath-school room.

"No one, however, would thus judge of Mr. Frelinghuysen. The living know the living. 'The spiritual man is judged of no one (who is not spiritual), while he himself judgeth all things.' But, aside from this, even the worldly and the irreligious have a faculty for detecting the genuine here. They feel how much it differs from that which is either wholly false, or but a passing sentimental emotion. Mr. Frelinghuysen's soul was in these speeches. He was pleading for Christ his Savior. The religious aspects of the questions were to him the main aspects; the social and political had their value in subordination. Justice, humanity, national faith—ever to be esteemed the stronger when pledged to the weak—the forms of treaties, the substantial truth of covenants—all these were treated, not merely in their humanitarian economies, but as strictly religious—as having their sanctions from their never-to-be-sundered connection with the invisible and the eternal.

"It was, indeed, a noble effort, characterized, too, by the highest eloquence of thought and language. The next thing I read of Mr. Frelinghuysen's was an address before one of the national religious societies in New York. It was a very different theatre, but the same man unchanged in thought and utterance. Here, too, the mere politician has, now and then, put forth his patronizing platitudes; but here was Mr. Frelinghuysen especially at home—more at home than in the Senate of the United States. Never did the union of those two characters, the statesman and the Christian, seem so perfect. The man who had enchained the attention of the highest political audience now pleads the cause of missions and of Bible distribution with the soul of a martyr. It was no mere talk about the political economies of religion, the 'patriotism of Christianity,' its statistical and commercial benefits; it was no gracious presentation of thanks on the part of the State for the Church's good conduct, and its excellent police aid in the preservation of order and property; it was no mere harangue on the physical or secular good of the Sabbath, and the duty of all respectable people to respect it on that account; it was no empty laudation of missions and missionaries as the pioneers of civilization—its subject was none of these, except as lying far below in the scale of subordination, but 'life, life, eternal life' for perishing men and a perishing world. Instead of such cold secularities, his whole soul was on fire with the intensest spiritualities of the Christian argument. The union of the two characters was delightful. It raised my admiration of the man to the highest pitch. I read with eagerness every thing that fell from his mouth on every occasion, secular or religious. And this may be called my first phase of experience.

"In the year 1839 Mr. Frelinghuysen was appointed Chancellor of the New York University. I had been connected with the institution a few months before. It need not be said how strong was the interest felt at the thought of being associated with such a man. Nor was the first meeting a disappointment. The personal appearance was noble, commanding, equal to any thing that had been imagined respecting it. The inaugural address was worthy of the speaker's high reputation. But when we entered upon the daily routine of college life and discipline, I must confess some change of feeling. This man, who, I thought, would fill me with awe and reverence, was found to have his humanities, and close contact sometimes brought them out unpleasantly. We had expected one who would take the lead commandingly, and under whose influence the institution would immediately take the highest rank. Such an expectation was, of course, unreasonable. Colleges are of slow growth. We ought to know that this would be the case in our own country, when we remember that the universities of the Old World are the production of centuries. True education can not be accelerated by outward forcing, or by calling to its patronage the highest influence of great names. There was no disappointment in regard to his public efforts; but it is to his private intercourse with us that I have now chiefly reference. This was, indeed, of the most pleasant kind, viewed merely in its social aspects. Never shall I forget the beautiful harmony of our faculty meetings as they were weekly held for nearly eleven years. We were of various denominations in religion. There was Dr. C. F. Henry, a profound thinker, an admirable writer, a noble man in every way, but a churchman of towering altitude, even as his eloquent appeals now place him in the front rank for loyalty and patriotism. There was Professor Johnson, a man of the most precise New Englandism, but whose Latin and German scholarship are unsurpassed in our country. There was Professor Draper, of European celebrity; Nordheimer, the distinguished Orientalist, and 'an Israelite truly in whom there was no guile.' There was Presbyterian, Episcopalian, Dutch Reformed, Unitarian, Free-thinking (I use the term in no offensive sense), Old School, and New School; but in our weekly meetings there was the most perfect brotherhood of thought and action. Mr. Frelinghuysen presided so kindly, so genially, that there could be nothing sectional or sectarian in his presence. We all had our isms in theology, in philosophy, and even in pedagogy; but in our stated college associations there was the most perfect catholicity. Though formal to some extent in mode, they were wholly informal and social in their spirit. Mr. Frelinghuysen was fond of treating things in a familiar, conversational manner, though no one could be more impressively dignified when the occasion demanded it. He had a touch of humor, quite a fund of anecdote, and, in a word, that easy sociability, such a well-known trait of gentlemen of the bar, and which Mr. Frelinghuysen brought with him from his long practice in the courts of New Jersey. All this was very pleasant, but still not in exact accordance with my high expectations. It was not the commanding character imagination had pictured. I would not retract the word already used; it was, indeed, a fault in this great man and this pure Christian that he had a way of so constantly deferring to others. It was the carrying to excess the apostle's precept: 'Let each man esteem others better than himself.' There were times when he would rise, and we saw before us the man who had commanded the United States Senate; but he was not now with politicians and corrupt party schemers, and amid scenes that would arouse the eloquence of his indignant rebuke. Surrounded by a small company of literary men and teachers, he sat in our midst as *primus inter pares*, or, rather, as one who sought to learn from others rather than command, and who would substitute their professional knowledge for his own wide and catholic experience. In other things, too, there was that about him which disturbed the too enthusiastic prejudgment. How strong must this man be in Christian faith, I used to think! What a privilege to lean upon his steady arm, to have the benefit of his Christian counsels and Christian experience! Here was, at first, what must be acknowledged as a disappointment. He was fond of religious conversation, and frequently drew one or the other of us into it in the most familiar way. Often was it my privilege thus to converse with him, sometimes in his own scholastic apartment, sometimes sharing his long daily walk, and, on a few occasions, in his chamber of sickness. He imparted strength, but not in the way I had expected. He was an admirable illustration of the apostle's paradox: 'When he was weak, then was he strong;' and 'out of his weakness' were made strong those who enjoyed the privilege of this blessed Christian intercommunion. Mr. Frelinghuysen had difficulties in his religious life, in his personal experience, and he would freely tell them. His whole soul was in the pilgrimage to the New Jerusalem. Still, he was but a '*seeker of salvation*.' This was ever the form of his thought and the spirit of his language. He hardly dared to take to himself any other title. Of course, there was no allusion to the services he had rendered the cause of

Christ. He did not think of them. His mind was ever upon his demerits, his deficiencies. It was no mock humility. The prayer of the publican was ever in his heart and often upon his lips. He was continually asking others about their experience, their difficulties, the comforts and grounds of their faith. This was not for the obtaining comparative confidence, but because his true Christian soul loved thus to commune with others whom he esteemed as Christians, and to regard himself and them as a company of earth-weary, heaven-seeking pilgrims, marching hand in hand, and mutually holding each other up through 'sloughs of despondency' and over 'hills of difficulty,' and in evil-haunted vales of temptation, until at last the heavenly land is reached by all, the weakest as well as the strongest in the band.

"I have endeavored to give you my exact impression of the man,—an impression I would not now exchange for any former ideal of the statesman. The habit I have mentioned of his continual deference to others was a hinderance to his literary success; it prevented his having that commanding influence he might have exercised, and should have exercised on the faculty and the college, and therefore it was that the first contact with these failures of character, if I may so call them, produced disappointment. He fell in reverence, while he rose in love; and this is what I may call my second phase of experience respecting him.

"Still, the man of power was there; the man of eloquence; the believing soul, large and loving. As a Christian, he must, of course, be humble, but I had not looked for such a palpable exhibition of it. This feeling of disappointment was not of long continuance. It seems now, however, that it was necessary to a just appreciation of just such a character. I should never have known how true a Christian Mr. Frelinghuysen was had there been nothing but the first knowledge of him as a senator and a Christian orator. It was necessary to see how very human he was in some respects, if we would see the beauty of that divine life which shone through this humanity so conscious of its weakness, so ever seeking help even from others who needed for themselves his wiser and stronger guidance. This was the *third* phase of the writer's experience respecting him. Mr. Frelinghuysen was a great man, a statesman, an orator seldom surpassed at the bar or in the Senate. He was a Christian man, hearty and true. He was a very humble Christian man, and in this lies the very essence of his greatness and his strength.

"Yours truly, TAYLER LEWIS.

"Rev. T. W. Chambers, D.D."

CHAPTER VI.

PRESIDENT OF RUTGERS COLLEGE.

1850—1862.

Early History of the Institution.—Inauguration of Mr. Frelinghuysen.—Growth of the College.—The President's Diligence.—Letter from Dr. Crosby.—Death of the first Mrs. Frelinghuysen.—Baccalaureate Addresses.—Useful to the End.—Death.—Funeral.

THE old literary institution at New Brunswick was established by a charter from George III. in 1770, and was styled Queen's College. This charter was obtained and the college founded by the prayers and efforts of the earlier Frelinghuysens and Hardenberghs. It passed through many severe trials, and sometimes suffered a total suspension of service; but its friends persevered, and had the pleasure of seeing a complete and permanent revival of the institution in the year 1825, under the name of Rutgers College, when it entered upon a career of growing prosperity and usefulness. The first president of the revived institution was the learned and eloquent Dr. Milledoler, who at the same time held the chair of theology in the Theological Seminary of the Reformed Protestant Dutch Church. Dr. Milledoler withdrew from his position in the year 1841, and was succeeded by the Hon. A. B. Hasbrouck, LL.D., of Kingston, N. Y., who had achieved distinction at the bar and in Congress, and who, for a period of ten years, presided over the college with great dignity, efficiency, and success.

At the end of that time domestic circumstances induced Dr. Hasbrouck to resign his office and devote himself to his private affairs.

In looking for a gentleman to fill the responsible position thus vacated, it was natural for the trustees to turn their eyes toward the honored son of New Jersey, whose heart still beat so warmly toward his native state, whose earliest associations connected him with the institution at New Brunswick, and whose personal gifts and attainments had now been matured by many years' experience in academic instruction and government. They unanimously invited him to become their president. After seeking, according to his invariable custom, the Divine direction, he cheerfully accepted the appointment, and removed his residence to New Brunswick—the last remove he was destined to make on earth. At the annual Commencement, July 24th, 1850, he was formally inducted into office. His Excellency Daniel Haines, the governor of the state, acting in behalf of the Board of Trustees, introduced the president elect to the audience in a short and graceful speech. The venerable Dr. Cannon, the oldest member of the board, then welcomed the new officer to his position with fitly chosen words, which, spoken with the fire of youth, thrilled through the assembly, and gave just expression to the enthusiastic cordiality with which the accession of Mr. Frelinghuysen was regarded by the authorities and friends of the college. The exercises were closed by an inaugural address of the president, abounding with pertinent and instructive suggestions respecting the true aims of a collegiate education. The concluding paragraphs, containing a touching reference to his own feelings in view of his return to the scenes of his childhood, are here extracted:

"If I may be allowed a single personal allusion, it is matter of grateful interest that the revolutions of time have conducted my footsteps, in the evening of life's pilgrimage, to the cherished spot where its morning began; and that, notwithstanding the desolations of the past—and they are many and sad—a benignant Providence permits to-day the recognition of many living names whose early recollections harmonize with my own.

"And now may He whose blessing maketh rich, grant his constant favor that our college may continue to send forth a hallowed influence; that its sons may illustrate its fame by the light of a pure and upright example; and that, whatever else may befall them in a world of affliction and change, no one of them may be permitted, by the perversion of his powers, to impair the foundations of truth, or give countenance to the enemies of virtue."

Here Mr. Frelinghuysen continued to the end of his life, surrounded by the friends of his youth, and happy in the service of an institution endeared to him by precious ancestral recollections. The favorable auspices under which he began his administration of its affairs were fully confirmed by the result. The old friends of the college engaged with fresh zeal in its behalf, and many new ones were enlisted. The number of the students began at once to increase. The endowment funds were considerably augmented. The course of study became, in time, greatly enlarged. Valuable additions were made to the corps of professors. Pecuniary embarrassments were removed; philosophical and other apparatus was abundantly provided; and the institution, always respectable for its age, and history, and character, attained a still higher reputation at home and abroad.

Mr. Frelinghuysen's connection with it was far from being nominal. Notwithstanding his approach to the allotted term of human life, he entered into his work with conscientious fidelity and energy, carefully elaborating the special duties of his own department, and conducting the discipline of the institution with a gentleness, firmness, and impartiality which secured the happiest results. To the customary care of the mental progress of the students he added a parental concern for their moral and Christian advancement, for which many will have reason to thank him as long as they live. On this point the author is happy to present the following testimony of one who had rare opportunities of forming an intelligent opinion, the Rev. Dr. Crosby:

"New Brunswick, August 14, 1862.

"REV. TALBOT W. CHAMBERS, D.D.:

"DEAR SIR,—It gives me great pleasure to comply with your request, and record my impressions of the late Mr. Frelinghuysen in his official capacity as the presiding officer of a college, not only from my desire to contribute what I can to the general good in the exhibition of so bright a character, but also from a grateful sense of the benefits which I personally received from the official influence of the illustrious deceased. I had the good fortune to witness Mr. Frelinghuysen's administration of a college presidency from two distinct points of view, having been four years a student at the University of New York when he occupied its chancellorship, and having, fifteen years thereafter, become his colleague in the faculty of Rutgers College, where I enjoyed his intimacy three years until his death. Students uniformly loved and respected him. They knew he was their fast friend, and they also knew that his conduct was actuated by the purest and most exalted motives. Such a knowledge, of course, was accompanied by the fullest confidence, so that, however disappointed a student was made by the chancellor's denial of his request, the disappointment was never followed by a revengeful or rebellious spirit. I well recollect how, at my first admission to the Freshman class, I applied to Mr. Frelinghuysen for a dispensation from the exercise of public speaking. I promised double exertion in every other department if I could only be excused in this one. His reply was gentle in tone and manner, and yet a firm denial. He used the affectionate phrase 'my son,' and assured me that no better opportunity would ever be offered me for the removal of my diffidence, and for the attainment of ease and readiness in oratory. I ventured once after this to renew my request, and received the same answer, with a similar manifestation of regard for my welfare. Instead of repelling me, these interviews won my heart, and I felt ready from that time to meet his 'my son' with a responsive 'my father.' Four years after, when I delivered an oration in the University that possessed some merit, the chancellor came down from the rostra and greeted me warmly, saying, with clear memory of the interviews at my entrance upon college life, 'Are you not satisfied now that I did right in refusing you exemption from oratorical duties when you were a Freshman?'

"The respect which the students entertained for Mr. Frelinghuysen was always a guarantee of orderly behavior and attention in his class-room, so that severity was never needed, and he was relieved from the use of methods from which his mild nature would have shrunk, while their love for the chancellor often assumed the form of enthusiasm which gave vigor even to sluggish minds.

"In Rutgers College I noticed these same marks of Mr. Frelinghuysen's relations to the students, although they were somewhat modified by his advanced age. His intercourse with his colleagues was marked by modesty, simplicity, and gentleness, and whenever he differed with them in the details of discipline, it was easy to see that the kindly sympathies of his heart lay at the bottom of the difference.

Conspicuously, through all the attributes of his character, shone Mr. Frelinghuysen's Christian faith and devotion. No one could spend a day in his company without being impressed with his zeal in the Master's service. His colleagues saw that the love of Christ was the constraining principle of his life, and it was this consistent Christian example which rendered his influence over the young so precious, and to which an army of men of young and middle years now gratefully yield their testimony, as they feel that his character and counsels saved them from ruin, and guided their feet in the path of uprightness and Christian truth.

He took especial delight in addressing the four classes on Saturday mornings, founding his earnest exhortations to repentance and a godly life on some passage of Scripture read at the opening service of the chapel, and on the Sabbath the students were again assembled before him in the chapel to receive a systematic Biblical instruction.

To his view the student was, first of all, a sinner requiring the atoning blood of Jesus, and all learning and discipline were subordinate, and to be made subsidiary, to the great end of spiritual conversion and renewal. Education was a training of the *whole man*, and thus the fear of the Lord was recognized as the beginning of wisdom. Oh that all our instructors felt this truth as did the distinguished saint whose death has put the whole Church in mourning. His legacy to us all is the example of a consecrated life. As we honor his memory, may we follow that example.

"Yours faithfully, HOWARD CROSBY."

While thus assiduously and successfully engaged in the appropriate duties of his office, his home was desolated and his heart bereaved in April, 1854, by the death of Mrs. Frelinghuysen. "From an early period of her life she was an exemplary member of the Church of Christ, and enjoyed beyond most the comforts resulting from a firm trust in God and hope in his mercy through his beloved Son. She retained her consciousness until near the close of life, and anticipated death with the composure and peace which nothing but faith in the glorious Gospel of the grace of God can inspire." Three years afterward Mr. Frelinghuysen repaired the breach in his domestic relations by a union with Miss Harriet Pompelly, of Owego, N.Y., a lady of great intellectual and moral worth, who, after ministering largely to his comfort and usefulness during the closing years of his life, still survives to bear his name and cherish the memory of his many virtues.

In New Brunswick, as in New York, Mr. Frelinghuysen always delivered, at the annual Commencement, a baccalaureate address to the members of the graduating class. These addresses bore the stamp of their author. Nothing was said for display or sensational effect, but all for personal and practical use. Such themes were chosen as pertained most directly to the interesting situation of the young men, and weighty thoughts and wise counsels were urged with the affectionate earnestness becoming his years and position. These addresses were never long, much less wearisome. Their author studied a compact brevity, and a simplicity of statement and illustration which enchained and rewarded attention. His suggestions covered a wide range, extending to all the relations of his hearers, personal and social, for time and eternity. In times of political excitement he did not fail to inculcate a pure and lofty patriotism. Shunning all mere partisanship, he gave the whole weight of his experience and character to uphold the Constitution and the Union, recurring to the character of their founders, and pleading with a pathetic earnestness that the children should cherish with ceaseless vigilance this honored legacy of their fathers. He delighted to invoke afresh, as he said in 1855, "the fraternal feelings that formed the American Constitution, which has so long and so illustriously shown how much of human wisdom and forecast, and how much more of divine benignity, crowned this first great experiment of a free and self-governed people. May it be perpetual! May no rash hand mar its glory or dare disturb its foundations!"

The last years of Mr. Frelinghuysen's life, spent in New Brunswick, were attended with better health than he had enjoyed in New York. And he was, in consequence, even more active than before in rendering occasional services to such benevolent enterprises as made a claim upon him for counsel or for public addresses. Usefulness was a passion with him, and there was no sphere, however humble, which he was not ready to fill when called upon. It was a matter of thankful joy to him and to his friends that, after so long a period spent in exhausting cares and duties, he was still able faithfully to perform the regular duties of his office, and, at the same time, in other ways actively contribute to the general good of his fellow-men. Yet, in the case of one who had lived three quarters of a century, this could not be expected to continue very long. In this view the occurrence of his death was marked by a providential fitness. He had filled the probable measure of his activity. He had served his generation faithfully by the will of God. He had left his enduring mark upon all the stations in which he had been placed. He had illustrated all the various phases of Christian character in the scenes of active life. It was well that he should pass with small delay from his work to his reward; that there should be no lengthened period of enforced seclusion and gradual decay between his usual efficiency and his final rest; but that, when called away in the fullness of his days, honors, and labors, it might be said of him as of the old Roman, "Felix, non vitæ tantùm claritate, sed etiam opportunitate mortis."

He died on the 12th of April, 1861, after an illness slightly protracted, the details of which will be furnished in a subsequent chapter. His death, although not unexpected, produced a deep sensation throughout the community. Resolutions complimentary to his memory were passed by the Faculty of the College, the Council of the University of the city of New York, the Bar of Essex County, and various other bodies with which he had been connected; and his funeral, on the fourth day following his decease, was attended by a large concourse of persons from different parts of his own state, and also from New York and Pennsylvania. Brief and appropriate services were held at his recent residence, the Rev. Professor Woodbridge and the Rev. Dr. H. N. Wilson officiating. Afterward a long procession proceeded to the First Reformed Protestant Dutch Church, following the bier, the pall of which was borne by the governor, chancellor, and chief justice of the state, the president of the College of New Jersey, and twelve other distinguished gentlemen. The flags of the city were at half-mast, the bells of the churches were tolled, and the places of business along the route to the church were closed; every possible sign of respect and grief was shown by his fellow-citizens. The services in the church were opened by the Rev. Dr. J. Few Smith, of Newark, with the announcement of Wesley's beautiful hymn, "Jesus, lover of my soul," etc., and the reading of the fifteenth chapter of the First Epistle to the Corinthians. The Rev. Dr. Hodge, of Princeton, the friend of Mr. Frelinghuysen from boyhood, followed in an earnest, humble, simple, and impressive prayer. A carefully prepared and eloquent minute, adopted by the trustees of the college in reference to the life and character of the deceased, was read by their secretary, the Rev. Dr. T. C. Strong, of New York. The address of the occasion was pronounced by the venerable Dr. De Witt, of the Collegiate Church, New York, who, in fitly-chosen words, and with a voice and manner fraught with emotion, portrayed something of the life and character of his departed friend, and gave appropriate utterance to the feelings which animated the whole of the vast assembly. The Rev. Professor Campbell closed the services in the church, after which the remains were removed to the adjoining grounds, where already so many of the former presidents and professors of the institutions at New Brunswick lie sleeping in Jesus. Here the Rev. Dr. Neville, of Newark, N. J., read a portion of the funeral service of the Protestant Episcopal Church, and then, beneath the lingering rays of the setting sun, all that was mortal of Theodore Frelinghuysen was committed to the tomb.

CHAPTER VII.

PERSONAL TRAITS AND HABITS.

His Person.—Social and Domestic Habits.—Hospitality.—Popularity.—Mental Traits: Insight, Judgment, Imagination.—Reading.—Style.—Speeches.—Eloquence.—Instances.—Reminiscence of Dr. Magie.

MR. FRELINGHUYSEN was a man a little under six feet in height, with a sinewy and well-proportioned frame. In time the weight of years and the inroads of disease somewhat bent his erect form and lessened his flesh. A broad expansive forehead towered over a pair of eyes which, soft and dreamy in repose, when he was aroused gleamed and flashed with strange power. The lines of his mouth and chin gave a tone of decision and firmness to his habitual expression, which, however, when he was conversing with friends, gave way to a very fascinating smile. His whole appearance, when in the flush of early manhood, was of a commanding yet attractive character.

In natural disposition Mr. Frelinghuysen was amiable and kind, with a marked tendency to mirth. The old men in Somerset, N. J., who knew him when they all were boys together, concur in describing him as a lively, pleasant companion, full of sport, ready to give and take a sharp jest, and a general favorite in the community. The same traits marked him in maturer years. Even when most burdened with cares and responsibilities, he knew how *desipere in loco*. He enjoyed society greatly. The company of congenial friends was his best earthly relief from continued and exhausting labors. He entered without reserve into the spirit of the occasion. Never forgetting, even for a moment, what was becoming to his own character and station, he yet could so adapt himself to those who were around him that stiffness and formality vanished, the timid became emboldened, and the young found themselves quite at their ease. Although not a professed wit, he had a keen sense of the ludicrous, and not unfrequently enlivened conversation with sparkling turns of thought. Thus, on one occasion, many years ago, a lawyer who was notorious for pecuniary shifts drove a very handsome equipage to the Somerset courts, and, as he was displaying his carriage and horses, challenged Mr. Frelinghuysen to tell what he gave for them. "Oh! that is not hard to say," was the reply; "I have no doubt you gave your *note* for them." He had great skill and tact in narration and recital, seizing at once the salient points of the story, and stating them with few and expressive words. His conversational resources were large and varied. Having mingled much with men of every class, and having, by his professional and political associations, acquired great familiarity with human life in all its aspects, he was fitted to inform and interest others on almost any topic. A store of reflection, incident, anecdote, was ready at hand whenever needed. He knew how to listen as well as talk, and his sympathetic nature, habitual kindness, and unflagging courtesy left his companions nothing to desire.

His society was always, even in his advanced years,

pleasing to the young. Notwithstanding the pressure of cares and the increase of infirmities, he was to the end youthful in his feelings. This he used pleasantly to attribute to the fact that he had so many young nieces and nephews, whose society aroused his sympathies and precluded the rust of age. Nothing gave him more pleasure than to have them in his family, to see them around his board, and elicit their various traits of character and phases of feeling. He often spoke of the beneficence of Providence in giving "an undergrowth of affection" to the moral world as to the "natural forest," and quoted with great feeling some characteristic lines of Wordsworth on the subject. He felt, with the author of the Excursion, that while

> "The primal duties shine aloft like stars,
> The charities that soothe, and heal, and bless,
> Are scattered at the feet of man like flowers;
> The generous inclination, the just rule,
> Kind wishes, and good actions, and pure thoughts.
> No mystery is here; no special boon
> For high and not for low, for proudly graced
> And not for meek of heart."

Mr. Frelinghuysen's interest in the young extended even to little children. In his daily walks in New Brunswick, he could scarcely ever meet them in the street without pausing to look in their smiling faces and engage them in suitable conversation. Not unfrequently, when he saw them flattening their noses against the windows of a toy-shop in their eager desire to scan its treasures, the childless man would find out what they most coveted, and then gratify himself by gratifying them.

He was a whole man with a rich and generous nature. He enjoyed life, and wished others to have the same pleasure. Without degenerating into a mere animal, he appreciated a bountiful table, and, with the apostle, counted that "every creature of God is good, and nothing to be refused, if it be received with thanksgiving; for it is sanctified by the word of God and prayer." His hospitality was uniform, and profuse, and cordial. Caring nothing for fashion, opposed on principle to waste and extravagance, and attentive to the minor duties of domestic economy, he yet carried the largeness of his own soul into all his social arrangements. Nothing mean or petty was ever suffered to disfigure his household. It was conducted on the scale of one who could use this world without abusing it, and who, while duly prizing the unspeakable spiritual gifts of the Lord, could yet thankfully receive and heartily enjoy his temporal bounties.

The personal popularity of Mr. Frelinghuysen with many men in political life who had little or no sympathy with his religious opinions can scarcely be accounted for without supposing something in the inherent nature of the man, a sort of magnetism, such as existed so remarkably in his great friend and compatriot, Henry Clay, which grappled admirers as with hooks of steel, and held them by a willing but invincible bond. He had a chivalrous nature. He was the soul of honor. He could not do small things or mean things. There was in him a strange combination of fearless courage and melting tenderness. He was frank and open-hearted, yet always retaining his personal dignity. He was devoid of reserve or cunning. He never sought an end through indirection.

And he was thoroughly trustworthy. Truth and candor beamed in his countenance, and characterized every word and act. Rigid adherence to principle was unaccompanied by any narrowness of views, or sourness of disposition, or uncharitableness of opinions. His catholic sympathies took in men of all sections, and classes, and parties; and the nobleness of his nature commanded respect and won affection even among those who dissented most decidedly from his political or religious convictions. It was doubtless the rare blending of deep Christian humility and conscientiousness with a cheerful, buoyant, manly, generous, fearless deportment in all the varied phases of life, which attracted the good will of many who otherwise would have been repelled by the strictness of his course and character.

The prominent feature of his intellectual character was insight. He had a quick, keen perception. His mind moved rapidly. Naturally alert and agile, it was disciplined to strike right at the heart of things. He had no relish for cloudland. He could not endure mist and fog. His masculine understanding craved the solid truth, and this he commonly grasped as if by a sort of intuition. He reached his end by a much shorter process than the repeated and painful tentatives by which most men arrive at their conclusions. Nor was this because he looked only at the surface. He saw clearly and he saw far. His comprehensive glance took in all the relations of a subject at the same time. The connections of truth, the bearings of facts, the springs of action, the developments of character, were apprehended by him with peculiar facility and promptness. He was not often or easily blinded by mere appearances, but pierced at once to the reality. His friends and students were often amazed at the rapidity of his mental operations. He would take a law-book down from the shelf, and, turning a few leaves, would gain, in what appeared an incredibly short time, an accurate comprehension of its contents. The same was true in human character. At his first interview with a man, he would, without betraying the fact either by look or motion, thoroughly measure his visitor, and form an opinion which he rarely, if ever, found occasion to revise or alter.

This sharpness of perception was accompanied by a very sound and accurate judgment. He was cool, cautious, and dispassionate, not wedded to theories, not attracted by startling novelties, not misled by any love of paradox. He could discriminate nicely, could weigh differences, and feel the force of objections. In all matters, personal, social, professional, political, and ecclesiastical, it was his habit to consider both sides of a contested point, and then impartially adjust their respective claims. However intense his convictions on any subject, they never led him into extravagance or fanaticism. He never avoided one error only to fall into another of the opposite class. This exquisite balance of his mind appeared alike in arguments, in addresses, in counsel on different questions, and in the general conduct of his life. His "large, roundabout sense" gave to the advice often solicited from him a force like that of inspiration. He was singularly free from prejudice, precipitancy, and partiality, and seemed to know instinctively what to say and how to say it.

His imagination was lively and fertile, but it was not a primary power. It was not remarkably originative, but in an uncommon degree receptive, having a capacity of realizing the conceptions of others, and through them bodying forth the unseen. When exalted by the understanding and heated by the affections, it burst out with great force, but always as a servant, not master. Nor did it ever exhibit traces of any unusual or careful cultivation. In preparing for an audience, his attention was concentrated mainly on the matter and order of the thoughts; all the rest was left to the natural workings of his mind under the spur of the occasion. Its main use to him was in jury-trials, when by its aid he was able to bring up the past and the distant so as to make them live in the present before the men whose verdict he sought to gain. His interest in the grave themes he was accustomed to handle did not allow him to go out of the way for mere ornament. Whatever flights of fancy would contribute to the end he had in view were freely indulged, but nothing for purposes of display.

Although he never undertook to versify, he seems to have had a great deal of poetic sensibility. "This," as one of his near friends remarks, "caused him to feel an indescribable charm in all the scenes of rural life. To him there was a grace in the laborer's cheerful toil, the singing of birds, the hum of the insect world. A snow-storm gave him great pleasure; he stood gazing upon the whitening landscape with ever new delight."

His reading throughout life was careful and select rather than extensive. Gibbon among historians, and

Burke among philosophical and political writers, were his chief favorites. The leisure he enjoyed in the early years of his professional life was spent in familiarizing himself with the best English classics. Sir Roger de Coverly was a character he always greatly admired, and Dr. Johnson's Life and Works were subjects of abiding interest to his mind. Like every other man of taste, he highly appreciated Milton and Shakspeare, but his warmest affection was for Cowper, Montgomery, and Wordsworth. From "The Excursion" the inmates of his household often heard him read aloud with very great sensibility and pathos. For light literature he never had any taste. He could gain sufficient relaxation from the burden of professional toils by solid reading or in the social circle, without reducing his mental and moral stamina by a weak, washy flood of ephemeral fiction. This taste continued to the end. As his cares increased there was less opportunity for miscellaneous reading, but what time he could redeem for the purpose was carefully improved. He kept in some degree abreast of the literature of the age, yet habitually preferred to refresh his mind with those productions upon which time had set its unerring seal.

For devotional reading he was accustomed to resort to the Morning and Evening Exercises of Jay, the Sacra Privata of Bishop Wilson, and particularly to the practical works of Baxter, whose Saint's Rest he esteemed next to the Bible. He found the habitual perusal, from day to day, of such works greatly conducive to his spirituality and comfort. But, according to the testimony of his last pastor, the Rev. Dr.

Wilson, of New Brunswick, his advancing years led him to a more exclusive attachment to the Word of God as the means of growing in personal holiness.

Mr. Frelinghuysen's diction in oral and written productions was terse, chaste, and perspicuous. His style indicated a familiarity with the older models of English, and sometimes betrayed the influence which Dr. Johnson's sonorous periods exerted upon writers in both hemispheres at the beginning of this century. There was nothing elaborate in Mr. Frelinghuysen's mode of expression, no *curiosa felicitas*, no attempts at word-painting, but rather a careless ease and grace, which seemed to seek only a transparent medium for the thought, and postponed all other considerations to the one object of conveying his own views and carrying conviction to the minds of his hearers.

His speeches were all remarkable for compactness and brevity. His great effort in the Senate on the Indian Bill, which occupied parts of three days, and consumed about five hours altogether, was an exception which was due to the importance of the subject and to the large mass of documentary evidence which the nature of his argument required him to introduce. But in general he rarely exceeded an hour. When at the bar he studied principles rather than cases, and shunned the risk of being smothered under the weight of accumulated authorities. The peculiarities of his mind enabled him to seize upon the strong points of a case, and these he pressed home with resistless power. He scorned tricks, sharp practice, and unfair advantages, and won a cause honorably or not at all. His main reliance was upon solid reasoning addressed neither to the prejudices nor the passions of his hearers, but to their judgment. Yet, like every other speaker who has a point to gain, he employed all the subsidiary means which Nature put into his hands to arrest attention, to awaken interest, to conciliate favor, to stir the fountains of laughter or of tears. It is related that once, when urging the conviction of a notorious counterfeiter, he had occasion to represent the way in which the accused passed off the spurious notes upon a neighbor, the statement was so comical that the entire court and jury broke into a peal of laughter, in which the prisoner at the bar joined as heartily as any of the rest. Yet, on the other hand, many years later, precisely the opposite effect was produced in the same city. In 1837 the American Board held its annual meeting in Newark under circumstances of deep interest. The commercial revulsion of that memorable year had greatly impaired the receipts of the Board, and threatened to leave it embarrassed with a very heavy and unmanageable debt. At one stage of the anxious discussions produced by this state of things, Mr. Frelinghuysen, who was sitting among the audience in the body of the house, suddenly arose to speak. He had been deeply moved by some of the representations made, and he stood up to pour out an overflowing heart. For half an hour he held the crowded house spellbound. His speech, wholly unpremeditated, ran on in a strain of the loftiest eloquence. The speaker was lost in his theme. His animated appeals for the Savior's honor and the salvation of a perishing world overwhelmed the entire audience with a flood of sacred emotion. Old and young were melted under the orator, so that hardly a dry eye was to be found in the house. A similar instance is mentioned by the Rev. Dr. W. J. R. Taylor, in a sermon preached on occasion of Mr. Frelinghuysen's death. In illustration of his "peculiar powers of eloquent speech," the preacher says, "Thus I remember how, a few years ago, when some converted Indians were introduced at one of the sessions of the American Board of Foreign Missions, he welcomed them in an impromptu address which thrilled the vast assembly, and so paralyzed the utterance of others, that even one of the most eminent pulpit orators of our time, who was to follow him, only apologized, and exclaiming, 'But who can come after the king?' sat down among the tearful multitude."

His reported speeches are not a fair expression of his oratorical powers. His mind, strong and richly furnished as it was, needed the spur of opposition or provocation to bring out its full capacity. It is true that, when he spoke on set occasions, after preparation in the calmness of the closet, what he said was always appropriate, judicious, and instructive; but these productions bore no comparison to the utterances of the same man when upon his feet before a popular assembly, with his whole soul aroused and a vehement inward impulse urging him to speak. Then he seemed to rise with the magnitude of the subject or the occasion. Thoughts marshaled themselves in the order of a natural logic, and words tripped like nimble servitors at a master's bidding. At such times he was every inch an orator. His whole frame was moved. His voice responded accurately to every phase of his feelings. He was vehement, yet not overstrained; earnest, yet by no means frantic. In the very whirl of excitement he was master of himself, and therefore of his audience, whom he electrified and carried away as if with a magician's spell.

He usually began to speak in a slow, simple style, gradually warming as he proceeded. He never was at a loss for words, but went on with increasing fluency to the end. He was animated and impassioned, and at times overwhelming. His eloquence was of that kind to which no report ever does or can do justice. The kindling eye, the heaving form, the expressive tones, the impetuous emotion, can not be transferred to paper. The outward man responded in every muscle and fibre to the inward passion. The earnestness of the speaker, and his intense conviction of the truth and importance of what he was saying, took full hold of his audience, and made an impression which long outlasted the occasion. Men often admired and praised the speaker, but still oftener they forgot him and thought only of what they were to do.

In speaking before benevolent and religious institutions, the effect produced depended almost entirely upon the frame of mind in which he happened to be at the time. If called upon at the first, or in an ordinary state of mind, he never came up to his reputation. But if suddenly stirred by some perilous crisis, or roused by the energy of some preceding speaker, he seemed to break loose from all fetters, and soar at once into the region of natural and vehement eloquence. His soul took fire. His logic was red-hot. His appeals were irresistible. Before the audience were aware, they found themselves borne away at a master's will, and every thought and feeling absorbed in the rushing flow of the orator's voice.

> "And when the stream
> Which overflowed the soul was passed away,
> A consciousness remained that it had left
> Deposited upon the silent shore
> Of memory, images and precious thoughts
> That shall not die and can not be destroyed."

The following interesting reminiscence of Mr. Frelinghuysen's ability as a persuasive speaker has been kindly furnished to the author by the Rev. Dr. Magie, of Elizabeth, N. J.:

"You ask me to give you a little incident which I mentioned at our recent Sabbath-school Convention of a man whom I never think of but with respect and love. Christians owe it to themselves, as well as to the cause of Christ, not to forget the late Theodore Frelinghuysen. To whom can parents better recommend their children as an example of all that is bright and beautiful in character; and of whom can the Church speak to her members better suited to encourage high aims and efforts in her service? I hope you will be enabled to embalm his memory, and render it fragrant for ages to come.

"The incident, with its associations, was this: A good brother had just pronounced a brief and touching eulogy upon that incomparable man, in connection with Sabbath-schools, and telling us that when chosen to the office of superintendent of a school in the Church to which he belonged, he prevented all apology for putting so much additional work upon hands already full by declaring that he regarded the post as, on some accounts, more honorable than that of senator of the United States. My heart was moved, as was every other heart present, and, in a moment, a crowd of tender recollections came pouring in upon me. No other person present had enjoyed the privilege of an acquaintance with him for so many years, and I confess to some rising of desire, just then and there, to appear in connection with a name so esteemed and illustrious.

"Mr. Frelinghuysen was in attendance as an elder of the Second Church of Newark upon the sessions of the Synod of New Jersey, held in my lecture-room. A minute was under consideration recommending the cause of African Colonization to the confidence of our churches, but it was opposed by an aged and venerable minister present on the ground that this was no cure for the evils of slavery, and, indeed, was adapted in his opinion to rivet the chains of the poor blacks still more firmly. The speech was able, and was listened to by many with feelings of deep regret. At its close all eyes were turned to Mr. Frelinghuysen. His eloquence as a speaker, the influence he was rapidly gaining in the community as a man of enlightened and generous philanthropy, and especially the deep interest he had begun to manifest in the welfare of the poor blacks, all pointed to him as the person who must put things right before the Synod. In a few minutes he rose with a face shining like the face of an angel, and for twenty minutes he held us all completely entranced.

"The tones of his voice seem still to ring in my ears as he pleaded for doing what we could, even if we could not do every thing. Referring to the preaching of John the Baptist, when first the people generally, then the publicans, and last the soldiers, crowded around him, saying, 'What shall we do?' he repeated the words of the bold man in tones that awakened the response of gushing tears. I need not say that the resolution was adopted with but a single dissenting voice.

"This scene, let me add, brought to me and to several members of the Synod another rich treat. Dr.

Archibald Alexander was staying at my house, and never shall I forget his manner as, laying off his coat, he entered the parlor, exclaiming, 'This is wonderful; I have long esteemed Mr. Frelinghuysen, and considered him a most excellent man, but never till this afternoon was I aware of his power. I have been reminded of some of the very best efforts of Patrick Henry.' The good old man then went on to give us some delightful reminiscences of that prodigy of ready eloquence as witnessed by himself.

"But I must not go farther. The mention of the name of Theodore Frelinghuysen touched a chord in my heart which must vibrate so long as it is in me to revere unsullied purity of character, venerate exalted station, and love mild and childlike Christian piety. Heaven seems to me more attractive for the hope that I shall meet the beloved man there."

CHAPTER VIII.

ORIGIN AND CHARACTER OF HIS PIETY.

Early Impressions.—Conversion at Newark.—Influence of his Brother's Death.—Eminence of his Piety.—Its Elements: 1. Simplicity of Faith; 2. Humility; 3. Devotional Habits; 4. Geniality; 5. Tendernesss of Conscience; 6. Completeness; 7. The Fruit of Culture.—Letter from Dr. Woodbridge.

MR. FRELINGHUYSEN was born within the pale of the Christian Church, and in infancy received the baptismal seal of his birthright. He was carefully trained in the nurture and admonition of the Lord, and while yet young manifested the same tenderness of conscience which characterized all his mature years. His deepest religious impressions were traced by himself to the influence of his pious grandmother, the Jufvrouw Hardenbergh, who took particular pains to lead him to the Savior. Deservedly eminent for her piety, she was far from being austere, but, on the contrary, gracious and winning. Her heart was set on seeing the ministry recruited from her own family, and, though disappointed in this respect in the career of her oldest son, she renewed her desire in the case of his children. Theodore, in his advanced years, gratefully acknowledged his indebtedness to her pious counsels, which, although they did not attain their end at once, yet sank deep into his memory and heart, and laid the foundation for the solid and symmetrical Christian character which he afterward exhibited.

There is no reason to suppose that his religious views and sensibilities suffered any deterioration while at school in Basking Ridge. Dr. Finley was remarkable for the attention which he paid to the spiritual culture of his pupils. The Rev. Dr. Studdiford, of Lambertville, N. J., speaks very warmly of his holy earnestness in this work, and of his success in bringing truth forcibly home to the minds of youth. And Mr. Frelinghuysen's younger brother, Frederick, who was also one of Dr. Finley's scholars, bore witness on his dying bed to the fidelity of "that good man," through whose instrumentality "the Lord began to be gracious to his soul, and to sow the good seed in his young and tender heart." Still, no such change appears to have been wrought as yet upon the mind of Theodore. He was correct, moral, conscientious, and studiously observant of the outward duties of religion, but nothing more; nor did he reach the final decision until he came to reside in Newark.

Here he became interested in the founding of the Second Presbyterian Church, and was elected a member of its first Board of Trustees in January, 1811. He was received into the full communion of the Church in September, 1817, under the pastoral care of the Rev. Dr. Griffin, of whose ministrations he was always accustomed to speak in terms of the highest respect and gratitude. Not many months before his death, when writing to the Rev. Dr. Few Smith, in acknowledgment of his discourse on the fiftieth anniversary of the Second Church, he used this expression in reference to his coming to Christ: "I feel a strong interest in that dear sanctuary where my own hopes of salvation first trembled into experience." This "sweet and characteristic" expression well describes the prevailing type of his religious experience. The *law-work*, as the old-fashioned divines express it, was wrought upon his soul with great power. He had a deep sense of the evil of sin, of the justice of God, of the deceitfulness of the heart, of the perils of temptation; and he habitually trembled under the fear of offending his gracious Savior.

A few years after his connection with the Second Church, his seriousness and spirituality were greatly increased by the dealings of the Lord with his brother Frederick, who, after five weeks of illness, was removed by death in November, 1820. This brother had been, while yet young, brought very nigh to the kingdom, but afterward strayed into forbidden paths, so much so as to be even infected with deistical sentiments. He was, however, graciously restored, and, but a few months before his death, delivered an eloquent address before the Somerset County Bible Society. At the last communion season of the Church in Millstone, N. J., which he attended, he was greatly inclined to join himself to the number of God's professed people, but, through fear of unfitness, and dread of subsequently becoming a reproach to the cause, determined to postpone the matter. When overtaken by disease he saw his error, confessed his sin, and sought earnestly, as a new sacramental season was approaching, to be examined and received by the officers of the Church. His request was granted, and in his sick-room he made a noble confession of Christ. Henceforward he spent his whole time in prayer and praise, in sweet expressions of submission to the Divine will, in earnest entreaties to his impenitent friends and neighbors to seek the salvation of their souls, and in pious communion with the Christian friends around his bedside. The printed narrative of his exercises states that on one occasion, "his second brother [Theodore] went to him and said, 'Frederick, the Savior must appear very precious to you now.' He raised his hands, his countenance beaming with inexpressible joy and serenity, and said, 'Oh, Theodore, Theodore, I have not language to describe it. The enjoyment of this hour is greater than that of my whole life.'" At other times, when urged to desist from speaking, and seek, if possible, to get some sleep, he answered, "Why? I am much happier than if I were asleep, and what I say may do good hereafter."

The whole scene is described by those who witnessed it, some of whom, after the lapse of forty years, still retain a vivid recollection of it, as most affecting. The impression it made upon Theodore was decided and indelible. It was so pervading as to render him, in the judgment of his friends, almost another man. He seemed to ascend at once to a higher plane of the Christian life, to make a new and entire consecration of himself to the Savior, and to walk henceforth as in the continual presence of things unseen and eternal.

Nor was this a short-lived impulse. It ended only with his life. There have been few believers in any age whose course and character have been marked by so little that is fitful and evanescent. His course was literally like the shining light, which shineth more and more unto the perfect day. There was no obvious abatement or pause in his steady walk with God. While *in* the world he was not *of* it, but overcame it, often in circumstances sufficiently difficult and perplexing. His religion was not a thing of time and place, an appendage, a separable part of the man. It was the man himself. It pervaded his whole character, shaped his course, entered into the very elements of his being, and made him what he was. Like Joseph of Arimathea, he was an honorable counselor, but, like him also, he was a good man and a just.

His piety did not derive its eminence simply from the force of contrast, from the fact that it is so rare to find any spiritual Christianity at all among those who are embarked upon the troubled sea of politics. On the contrary, it was great absolutely as well as relatively. Had he been confined to private life, wholly unknown beyond a narrow circle, still within that circle he would have been a Christian of mark, eminent for spirituality, self-denial, heavenly-mindedness, consistency, purity, and usefulness. There was such a completeness in his character, such a harmony between the inward and the outward, such an attention to the greater duties without the neglect of the lesser, such an evident candor and sincerity, such an earnestness and meekness of spirit, that all who knew him even slightly, much more those who enjoyed his familiar intercourse, felt that he was a man after God's own heart.

1. In considering the characteristic elements of his piety, those who knew him well were most struck by the great *simplicity of his faith.* While he was well grounded in the abstruser doctrines of the Christian

system and thoroughly versed in its evidences, he had a spiritual perception of the truth as it is in Jesus. He saw his own wants, and the admirable provision made for them in the Savior's finished work. He was willing to count all things but loss for the excellent knowledge of Christ, because his own experience taught him its inexpressible value. He rested, therefore, upon the revelations and promises of the written Word with a confiding, childlike faith, the very simplicity of which made it invincible to all the assaults of skepticism or worldliness. It was not necessary for him to be able logically to refute any of the various charges which human or diabolic subtlety has brought against the Gospel. He had the witness in himself, and therefore stood unmoved amid all the clamor of skeptics and scoffers. His natural intelligence inclined him at times to investigate the more recondite parts of theology, and in mature years he refreshed his early classical studies for the sake of studying the New Testament in the original, yet the prevailing type of his religious thoughts and meditations was of a simpler cast.

This view of his faith is pleasantly confirmed by the following statement in his own words, for which I am indebted to my friend and colleague, the Rev. J. T. Duryea, who was present on the occasion referred to:

"President Frelinghuysen was addressing a little company of the friends of Sabbath-schools in New Brunswick, and encouraging them to hope for the early conversion of children, because of the simplicity of the way of life, and its adaptedness to the comprehension of the most youthful minds.

"He said, 'After all, we must, however wise or great in our own estimation or in the estimation of others, become as little children in order to enter the kingdom of heaven. The simple facts of the Gospel are the foundation of our hope. This is my experience. I have tried to study the mysteries of our religion. I have read the great apostle's writings, and meditated upon them with much satisfaction, and have endeavored to trace his arguments and fathom his meaning. But when I think of myself, a sinner before God — when I look forward to death, and the judgment, and eternity, I forget these deep things of God; faith clings to one precious truth, and hope adds to it another, and they are these: Jesus Christ loved me and died for me, and I feel in my poor sinful heart a responsive throb of love to him.'"

2. *Humility* was another eminently characteristic feature of Mr. Frelinghuysen's character. His lowliness was profound and unaffected. It sprang from the deep sense which he had, on the one hand, of the Divine holiness, and, on the other, of human depravity. Measuring himself by the lofty standard of the Scriptures, he continually saw enough of defect, even in his best services and holiest exercises, to keep him in a low place before God. Hence the permanency of this trait. He grew in grace, in knowledge, in wisdom, in usefulness, and could scarcely fail to have some consciousness of the fact; but at the same time he grew in his perception of the strictness and spirituality of the Divine law, and thus there was always maintained the same relative distance between his attainments and the mark at which he aimed.

This humility was rendered more remarkable by the circumstances which surrounded him. He had to contend not only with the ordinary temptations to pride arising from his birth, connections, professional success, and personal popularity, but also with the keener and more insidious allurements suggested by the general recognition of his position as a prominent Christian leader. This recognition came before him in various ways, in his presence on the platform, by letter, in the public prints, and by the action of corporate bodies, as well as in ordinary social intercourse. When expressed in gross and obvious forms, it gave him great displeasure and encountered severe rebuke. Once, in Newark, a lady who belonged to the Church he served as elder said to him, "I went to the prayer-meeting this morning to meet you and hear you pray, and you were not there!" With mournful severity he replied, "Was not God there? I thought you went to meet *Him*." Frequently, at public meetings, his countenance has testified the great pain he felt in being obliged to sit and listen to personal adulation. On one of these occasions, the offensive speaker, after the exercises were ended, called at Mr. Frelinghuysen's house, and immediately received a severe reproof, in which the good man declared, with godly sorrow and deep humility, that such utterances desecrated God's house and service, and were very abhorrent to all his feelings. The unanimous testimony of all who were in occasional or habitual intercourse with him is that they never saw any appearance of elation in his deportment or conversation. Whether he had such feelings only the Searcher of hearts can say, but that he never manifested them is very certain. Growing honors seemed only to drive him back closer to the mercy-seat. The praise of men only made him more sensible how little he deserved the praise of God. And so it continued through life. As the full head of ripened grain bends lower than the immature or empty stalk, so he, in the maturity of his years and fame, bowed only the more humbly in his Maker's presence. To the last he received the kingdom of God "as a little child." He had nothing, he was nothing, but Christ was all and in all.

This trait was so marked in him that it attracted the attention and admiration even of worldly men. It is said that the celebrated John Randolph, of Roanoke, once speaking in his sarcastic way of certain pretenders to righteousness, suddenly turned to Mr. Frelinghuysen, and pointing toward him, said, "This man does not boast of religion, but he has it, he *has* it."

Perhaps there never lived a more unassuming man. He never struggled for pre-eminence any where or in any relation. The civil honors or offices bestowed upon him were in all cases unsolicited, even where they were such as might be justly esteemed the worthy aims of an honorable ambition. The same remark is true in reference to academic, social, or religious distinctions. All came to him without the least hint or suggestion on his part. He had successfully schooled himself to obey the apostolic injunctions, "In honor preferring one another;" "Let each esteem other better than himself." Habitually he deferred to others, not through weakness, cowardice, or a desire to escape responsibility, but from a desire in this way to illustrate and adorn the doctrine of Christ.

Some have deemed that he pushed this rare and amiable trait to an excess, so that it became a weakness. Yet this may well be doubted. When circumstances required, Mr. Frelinghuysen stood firm as a rock in support of a principle or a duty, but in all cases where only personal considerations were concerned he regarded the rule, "Let every one of us please his neighbor for his good to edification," and imitated, as far as mortal man could, the example of Him of whom it is written, "For even Christ pleased not himself." It is hard for those who knew his dignity, independence, firmness, and courage, to conceive how his close following of his Divine Master in this most difficult and characteristic grace could degenerate into an infirmity, or be confounded with the timidity which surrenders honest convictions out of an unbecoming deference to the opinion or will of others.

3. Mr. Frelinghuysen's faith and humility were nurtured by his life-long habits of *devotion*. He was by eminence a man of prayer. It was his "native breath." He not only felt it as a necessity, but rejoiced in it as a privilege. In the busiest period of his life, when worldly cares pressed hardest upon him, it was his custom to imitate the Psalmist, who said, "Evening and morning, and at noon, will I pray." His profession and his practice corresponded here as beautifully as they did in other matters. At an early period of his Christian course he formed the habit of devoting a quarter of an hour in the middle of the day to prayer. And this he never relinquished. Sometimes circumstances prevented him from retiring to his closet at the exact time, but the service was not

therefore omitted. The earliest subsequent leisure he could command, even if it did not occur before nightfall, was carefully appropriated to the purpose. And it is believed that this devotional service was not intermitted even once in the course of more than forty years. It may be added here that his custom was, in his private devotions, to pray aloud, because, as he said, he found it the best way to prevent wandering thoughts. Robert Hall, who had the same habit of oral, audible private prayer, pursued it from the conviction "that silent prayer was apt to degenerate into meditation, while, from our compound nature, a man can not but be affected by the sound of his own voice when adequately expressing what is really felt." Nor was he a stranger to the custom of observing extraordinary and protracted seasons of prayer, accompanied with abstinence from food. The notion which obtains so extensively in our day that fasting, when enjoined by the Scriptures, is to be understood figuratively, and does not involve the omission of a single meal, did not commend itself to his old-fashioned piety. Although no ascetic, and no believer in the propriety of bodily mortification for its own sake, he yet cherished occasional fasting as an appropriate expression of a penitential spirit, and an admirable help in the cultivation of a devotional frame of mind. It need hardly be added that this was always done, so far as possible, in such a way that he would "not seem unto men to fast."

His prayerfulness was intimately connected with the study of the Word of God. This study was conducted, not as a philological exercise, nor to solve theological problems, nor to refresh his taste with the highest models of literary excellence, but as a means of his own growth in grace. One who was for many years a member of his household writes to the author as follows: "From every thing he turned with new interest to the Bible. I never knew so constant a student of it—not as a duty, but from real pleasure. So that I often said to him, 'Uncle, you must know it by heart.' 'Oh no,' he would say, 'I see new beauties every time I open it.' He was in the habit, as long as I can remember, of taking, after dinner, his Bible and a little manual of prayer, and spending half an hour or more in reading. So a little text-book of Scripture was laid near his best razor, and I don't believe he would have considered the shaving properly done without the morning's text to meditate upon." Another intimate acquaintance says, "He studied the Scripture with ever new delight. Its style, he used to say, was the perfection of beauty and simplicity. It was no unusual thing to see him reading the Word throughout a long winter evening, never taking up any other book, although many were lying beside him on the table."

It was this habit of constant devotional study of the Scripture which caused his uniform spiritually-mindedness. There were seasons when his nervous temperament, or the irritability caused by bodily disease, led him to speak with what afterward seemed to be undue harshness; but this never occurred without giving him infinite grief in the retrospect, and sending him anew, with strong crying and tears, to the mercy-seat. In every emergency of every kind, as well as on set occasions from day to day, he resorted to the Bible and prayer. In the one God spoke to him, in the other he spoke to God; and this unbroken communion with the Most High lay at the foundation of his extremely thorough Christian character. It continually refreshed him when worn and wearied by professional toil. It kept him from being absorbed in temporal duties and interests. It enabled him to carry a heavenly temper into all the scenes and associations of daily life. This was very apparent in his treatment of such as trespassed on his rights or feelings. He rarely manifested displeasure, although his sensibility was keen; and when he did, was always ready and eager to accept any explanation and extend the most cordial forgiveness. A friend once said to him, "I have forgiven the offense, but can't forget it." His answer was, "That kind of forgiveness will not bear the light of heaven. You are deceiving yourself." He once received a letter, written under a mistaken sense of duty, the contents of which wounded him deeply. After his death that letter was found among his papers, bearing this endorsement in his own handwriting: "And be ye kind to one another, tender-hearted, forgiving one another, even as God, for Christ's sake, hath forgiven you."

4. Yet his piety was of a decidedly *genial* cast. With all its strictness and spirituality, it never degenerated into sanctimoniousness or gloom. Naturally of a buoyant temperament, with a large capacity for mirth and innocent enjoyment, these qualities were enhanced and refined by the grace which was in him. He had his trials indeed, and there was one source of

anxious thought, to which I shall advert in a subsequent chapter, which he carried with him through life; but these were borne with patience and meekness of wisdom; nor did they hinder him from being, in the main, a serene, happy Christian. Sometimes ill health and other similar causes depressed his spirits, but, in general, the habit of his mind was a playful gayety, which, so far from being extinguished, was rather heightened and purified by his religious faith and hope. There was nothing sour or morose about him. He delighted in the play of the social and domestic affections. He enjoyed the society of kindred and friends. Having himself a vein of humor and a keen sense of the ludicrous, he greatly relished those qualities in others, and his contagious laugh quickly responded to any amusing tale. And this is one cause why the young always found him such an agreeable companion. But while thus cheerful, it was always in reason and moderation. The proprieties of time and place were sedulously regarded, and even amid sallies of mirth and sparkling jests there was an under tone of seriousness such as becometh saints.

His faith concurred with his constitutional peculiarities to maintain this pleasant, attractive type of character. He was accustomed to seek for and observe the hand of Providence in all the events of life, and therefore found a double charm in every temporal blessing, while he had a sure resource in the time of trial or disaster. Besides, he had in his own soul the peace which passeth understanding. He enjoyed the service of God. The Divine thoughts were precious to him. His meditations on sacred themes were often very, very sweet. And so the joy of the Lord was the strength of his soul. Men found in him an unbending integrity which commanded respect, but also a refined humanity which won their affection. His life showed that the most inflexible adherence to the rule of right did not require the abridgment of a single rational pleasure.

5. *Tenderness of conscience* was another eminently characteristic feature of his piety. He carried his Christian principles into every walk of life. He regarded all things from a religious point of view, and conscience maintained a supreme and unchallenged dominion over his entire course. His one great desire in things small and great, public or private, was to do what was right. Few men have ever lived who so carefully and constantly canvassed the correctness of their deportment in every minute particular. Nor did this degenerate into scrupulosity, a morbid sensitiveness which makes offenses where none really exist, and poisons peace without promoting holiness. Mr. Frelinghuysen's piety was too intelligent and healthy to waste its energies on chimeras. Yet it was studiously careful in respect to real difficulties. He was not content with first impressions or hasty conclusions, but, as if well aware of the unequaled deceitfulness of the heart, subjected acts and motives to the most rigid ordeal, so as to preserve a conscience void of offense toward God and toward man. He was in the fear of the Lord all the day long, and lived "as ever in his great Taskmaster's eye."

The consequence was an unparalleled rectitude of

life, such a degree of blameless integrity as excited the amazement and admiration of all who knew him. An instance or two may be mentioned as illustrations. He was very fond of game, which was regularly supplied to him by an old colored man named York; but when York sent any at the time when the law of the land forbade them to be killed, no persuasion could prevail upon him to eat them. Even during his last sickness, when his appetite was delicate and capricious, and it was almost impossible to obtain any food which he could take, his reverence for law prevailed, and the quails which had been provided were sent away untouched. These were little things, but they were such trifles as indicate character. Mr. Frelinghuysen's unbending rule of right recognized no distinction of great and small in moral questions.

6. Another feature of his piety was its *completeness.* It was in no respect fragmentary, or fitful, or one-sided, but full-orbed—a complete, rounded whole. In the case of most believers, it is certain features of their character, or particular portions of their lives upon which the thoughts of their friends love to linger, and from which incitements to Christian excellence may draw an animating example. But it was not so with Theodore Frelinghuysen. His whole course, from first to last, was of one texture. Fervid as his piety was, it never ran into enthusiastic extravagance. Active as he was in any one form of Christian duty or beneficence, he never forgot that there were others. No one trait in his character stands out so prominently as to dwarf all the rest in comparison, but the entire sisterhood of Christian graces seemed to grow to-

gether, mutually supporting each other, and constituting, in their combined effect, the exquisite symmetry and fullness of the perfect man in Christ Jesus. More than thirty years ago, that shrewd observer of men and manners, the Rev. Dr. James W. Alexander, wrote from Trenton, N. J., to a friend, "Mr. Frelinghuysen is here at this time, full of the subject of Temperance. He is a singular instance of a man zealously devoted to every good enterprise, without the slightest eccentricity."

There were, of course, defects in his walk, infirmities which cost him many a tear; but, despite these, there was that in him which brings up vividly to mind Mr. Clay's descriptive epithet that he was "self-poised." He passed through seasons of religious awakening when whole communities were bowed by the presence of the Spirit, and he himself was deeply moved; he engaged in schemes of social and personal amelioration very absorbing to a humane or Christian mind; he was closely allied with organizations literary, charitable, and religious, which are prone to engross all the thoughts of their agents and advocates; but he never appeared to swing from his moorings, or lose the admirable balance of his character. Every where, and at all times, he was an humble, earnest Christian, sweetly blending contemplation and action, full of love to God and love to man, abounding in the graces which are distinctively evangelical, yet without rant or cant, without turbulence or rashness, filling the position the Lord had assigned him without encroaching on others, happy when success crowned his efforts, yet never bitter or impatient because of delay or failure.

His piety was not absolutely complete, but it made as near an approach to that excellence as the present generation has seen.

7. Many who saw Mr. Frelinghuysen's Christian excellence only at a distance, or knew it only by report, have supposed that he made an exceptional case to the ordinary lot of believers; that he had some special facilities, some happy peculiarities of constitution, which rendered holy living easy and natural to him. This is far from being the case. His piety was the *fruit of assiduous culture.* He had difficulties to contend with both within and without. Although naturally of an amiable disposition, and from early youth possessed of an active and sensitive conscience, yet he had native infirmities of temper and temperament which it required a constant struggle to subdue. His own experience gave him insight into the inward contest between flesh and spirit, sense and faith, so often alluded to in the apostolic epistles. He needed to watch, and fight, and pray as much as the weakest or obscurest believer in the land. He used the various means of grace, private, social, and public, with eagerness and constancy, as one to whom they were not only attractive, but necessary. The care with which he sought to benefit by the preaching of the Word is shown by the fact that he uniformly, on returning home from public worship, retired to his room to pray for a blessing upon the service. He studied his own heart, he learned by experience, he guarded against temptation, he gave all diligence to make his calling and election sure. He was, in the old sense of the term, a *painful* Christian; that is, one who took pains

to reach and preserve a high standard of character. His exquisite consistency, and purity, and maturity were not the result of some happy accident or of some semi-miraculous endowment, but the natural outgrowth of seed planted, watered, and ripened under the blessing of the Good Spirit. No help toward a close walk with God was so small that he did not diligently use it; no temptation or infirmity was so trifling that he did not deplore and fight against it. If there be a royal road to eminent holiness, assuredly he did not walk in it; on the contrary, his route was through the strait gate and on the narrow way, with many a cross and many a conflict. It would be sad were the lustre of his course and character to blind any to the incessant vigilance and effort by which, with the Divine favor, he obtained such good report among the people of God.

The reader will observe a remarkable confirmation of many of the foregoing statements in the following letter from the Rev. Dr. Woodbridge, professor in the Theological Seminary of the Reformed Dutch Church, written at the author's request:

"New Brunswick, September 3, 1862.

"DEAR BROTHER,—For nine years immediately preceding the death of Mr. Frelinghuysen I was brought into near relations with him, chiefly as his pastor, and during all this time I had increasing conviction that there was in him, to a remarkable degree, the elements which constitute greatness in the kingdom of God.

"The feature of his character which first struck a stranger aware of his position and national reputation was his extreme simplicity. He illustrated more fully than any man I ever knew the language of Christ, that he who would receive the kingdom of God must become 'as a little child.' His prayers, his addresses, his intercourse with Christians, all partook of this childlike spirit. It was not assumed, but seemed perfectly natural, an essential part of his character. Nor did it give to him any appearance of weakness. The language he uttered might be pure and simple, but the thoughts were the great revelations of the Gospel of God. He seemed to be entirely unconscious of possessing any remarkable degree of grace; upon the contrary, he constantly manifested a profound *humility*. He appeared to be deeply sensible of the plague of his own heart—so sensible of it that not unfrequently, while the light that was in him was shining forth so that all saw it, and many were rejoicing in his pious words and generous acts, he was doubting whether the enlightening influence of the Spirit of grace had ever entered his heart. His clear and habitual views of the greatness and holiness of God seemed to repress and banish self-confidence and spiritual pride. He shrank from adulation; he was afraid of self-righteousness as a foe to his peace and to God; and even in his last sickness, when one recalled to his memory the useful life he had lived, he begged all present to remember that he was the chief of sinners. Not one ray would he detract, even in thought, from the glory of God's grace.

"One could not be with him long without discovering *how strong was his faith*. The time for reasoning and doubt had long since passed away. Christianity was not *put on*, but was interwoven, as it were, with all the faculties of his mind and heart—with his very being; it spoke out spontaneously in his language; the idea of the kingdom of God entered wholly into all his conceptions and plans of life. I often felt, when with him, how utterly impossible it would be for any power on earth to shake his faith in the Word of God; he 'seemed to be a pillar' in the house of the Lord; his heart was fixed; he might have conflicts, but he could no more fall away from the Gospel of Christ than from any other essential condition of human existence. This impression arose, I think, from the spontaneousness with which he uttered the language of the Christian.

"I have more than once admitted the exceeding clearness of his views of truth. To many of the modern works of error he had evidently given no special reading, but it was in vain that any errorist attempted to deceive him. As if by a kind of Christian instinct, his soul refused to receive any thing but the pure milk or the strong meat of the Lord. He did not love controversy, but he detected in a moment what was contrary to sound doctrine, and without censoriousness, with a few simple words, usually drawn from Scripture, he set aside the fallacy.

"That a beautifully consistent life should flow from such a faith was a necessity. Of his constant study of the Scripture in his home, and his long communings with God, there are friends enough to testify. In public he was where duty called him, among the first at the weekly prayer-meeting and lecture, frequently speaking words of kindly Christian warning to such as had no hope, not only to the students in the college, but to the thoughtless in the street, and irrespective of their condition in society; and where the honor of Christ was concerned, I verily believe, never fearing the face of man; ever ready to relieve the distressed, to comfort the mourner, to advise the doubting. He was a true man, in every respect true, in word never exaggerating; in action, in all his life, conscientious to a degree that often occasioned remark. He was kind and gentle, one who attracted to confidence, and to whom you would go in the day of trouble. I have many a time thought that, were a skeptic to ask for the living testimony of the power of the Gospel on the heart and life of man to make him true, and honest, and lovely, and of good report, I would point him to Theodore Frelinghuysen, and ask an explanation of such a life and death. His path was that of the just, shining more and more unto the perfect day.

"Yours in the Gospel, S. M. WOODBRIDGE."

CHAPTER IX.

HIS RELIGIOUS LIFE.

At Home—at the Bar—in Washington—in Church Relations—Sunday-school.—Charity.—Catholicity of Feeling.

THE piety, the origin and leading features of which have just been described, manifested itself in every appropriate way in Mr. Frelinghuysen's life. It controlled his entire conduct at home and abroad, in private and in public. Gentle, and courteous, and conciliating, he yet never shrank from carrying out his principles to the very letter. Whatever it might cost, he stood immovably for the right, not only as a man of integrity and honor, but as a disciple of the Lord Jesus Christ.

He was careful, in accordance with the apostolic precept, "to show piety at home." Having no children, he adopted a nephew and niece of his own, also a nephew of Mrs. Frelinghuysen, who continued with him until they were settled in life. Besides these, he took a paternal interest in the numerous children of his brothers and sisters and those of his wife, all of whom were cordially welcomed to his house, and received his best aid and counsel in their temporal and their spiritual interests. Although always free from nepotism in any official trust, he never forgot the claims of kindred, but held his heart and hand open to them as a sacred duty.

He was "given to hospitality," and being a generous liver, as far from asceticism as he was from riotous prodigality, he delighted to gather congenial associates around his table. The company was always a cheerful one. The refined courtesy, buoyant spirits, and genial tact of the host and hostess, put all at their ease, and made old and young equal participants in the enjoyment of the occasion. Yet, with all this, the household was a Christian one. Not only did the fire never go out on the domestic altar, but there was a pervading sense of holy things which filled the house like an atmosphere, and shed its mellowing influence on even the commonest relations and duties. Here the character of the man came out in a thousand incidental ways, indicating his largeness of heart, his sensibility, his appreciation of social excellence, his careful consideration for others, his benevolence in little things, his thankful enjoyment of God's temporal goodness, and his supreme regard for the Divine will in all things. His domestic life was a picture of piety without austerity, of purity without affectation. The voice of rejoicing and salvation was heard in his tabernacle. His own innocent hilarity was contagious. The peace of a good conscience, and the love of man springing from the love of God, opened and expanded every fountain of natural affection, and sweetly developed the ordinary contrasts of age, sex, and character. It is said that the skeptic who once passed a week in the home of the eminent and pious London physician, Dr. Hope, was converted by the beautiful exhibition of cheerful godliness which he there witnessed. A similar result might easily have been produced by a visit to the domestic circle of Mr. Frelinghuysen. His piety was peculiarly deep and spiritual, but it was in no degree sour or ungracious. So far from interfering with mirth or social enjoyment, it promoted both, and made him a companion as agreeable as he was edifying to persons of all ages and classes.

His hospitality had its foundation not only in social feeling, but in Christian principle, the Scripture inculcations of the duty being very familiar to his mind and his lips. Agents for benevolent institutions, Christian laymen, traveling ministers of any denomination, always found a welcome at his house. Sometimes the influx of visitors was so great and unexpected that it required no little ingenuity to meet the demand, but in some way it always was met. The sorrowful and necessitous so often found a temporary asylum in his family, that a lady once said, "Why, Mr. Frelinghuysen is making his house a house of refuge." "Such," he replied, "I would have it to be." This was his habitual feeling, although at the very time he was under the pressure of heavy professional duties and responsibilities, and had but little leisure to enjoy the society of his household. If the thought ever arose in his mind that the demands upon his hospitality were rapidly enlarging, or encroaching upon his domestic comfort, he instantly put it down with the remark which he was often heard to make, "I may be entertaining angels unawares."

The bar is not usually considered favorable to the culture of the Christian graces. Indeed, a high legal authority has said, "There is no profession in which so many temptations beset the path to swerve from the line of strict integrity—in which so many delicate and difficult questions are continually arising. There are pitfalls and mantraps at every step; and the mere youth, at the outset of his career, needs often the prudence and self-denial, as well as the moral courage, which belong commonly to riper years. High moral principle is his only safe guide—the only torch to light his way amid darkness and obstruction."* Popular opinion, indeed, goes farther than this, and multitudes seem to be persuaded not only that the legal profession offers great difficulties in the way of a pure morality, but that these difficulties are rarely, if ever, surmounted. Without assenting to this extravagant view, it may yet be said that it requires a constant struggle, amid all the excitements and perplexities of a large practice, to maintain an unsullied Christian character. And Mr. Frelinghuysen felt this. When appointed attorney general, he remarked, as one of the felicities of the position, that it relieved him from the constant pressure of a client at his elbow urging him to go farther than his own sense of right would warrant. Still, difficult as it was to maintain a conscience void of offense, he seems habitually to have succeeded in the effort. He happily reconciled his professional and his Christian duties. The growth of his practice indicates that no interest suffered that was put into his hands, and yet, in the judgment of all his contemporaries, his religious integrity was without a stain. Indeed, in the pamphlet of Mr. Courtlandt Parker, before alluded to, it is said that "his consistent morality in his profession, his scorn for petty artifice

* Professional Ethics, by Judge SHARSWOOD, Philadelphia, 1860.

and chicanery, his desire to settle rather than protract disputes, and his strict integrity in the conduct of legal difficulties, won for him such a reputation for honesty, that his brother lawyers soon complained that juries would believe any thing Mr. Frelinghuysen contended for simply because he did so."

His old classmate and friend, the Rev. Dr. Kirkpatrick, informs the author that he once asked Mr. Frelinghuysen how he managed to keep a clear conscience, seeing he must sometimes have to plead in justification of the rogue. The answer was, "If a man comes to me as a client, I catechise him as much as I can. If I think him in the wrong, I send him to another lawyer. If I believe he is in the right, I do all I can for him." But it is perfectly certain that this was not his rule in later life. We may therefore suppose that his mind underwent the same change which is recorded by Bishop Burnet respecting Sir Matthew Hale, a man whom our American lawyer greatly resembled: "If he saw a cause was unjust, he for a great while would not meddle farther in it but to give his advice that *it was so*. If the parties, after that, would go on, they were to seek another counselor, for he would assist none in acts of injustice. If he found the cause doubtful or weak in point of law, he always advised his clients to agree their business. Yet afterward he abated much of the scurpulosity he had about causes that appeared at first unjust, upon this occasion: there were two causes brought him, which, by the ignorance of the party or their attorney, were so ill represented to him that they seemed to be very bad; but he, inquiring more narrowly into them, found they were really very good and just. So after this he slackened much of his former strictness of refusing to meddle in causes upon the ill circumstances that appeared in them at first."

Mr. Frelinghuysen never in word or act assented to the monstrous dictum of Lord Brougham, that "an advocate, in the discharge of his duty, knows but one pesron in all the world, and that person is his client." He knew and performed what was due to the court, to the bar, and to honor and justice, as well as what his client required. At the same time, he early renounced what Lord Campbell calls "the specious but impracticable rule of never pleading except on the right side, which would make the counsel to decide without knowing either facts or law, and would put an end to the administration of justice."

He was studiously careful of the proprieties of the Christian profession in his office and in the court-room. Once, a wealthy client, in stating his case, incautiously uttered an oath. Mr. Frelinghuysen immediately arose, and said with deep feeling, "Sir, if you use such language again, I will immediately throw up your case." The offense was not repeated.

When Mr. Frelinghuysen was transferred to the Senate of the United States, he was subjected to a still more trying ordeal. Not a few of his compeers were either hopelessly ruined or sadly injured by the vices of the capital. But he not only escaped contamination from prevailing immoralities, but maintained throughout his whole term the same cheerful, simple, unobtrusive, but uncompromising godliness. The state of his mind, even at a time of the very highest political excitement, may be learned from some extracts from a letter written to his brother in the confidence of fraternal intercourse. It is dated December 18, 1832:

"Your letter finds us in good health, through the blessing of our heavenly Father, who has kindly watched over us. We have been much excited here by the doings of South Carolina. She seems resolved on dreadful extremities. The President, I rejoice to perceive, meets the crisis as becomes the chief magistrate of the country. But still our situation is very perilous. * * * I never more deeply realized our entire dependence on God, who hath the hearts of rulers and people in His control, who buildeth up and casteth down. May we look to His infinite riches of mercy and grace, and bear in faith the interests of our beloved country to His holy keeping. It is a season of peculiar claim on the Christian; he has an interest with a prayer-hearing God; and if the Lord leaves us to confusion of counsel, and to the curse of selfish and ambitious desires and purposes, we will be a ruined people. * * *

"We have peculiar trials in these high places of fashion. We have established a Congressional prayer-meeting on Thursday evening weekly. There were eight at the last meeting. More than twenty have agreed to attend. I hope to be strengthened by this waiting upon our Father and Redeemer."

The Congressional prayer-meeting thus modestly referred to was, it is believed, originated by Mr. Frelinghuysen. Certainly he was its most efficient supporter during his senatorial term. To him, and the late Governor Briggs, of Massachusetts, and others of the like stamp, it was a great source of comfort and strength; nor may we doubt that prayers were offered there, the answers to which brought down blessings upon the nation.

Congressional life is known to be very unfriendly to the maintenance of a pure and spiritual Christian character. Men are, for a large portion of the year, removed from their homes and the healthful associations which cluster there. They are embarked upon a sea of excitement roused by purely temporal interests. As members of a political party, they are brought into frequent and sometimes close contact with persons who, however eminent for other attainments, have no religious character. They are often solicited to engage in pursuits and amusements which they know to be inconsistent with a good conscience. At other times they encounter flings at piety and scoffing insinuations which it is extremely hard to bear. Besides, their very devotion to what they deem to be the true interests of their country leads to a stress of thought and feeling upon worldly things which is apt to become absorbing. Thus there is a variety of influences concurring from all quarters to lower the tone of the Christian's piety, to undermine his religious habits, to lead him away from communion with God, and to bring him down to the level of mere worldly men. It is one of the peculiarities of Mr. Frelinghuysen's life at Washington that he was enabled to resist these influences steadily to the end. He knew his danger, as is evident from the allusion to "peculiar trials" in the letter to his brother, and from other testimonies, and he set a double watch upon himself. Without secluding himself from society, or neglecting any public duty, he yet walked unhurt through all the pollution and corruption of the capital. He guarded against the beginnings of evil. He was more inflexible than ever in his habits of devotion. He was diligent and regular in using the ordinances of worship, whether public or social. While he never paraded, he never cloaked his Christian profession. The lustre of his example seems never to have been tarnished in a single instance. He left Washington the same man that he entered it, or, if altered, only in so far as his faith was ripened by experience, and his holy living confirmed and strengthened by trial.

The manifestations of his piety in connection with the Church were very decided and uniform. For forty-five years he was a professed follower of the Savior, and for the greater part of that time held the official station of ruling elder. His example in both these relations was irreproachable. He was a devout and regular attendant upon the means of grace, both on the Lord's day and during the week. He went to the assemblies of God's people, not as a matter of form, nor for intellectual entertainment, nor yet as a mere discharge of duty, but hungering and thirsting after righteousness. He could appreciate pulpit ability; he admired eloquence, logical force, originality, research, power of illustration, freshness of statement in his ministers; yet his great desire was habitually to hear the simple truth, to be built up and stimulated in the Divine life. No pastor ever had a more intelligent, attentive, and sympathetic hearer. He came to be fed with the pure milk of the Word, and, so long as this was given without dilution and without affectation, he was satisfied.

Owing to his own changes of residence and other circumstances, he became the parishioner of many clergymen in succession, with all of whom he maintained the most friendly personal relations. He was studious of their comfort, their reputation, and their sensibilities, delighting to serve them in any way and at any time, yet careful never to obtrude, to embarrass, or to oppress by the appearance of condescension. Among his earlier pastors (from 1822 to 1833) was the Rev. Dr. Hay, with whom he preserved a very close and affectionate intimacy down to the last month of the year 1860, when death sundered the tie for this world. Of his later pastors, the one to whom he was most attached, and whose ministrations he most enjoyed, was the Rev. Dr. De Witt, senior minister of the Collegiate Church, New York. Yet this, perhaps, was owing, not so much to the rare gifts and natural eloquence of his friend, as to the fine simplicity of his character, the evangelical richness and fervor of his discourses, and their luminous illustrations of all phases of Christian experience. The same feeling was cherished by his elder brother, John, in an equal degree, down to the day of his death.

He took particular pleasure in social meetings for worship on the evening of secular days. They formed a pleasant interruption to the constant stream of secular engagements, and he found them of great use in fanning and preserving the flame of his own devotion. He was accustomed to lead the devotions of others, and never without impressing all present with his humility, and reverence, and faith, and fervor. There was a plaintiveness in his tones, and a subdued earnestness in his manner, which rarely failed to bear all hearts along with his own up to the very presence of the mercy-seat. Not unfrequently he would use his gifts in offering remarks in the course of the meeting, and always to edification. He spoke because he had something to say, and he said it with simplicity and directness.

As a Church officer he rendered excellent service. His native shrewdness, insight, and practical wisdom here co-operated with his single-hearted devotion to the Master to render him invaluable in the councils of the Church. There were two functions of the elder's office in which he was very happy and useful. One was visiting the sick and sorrowing. His own delicate sensibility enabled him to enter into the feelings of God's afflicted children, and he delighted to render to them the proper offices of fraternal Christian sympathy. The other was watching for peace. He was quick to perceive alienations and difficulties which threatened to mar the harmony of the Church, and was wise to meet them (to use the Rev. Mr. E. Cheever's words) "as no other man could," so as not only to remove the trouble, but even promote Christian affection between the parties. The blessing pronounced upon the peace-makers fell richly upon his head.

But he was a man of action as well as counsel, and engaged with energy and perseverance in every good work. From the first he took great interest in the instruction of the young. During the whole time he was connected with the Second Church in Newark, he was superintendent of the Sunday-school attached to it. When he was in Washington, he regularly taught a class every Lord's day, and frequently made the assertion that he deemed this employment more truly honorable than the high official position he held in the Congress of the nation. After coming to New York in 1839 to reside, he resumed the same work, and met, in the church where he worshiped, a Bible-class of young men, many of whom attribute their deepest and most abiding impressions to his persuasive counsels. Along with this, he, especially in the latter period of his life, performed much work in delivering addresses before the schools of other churches, or at anniversary meetings. At a time when no other motive than the desire of doing good could have actuated him, he made considerable sacrifices of time and ease, in order in this way to cheer those who were engaged in this important form of Christian beneficence. The audience might be gathered in a rural church or a retired grove, or in the suburbs of a city, but he was equally willing there or any where else to do what he could for the welfare of the young; and it could be said of him as it was of his Master, that the common people heard him gladly. His shining consistency of character, added to his former professional and political distinction, gave to all that he said a weight and power not easy of estimation; and, although not a parent himself, his life-long experience in the Sunday-school, and his rooted convictions of the indispensable importance of the moral training of the youth to the stability of our free institutions, as well as to the solid growth of the Church, enabled him to speak with a peculiar fervor and unction.

But while thus interested for the spiritual wants of others, he was not less concerned for their temporal welfare. His hand was open as the day to melting charity. In the midst of the most exhausting period of his practice as a lawyer, it was his habit to spend every Saturday afternoon in searching out the poor and afflicted, and in ministering by sympathy as well as by pecuniary aid to their necessities, while in general he spared neither time nor means to relieve such children of sorrow as made their situation known to him. To the ordinary charities of the times which are administered by formal associations he was a regular and liberal contributor. An amusing instance of this is related by some who knew him well. He once heard a discourse upon systematic beneficence, the object of which was to enforce upon all Christians the duty of habitually giving to the Lord at least one tenth of their income, and, being very much impressed with the argument, determined to put the rule in practice. He had not gone far, however, before he found that this would require him greatly to abridge his usual charities, for these had far exceeded the tithe of his emoluments. Indeed, one who knew him well said that they amounted probably to the half of his income. "A long time since he remarked that, in view of the various calls of the Church, 'Christians might well fear to be rich.' He denied himself many things which other Christians of less means allow themselves, and he did so that he might have to give unto others. When one spoke to him upon the subject of increasing his comforts, he replied that it could only be done by increasing the necessities of others, and that he dared not do."—Dr. CAMPBELL'S *Funeral Sermon*.

His professional labors brought him a very large compensation. These gains were neither hoarded nor squandered, but lent to the Lord in a wise and liberal charity. It is related that, when he was a candidate for the Vice-presidency, a warm-hearted Christian woman said to a member of the Convention which nominated him, "Ah! sir, you have indeed done a good act in striving to elevate that man; he has been 'eyes to the blind and feet to the lame.'" His townsmen in Newark could justly pursue the quotation, and say, "When the ear heard him, then it blessed him; and when the eye saw him, it gave witness to him: because he remembered the poor that cried, and the fatherless, and him that had none to help him. The blessing of him that was ready to perish came upon him, and he caused the widow's heart to sing for joy." Not only did Mr. Frelinghuysen contribute regularly to public charities and to the poor in his neighborhood, but he also took pleasure in ministering to the comfort of many whose only claim upon him was very remote; and he did this in such a quiet and delicate way that the fact was rather inferred than known, even by the inmates of his household. Into what obscure channels his constant readiness "to do good and communicate" overflowed, only the great day will declare.

Catholicity of spirit was an eminent feature of Mr. Frelinghuysen's religious life. He loved all Christians who hold the Head, and was ready to manifest this fraternal affection at all times and under all circumstances. I have said "all who hold the Head," for this was a discrimination made by himself. He clung to the divinity of his Lord and Savior as a cardinal point, and he could not and did not recognize as brethren in faith and hope any who degraded the Redeemer into a mere creature, and repudiated His atoning blood. Such an error he regarded as vital, and he would never give place, no, not for an hour, to any who held the ruinous delusion. But within this rational and necessary limit his recognition of all believers was most hearty and general, and, as it were, spontaneous. His liberality was not the fruit of indifference, or ignorance, or indiscretion, but of an intelligent Christian spirit, which could overlook minor differences in a common love for all who are in Christ Jesus. He cherished a warm attachment for the ancestral Church in the communion of which he began and closed his days. This was the result not only of hereditary associations peculiarly strong and affecting, but also of a discriminating appreciation of her doctrine, and order, and discipline, and spirit. Hence, although he was first admitted to the Lord's Table in a Presbyterian Church, and continued long and happily in that connection, yet, as soon as Providence opened the way, he returned with alacrity and joy to the Church of his fathers. Hence, too, when, but a few years before his death, that Church felt itself called upon to carry on the work of Foreign Missions independently through a Board of its own appointment, and summoned him to preside over the Board, he promptly, although with no little pain, severed the ties which had long and pleasantly bound him to the American Board, and obeyed the summons.

Yet his love for his own branch of the one great family, while it was fervent and settled, resting alike upon the convictions of his understanding and the impulses of his heart, never degenerated into narrowness or bigotry. His expansive affection took in the whole Church of the redeemed. Their interests were dear to his heart. He rejoiced in their joy, and sorrowed in their sadness. He was ever ready to aid their enterprises by his counsel, and purse, and public addresses. He never paraded this catholicity of feeling. The reports of his numberless addresses before various benevolent associations furnish no instances of ostentatious assertion of superiority to denominational preferences or interests. *Prodesse quam conspici* marked him here as elsewhere. That absorbing devotion to Christ, which made him feel the whole world of Christians to be of kin to him, was shown in deed rather than in word. It was no grace cultivated with special pains for an occasion, but an unconscious, unstudied, instinctive efflorescence of that living principle which, like Elizabeth's babe in the presence of the mother of her Lord, leaps at once to acknowledge Christ's image wherever it is found, and hail His servants whatever livery they bear.

Hence the universal and spontaneous recognition of this feature of Mr. Frelinghuysen's character throughout the entire Christian community in this country. Believers of every name claimed a common property in him as a living representative of the whole body. His public and private worth, his eminent services, his steadfast and stainless consistency, his infinite remove from any petty denominational selfishness or exclusiveness, took him out of the category of local or denominational luminaries, and gave him a national and catholic position in the view of all the evangelical churches of America. Hence he was for years called to stand at the head of not only one, but several of the great national societies instituted for the promotion of religious and benevolent interests in this broad land and among the nations of the earth. Nor was the confidence thus reposed in him ever found to be misplaced. His administration of the trusts confided to him was such in every case as successfully to challenge criticism. Perhaps no layman has ever lived to whom all classes of believers would so readily and cordially point as a fitting representative to all the world of the best features and highest type of American Christianity.

CHAPTER X.

PERSONAL EFFORTS FOR THE SALVATION OF MEN.

Letter to Mr. Lincoln.—Consultation about entering the Ministry.—Dr. Spring's Letter.—Assiduity and Skill in speaking to impenitent Persons.—Grounds of his Success.—Letters.—Correspondence with Mr. Clay; with Mr. Webster; Governor Pennington; Judge Nevius.—Letter of Judge Chambers.—Other Examples.—Words of J. P. Jackson.—Perseverance.

IN the year 1853, the Rev. Dr. Wayland, of Providence, delivered a discourse in Rochester entitled *The Apostolic Ministry*, which excited much attention at the time, and was afterward widely circulated through the press. It was founded upon the text, *Go ye into all the world, and preach the Gospel to every creature;* and the preacher undertook to show, 1. What the Gospel is; 2. What is meant by preaching it; and, 3. Who are to preach it. Three fourths of the sermon are occupied in discussing the last point, in which the duty and responsibility of laymen in proclaiming the Gospel message are stated with great force and pungency. The Hon. Heman Lincoln, of Boston, sent a copy of this address to Mr. Frelinghuysen, and received from him the following reply:

"New Brunswick, January 8th, 1855.

"MY DEAR SIR,—I duly received your kind note and Dr. Wayland's excellent thoughts on the Apostolic Ministry. I have read this address with special interest, and I hope much profit. Like all that I have seen from his pen, it is sound, judicious, and of high moral excellence. I can not but think that his opinions on the duty of others besides 'ministers' preaching will yet become a prevailing sentiment in all our churches. How else shall the work of saving men prosper, as prophecy leads us to believe it will? I have often noted the case of the man possessed, whom our Savior restored to his right mind. His desire was to remain with his blessed Benefactor; but the Lord sent him home to tell how great things God had done unto him. 'And he went his way, and published throughout the whole city how great things Jesus had done unto him.' Now he was a preacher, and an effective one too, for the people marveled at his words. And the woman of Samaria, who left the Savior at the well and went into the city to report of the wonderful Being who had led her to a better knowledge of her own heart and life, preached also to good purpose. I suppose, my dear sir, that while, for the more solemn duties of the sanctuary and its worship, and for the governance and order of Christ's Church, the ministers are to 'be called' and set apart, yet for exhortation, and prayer, and witnessing for the truth, and warning sinners, and encouraging the trembling believer, we are all to labor for Christ, and have a heart and a tongue for His blessed service.

"I trust, my kind friend, that, through God's goodness, we may again be permitted to meet at the American Bible House—a precious spot, where denominational names only draw brethren more closely together in the sweet bonds of love and unity.

"Very truly yours in the best relations,

"THEO. FRELINGHUYSEN.

"The Hon. H. Lincoln."

This letter states the opinion of its author in 1855, but it was not then formed for the first time. It had been held and acted upon for scores of years. From an early period he seems to have felt both the obligation and the desire "to labor for Christ" in every suitable way. Indeed, this led him at various times to canvass with great earnestness the question whether it was not his duty to forsake the bar and enter upon the ministry of the Gospel. His mind was long and seriously exercised upon the subject, and he often consulted the Christian friends in whom he had confidence as to the path of his duty. It is believed that the major portion of these concurred in the views presented by the Rev. Dr. Spring in the following letter. At all events, the practical issue was in accordance with the suggestions here presented:

"New York, 17th Nov., 1835.

"MY DEAR SIR, * * * I am not a little embarrassed by the inquiry you propose respecting leaving the bar. Not a little must depend upon your own state of mind. The great question is, How shall I ascertain the will of God in this matter? Your age is not against the contemplated change. You may labor, if God spare you and give you health, twenty years in the best of causes. Your present influence and standing at the bar and in civil life *are* against the change. Influence and character are plants of slow growth: sometimes they are so local and professional that they can not be successfully transplanted. You will find it a very different thing to plead the cause of a despised Savior before an opposing world, where every thing is unexcited and like adamant, from engaging in a cause between man and man, where every thing is excitable, every thing novel, and every thing exists to cherish your own sensibilities. Multitudes of men now in the ministry, who are not above mediocrity in the uniform routine of parochial labor, would be men of distinction under the excitements of a legal or parliamentary profession. I have my doubts whether you can do as much for the cause of the blessed Redeemer in the ministry of reconciliation as you can now do in your present and kindred relations. And yet I say this with great diffidence. I need not tell you that if you 'lack wisdom' to decide in this matter, there is a weighty promise on record to guide you. I left the bar because I got sick of it; I could not be happy in it; I panted for a better work. And yet mere impulse should not, and I am persuaded will not, guide you. Our Master needs laborers in Church and State. Such is the feeling and such are the institutions of this country that ministers of the Gospel can get very little influence on the state, and therefore there is the more need for men who are qualified and have the spirit of ministers to retain their political influence.

"If you *have made up your mind* to leave the bar and the varied scenes of public life, the pulpit is the place for you, and not an agency for any society. Forgive my haste, and believe me,

"Your affectionate friend, G. SPRING."

Satisfied by these and similar considerations that it was not his duty to seek ordination, Mr. Frelinghuysen was none the less active in such ways as lay open to him in advancing the Savior's kingdom. And his success was such as to show that his decision was right, and that there would have been a loss rather than a gain in his entering the clerical profession. The very fact that he was a layman gave additional power to the appeals which he was accustomed to make to his fellow-men on religious subjects.

The admirable combination of zeal and discretion which marked his conduct in other matters also manifested itself in the manner in which he discharged the difficult and delicate duty of dealing personally with individuals in relation to their eternal interests.

Some believers, through timidity, reserve, unconquerable diffidence, coldness of temperament, or the imperfection of their faith, rarely or never open their mouths to warn the sinner or encourage the trembling disciple. They turn the whole work over to the ministry, and act as if they supposed that example were the only means they were to use for the extension of Christ's kingdom. Others, who are more intelligent and more conscientious than these, often fail by a lack of practical wisdom in adapting their efforts to persons and circumstances. They speak at the wrong time, or in an unbecoming spirit, or in an unfavorable situation; and the effort, however well intended, leads to no good result, if it does not do positive harm.

Mr. Frelinghuysen avoided both evils. He labored, and his labor was skillfully directed. His course continually exemplified the Scripture maxim, "He that winneth souls is *wise*." He sowed beside all waters, but the seeding was adjusted to the soil. He addressed persons at the top and also at the bottom of the social scale, but in each case with a divine discretion which insured attention or at least precluded offense. None were so high, none so low as to be beyond the reach of his affectionate Christian sympathy. He would speak to the old and to the young, to his kinsmen and to servants, to the poor and to the rich, to ordinary citizens and to those who were distinguished by high social or official position. In doing this he was aided by several advantages, partly natural, partly gracious in their origin. Of the former class were his hereditary courage, a quality which shines out in all his ancestors, and which rendered him quite insensible to the fear of man, and his shrewd insight into human character, which enabled him accurately to measure every one with whom he came in contact, and learn the best way of approach. To the latter class belong his eminently consistent life, which forestalled the retort, "Physician, heal thyself;" his unfeigned humility, which prevented his speech from offending the pride of those whom he addressed; and, above all, his habitual fervor of piety, which enabled him to speak out of a full heart—not from a cold sense of duty, but from the irresistible impulse of one to whom eternal realities were always near. Among all the vast variety of persons whom he addressed on the subject of personal religion, not one is known ever to have taken offense; while, on the contrary, persons at opposite points of the social scale have united in saying that they would cheerfully bear from him what they would not bear from any one else. It was not necessary for him to wait for favored moments, or depend upon some extraordinary contingency. So close was his ordinary walk with God, so constant his sense of the Savior's presence and love, that he was always in the mood to talk naturally and without constraint of spiritual things. When retired to the country for recreation in the summer, he could drop a good word to the domestics of the house; and when walking at the funeral of some dignitary, he could call the attention of his companion in the procession to the claims of the merciful Redeemer. All times and places, all ages and sexes were alike to him in this respect. He had the heart to bear witness for Christ, and by God's grace he found the way. If any class of persons, by their situation in life, their social, professional, or political connections, were removed beyond the range of the usual means of bringing the truth to bear upon the conscience, he seemed to feel himself the more impelled to use the advantage of his social position to press the Savior's claims personally upon such. Sometimes, of course, he was heard with ill-concealed impatience; but at others his words fell as the dew of Hermon on the mountains of Zion, where the Lord commanded the blessing even life forevermore. And there are not a few public men, lawyers and statesmen, who will be found in the great day to have been led to Christ by Theodore Frelinghuysen.

When personal approach was not to be had, he resorted to the pen, and wrote to those in whom he felt interest. But few of his numerous letters of this character have been recovered; but those which are extant, though for the most part brief, are marked with great fidelity, propriety, and a pleading tenderness which it must have been hard to resist. But he did not confine himself to such set epistles, but in almost every letter, no matter what the subject, contrived to insinuate or express something about the great concern.

The full details of his activity in this form of doing good will never be known, but some instances casually revealed will indicate the wide extent of his sympathies and the great variety of classes to whom he performed the office of a faithful Christian friend.

Among the most prominent of the public men for whose spiritual welfare Mr. Frelinghuysen cherished a deep and tender solicitude was HENRY CLAY. He was attracted by Mr. Clay's large and generous nature, he admired his talents, he sympathized with his political views, and he enjoyed for many years a friendly intimacy with him. It was natural, therefore, that he should long to see him a possessor of like precious faith with himself. In his correspondence with him, therefore, whatever might be the special occasion or topic of a letter, Mr. Frelinghuysen always included a reference to the great question of the soul's relation to God.

At the close of the year 1835 Mr. Clay was bereaved very suddenly of a favorite daughter. Mr. Frelinghuysen addressed to him a letter of condolence, the tenor of which is easily inferred from the following reply, dated Washington, 16th January, 1836, in which, after thanking Mr. F. for attending to a commission for him, he proceeds:

"But I thank you, my dear friend, still more for the deep interest which you so kindly take in my spiritual welfare. I should be most happy to have the confidence and assurance which you feel on that serious subject. It is one on which, if I have given no evidence to the world of its having engaged my anxious thoughts, I have long and constantly reflected with the greatest solicitude, and I indulge the hope that I shall ultimately find the peace which you have attained. My late sad affliction has taught me an awful lesson, and impressed me with a solemn conviction of the utter vanity of all earthly things. If I had been asked six weeks ago to point to the two happiest beings that I knew, I should have designated my poor daughter and her bereaved husband. She is now, perhaps, still happier; but alas! how wretched is he, and how miserable am I! My dear wife derives great support under this severe dispensation from her faith and future hopes, and I have experienced some consolation from the numerous letters of condolence which I have received from good and pious friends.

"I remain, truly, your friend, H. CLAY.

"Theo. Frelinghuysen, Esq."

The succeeding letter was written in reference to the nomination of Clay and Frelinghuysen by the Whig National Convention in May, 1844:

T. Frelinghuysen to H. Clay.

"New York, May 11, 1844.

"MY DEAR SIR,—I have been rather impatiently waiting for my lame arm to write a few lines to my honored friend, that I might express to you the heartfelt gratification that I feel at the recent association of my humble name with yours—a distinction as honorable as it has been to me surprising. And should the result of the fall election confirm the nomination, of which there now seems to be very strong indications, it will, I assure you, be among my richest political privileges to contribute any mite of influence in my power to render prosperous and lasting in benefits the administration of a patriot whose elevation I have long desired. Our names have been brought together here by the voice of our fellow-men. My prayer for you and my own soul shall be fervent that, through the rich grace of our Savior, they may be found written in the Book of Life of the Lamb that was slain for our sins.

"My good wife, who has never ceased to cherish the hope of your eventual elevation to the chief magistracy, unites with me in kindest respects to Mrs. Clay and yourself.

"P.S.—My hand is still lame, and I can write only in irregular characters."

The following was written when the defeat of the Whigs was ascertained:

Theodore Frelinghuysen to Mr. Clay.

"New York, Nov. 9th, 1844.

"MY DEAR SIR,—I address you this morning with very different feelings from my expectations a few months ago. The alliance of the foreign votes and that most impracticable of all organizations, the Abolitionists, have defeated the strongest national vote ever given to a presidential candidate. The Whigs in this city and state have struggled most nobly. All classes of American citizens have ardently, cordially, and with the freest sacrifices contended for your just claims to patriotic confidence; and could you this morning behold the depression of spirits and sinking of hearts that pervade the community, I am sure that you would feel, 'Well, in very truth, my defeat has been the occasion of a more precious tribute and vindication than even the majority of numbers.'

"The Abolitionists were inimically obstinate, and seemed resolved to distinguish their importance, right or wrong. The combination of adverse circumstances has often struck me in the progress of the canvass. At the South I was denounced as an Abolitionist, rank and uncompromising. Here, the Abolitionists have been rancorous in their hostility. A short time since, William Jay (of illustrious name) assailed me in his anti-slavery prints by a harsh, unchristian article in the form of a letter addressed to me, but sent to the winds. Its object was, no doubt, to drive the party, and it had, I suppose, some influence that way, although it was too bitter and irrational to accomplish much. And then the foreign vote was tremendous. More than three thousand, it is confidently said, have been naturalized in this city alone since the first of October. It is an alarming fact that this foreign vote has decided the great questions of American policy and counteracted a nation's gratitude.

"But, my dear sir, leaving this painful subject, let us look away to brighter and better prospects and surer hopes in the promises and consolations of the Gospel of our Savior. As sinners who have rebelled against our Maker, we need a Savior or we must perish, and this Redeemer has been provided for us. Prophecy declared Him from the earliest period of our fall in Paradise, and the Gospel makes known the faithful fulfillment. 'Come unto me,' cries this exalted Savior, 'come unto me, all ye that are weary and heavy laden, and I will give you rest.' Let us then repair to Him. He will never fail us in the hour of peril and trial. Vain is the help of man, and frail and fatal all trust in the arm of flesh; but he that trusteth in the Lord shall be as Mount Zion itself, that can never be removed. I pray, my honored friend, that your heart may seek this blessed refuge, stable as the everlasting hills, and let this be the occasion to prompt an earnest, prayerful, and the Lord grant it may be a joyful search after truth as it is in Christ Jesus.

"With affectionate regards to Mrs. Clay, in which my good wife, sorely tried, heartily unites, I remain, with sincere esteem and best wishes, your friend."

To this letter Mr. Clay sent the following reply, showing the spirit in which he met his defeat, the way he accounted for it, and the cordiality with which he entertained Mr. Frelinghuysen's religious suggestions:

Mr. Clay to Mr. Frelinghuysen.

"Ashland, 2d December, 1844.

"My dear Sir,—I duly received your friendly letter of the 9th November. I fully share in the feelings under the influence of which it was written. The most unexpected result of the Presidential election has caused many patriotic hearts to bleed, and has greatly affected my own. Although I will not deny that I feel the shock of the sad event on my own account, it is far more to be deplored for our country and our friends. I had indulged the hope that I might be an humble instrument in the hands of Providence to endeavor to bring back our government to its former purity, and to contribute toward rendering justice to a large body of virtuous, able, and patriotic friends who have been cruelly persecuted and proscribed. That hope is now fled forever.

"The issue of the contest has been brought about by the most extraordinary combination of circumstances. If nativism had not sprung up, or if it had been more faithful to its own principles; or if the foreign vote had not been united against us; or if the Catholics had been more divided; or if the Abolitionists had been true to their own avowed principles; or if there had been no frauds, the triumph of the Whigs would have been secured. It required a union of all these discordant elements to defeat them, and, unfortunately, the union existed.

"It is highly gratifying to me to learn from you that the Whigs of the city and State of New York struggled nobly. The same praise is due to them, generally, throughout the Union.

"We have other consolations. Neither you nor I have done any thing to bring upon ourselves self-reproaches during the canvass, and both of us, by its result, have been saved a great responsibility. Let us also cherish the fond hope that the evils to our country, which we so much apprehend from the new administration, may not be realized.

"You have, my dear friend, however, kindly suggested the truest of all consolations in the resources of our holy religion. I have long been persuaded of that solemn truth; nor have I been entirely neglectful of exertions to secure to myself its benefit. I wish

I could add that I feel entire confidence that these exertions had been crowned with success. But they shall not be intermitted; and I trust that, by diligent searching, I shall yet find, in faith in our Lord Jesus, that solace which no earthly honors or possessions can give.

"Mrs. Clay unites with me in reciprocating affectionate regards to Mrs. F., and I remain ever faithfully and truly your friend, H. CLAY.

"Theo. Frelinghuysen, Esq."

In the year 1846, Mr. Clay, in answer to a letter from Mr. Frelinghuysen speaking of his continued ill health, wrote to him, under date of October 9, from Ashland, recommending a certain course of treatment which had been beneficial to himself in 1828, when almost broken down by his labors as Secretary of State. After speaking on this point very minutely, the writer proceeds:

"I am greatly obliged, my dear friend, by the kind interest you take in my spiritual welfare. I feel much more comfortable than I ever did on that subject. I hope and believe that I have improved in my religious feelings and in the performance of my religious duties. I attend the Episcopal Church regularly and with satisfaction, but I have not yet become a member of it. This I hope to do. I must own, however, with regret, that I do not yet feel that *absolute* confidence in my future salvation which some Christians profess to have in theirs."

The last letter of Mr. Frelinghuysen to his old friend was written not many months before Mr. Clay's death:

Theodore Frelinghuysen to Mr. Clay.

"New Brunswick, January 19, 1852.

"MY DEAR SIR,—I have heard, with great interest and anxiety, of your continued feeble health, and that it had been rather more feeble since your decided testimony in behalf of Washington's foreign policy. I was rejoiced to hear your words of soberness and truth on the exciting question of Hungarian politics, and I trust that a divine blessing will follow your counsels.

"In this time of impaired health, and sometimes trying despondency that ensues, it must be refreshing to look away to Him who is a helper near in trouble, and able and willing to sustain and comfort you. This blessed Gospel, that reveals the riches of God's grace in Jesus Christ, is a wonderful remedy, so suited to our condition and character, and so full of inexpressible consolation to us as sinners needing mercy, His blood cleansing us from the guilt of sin, His Spirit purifying our hearts, and restoring us to God's image and favor. May you, my dear friend, largely partake of its comforts, and, leaning all your hopes on the Almighty Savior's arm, hold on your way, for life and for death, for time and for eternity, in His name and strength."

In a eulogy which Mr. Frelinghuysen pronounced in Newark, New Jersey, shortly after Mr. Clay's death, he concluded by a reference to his religious relations, and, after quoting some passages from the letters of his friend, remarked that these extracts "show how universal is the need of a Gospel hope for the noblest and the humblest; that, however human distinctions exist, and usefully, yet before God there is but *one level;* and also how far more gloriously true greatness beams upon us from the foot of the Cross, seeking peace through the blood of Him who once died upon it for our sake."

None of Mr. Frelinghuysen's letters to Mr. Webster have been recovered, but, from the replies which he received, their tenor can easily be inferred. In the year 1840, Mr. Frelinghuysen, being then Chancellor of the University, wrote to Mr. Webster in behalf of the literary societies of that institution, requesting him to deliver the annual address before them, at the same time adding some words on what he deemed the most important of all subjects. The following is the answer:

"Washington, Feb. 24, 1840.

"MY DEAR SIR,—I can hardly expect to be pardoned for delaying so long an answer to your first letter, and for waiting to be reminded by a second. The truth is, my dear sir, your kind letter was interesting, and I was hoping for leisure to do something more than to make a reply to its particular request. I wanted to say something on the solemn subjects which, in so friendly a manner, you introduce; but I have found my time very much engrossed by the concerns of public and professional life, and have also had to suffer the inconvenience of a very long-continued cold.

"I can not possibly undertake to make an address to your societies. For some time I have been compelled to decline *all* such requests. The P. B. K. of Cambridge have a standing claim upon me, which I have put off from year to year, and must put off again. I wish heartily it were otherwise, because I should be glad to oblige you, but do not flatter myself I could speak edifyingly to your societies. For some years I have hardly kept up with the literature of the day. Rust is coming over my earlier acquisitions, and, if I can keep myself a little bright in matters of law and politics, while I yet pursue them, it is all I expect.

* * * * * * *

"Yours, D. WEBSTER."

Eight years afterward Mr. Frelinghuysen addressed a letter of condolence to this distinguished man, then suffering under a sore bereavement. He was thus answered:

"March 13th, 1848.

"In the midst of severe affliction, my dear friend, I hear your voice tendering condolence and sympathy, and uttering admonitions of resignation and submission. I feel that nothing else is left, and I pray God that I may receive the chastening with a penitent and a believing spirit. It is not for me to say whether He shall call me or my children first into His presence. I know that there we must all shortly appear. I thank you, my dear sir, for your affectionate kindness and remembrance, and assure you that your health and happiness are subjects of my sincere prayers.

"The sun of our lives is fast going down; my own, especially, is already near the horizon. I wish to consider all things earthly as held by a precarious tie, and that by a tie still more precarious I am held to those who love me.

"Mrs. Webster joins me in kind remembrances to you and Mrs. Frelinghuysen, and pray you to accept our affectionate regards. DANIEL WEBSTER.

"Mr. Frelinghuysen."

Mr. Frelinghuysen was for many years intimately associated with the Hon. William Pennington, for many years Governor and Chancellor of the State of New Jersey, and afterward Speaker of the House of Representatives during the troublous times of the Thirty-sixth Congress. He was always faithful to the soul of his friend, and at last had the pleasure of seeing him an avowed and consistent Christian. His agency in leading to this result is thus acknowledged by the governor in a letter written in April, 1858:

" * * * If any one thing has impressed me more than any other, it is this wonderful mercy that we should be permitted to go on in sin, and rebellion, and ingratitude for a long life, and yet be permitted to share in the blessings which appertain to all who are penitent and ask forgiveness at the hands of the Mediator.

"I wish to say to you, as a friend to whom I would confide my most secret thoughts, that I do not consider myself a subject of the present revival any farther than it may have led me to consummate a purpose long intended. And it is due from me to say that I ascribe much of my reverence for divine things, and, indeed, my strongest and firmest religious impressions, to your advice and example—the living example, that is the preacher, after all, with the conscience and the intellect.

"With many hopes and firm resolves, I still am, and always expect to be, a trembling, doubting Christian. Some people have much enthusiasm, much feeling and excitement; with me, I confide in the promises, and in the hope that I have made a full and humble surrender penitently to the blessed Redeemer of the world. * * *

"I am, ever, your friend, WM. PENNINGTON."

With the Hon. JAMES S. NEVIUS, long a prominent member of the New Jersey bar, and afterward one of the justices of the Supreme Court of the state, Mr. Frelinghuysen frequently, during a course of many years, held conversations and correspondence, in which he acted the part of a faithful Christian friend, and at last had the pleasure of seeing him become an avowed disciple of the Lord Jesus. One of the last letters written to him before he took this step was couched in these words:

"Dear Sir,—I have duly received and read your letters with great interest, and hope that I may give a thought, under the guidance of God's blessed Spirit, that may be of profit to your own anxious mind. It seems to me, after much reflection on the terms of your letter, that the only hinderance in your way is in the unwillingness of your heart to give up all its pleas and strivings, its regrets at unavailing and unsatisfied strivings to be better, and to fall down a poor, lost, wretched sinner at the Savior's feet, and to give Him *all the glory* of your deliverance from the power, pollution, and guilt of sin.

"And here you have stood for years, in the inner secrets of your heart fighting against God and His way of mercy, and wanting to make terms with Him—some little spot or speck of merit, no matter how small, the very least grain that will save pride, your pride, the humiliation of such unconditional submission as the Gospel and grace of God requires. If the matter could be settled by the most painful investigation of reason and philosophy—if it were allowed or even required of you to undergo the pains of bodily toil and suffering—if the tears you shed, the horrors you experience, the darkness, doubts, and conflicts you endure—if these, or any of these, might only have some place to draw Divine forbearance and make up the account to soften a single grain of Divine requirements, how willingly your heart would give in to such conditions. Here it is—believe it: there is no obstacle but in a proud heart that will not bow down all the way to dust and ashes before God, and exclaim, 'O Lord! I surrender.

"'A guilty, weak, and helpless worm,
On Thy kind arms I fall;
Be Thou my strength and righteousness,
My Jesus and my all.'

"Yes, my friend, you must come and ought to come. For *who* is this gracious Redeemer? Remember that He is God manifest in the flesh. The Lord of life and glory for our sakes took upon Him our nature and *suffered for us*—died on the cross to *atone* for our violations of His own blessed law; and now all He asks of you is, 'Son, give me thine heart,' and you have refused Him this small tribute for years and years. He says in His Word, To as many as received Him, to them gave He power to become the sons of God. You won't receive Him, and then mourn that you can't get religion. You never will until you fly to the Savior. Submit now, unreservedly, and all will be peace. Yours very truly,

"THEO. FRELINGHUYSEN.

"The Hon. James S. Nevius."

The Hon. E. F. CHAMBERS was a member of the Senate from Maryland during Mr. Frelinghuysen's term of service in that body. In a letter written from Chestertown, Maryland, in March, 1854, Judge Chambers bears this testimony to the character and course of his friend:

"It is truly gratifying to witness the continued kind feeling of an old friend, for whom I have never ceased to entertain a warm regard; whose kind, considerate, and Christian counsel has been willingly tendered when impatience of spirit or intemperance of excited feeling would mislead me, and whose amiable and disinterested aid was never withheld when needed. May you long continue, my friend, to fulfill the office you have so well performed—a pattern of the Christian graces, and a wise counselor to all who would cultivate them. * * *

"It will afford me great pleasure to see you once more before one or the other shall be called away; but, if not on earth, I humbly trust we may in heaven renew our greetings.

"Very faithfully and truly yours,

"E. F. CHAMBERS."

On one occasion, many years ago, the legal friend with whom he usually traveled when going to Trenton to attend the courts was accompanied by his son, then a young man just about to make his appearance at the bar of the Supreme Court. The next morning Mr. Frelinghuysen invited the youth to join him in an early walk. While they were together the subject of personal religion was introduced, and urged by one so evidently taught by the Holy Spirit that that interview was a benediction. And when the good man lay upon his death-bed, the companion of his walk forty years before called at the house, and sent a message of thanks acknowledging the life-long benefit derived from the conversation then held. It elicited from the dying saint the characteristic response, "Give God the praise."

At this early period of his conversion he was often tried by temptations to forbear speaking to the worldly upon their spiritual condition. There was one eminent member of the bar for whom he had felt much concern, but whom he found it quite a trial to address on the matter, and accordingly deferred it from time to time. At last, in one of his morning walks, his mind became so troubled that he turned his steps homeward and at once sought the lawyer, saying, "There is a subject of which I have long wanted to speak to you, but have been afraid." "Why, Frelinghuysen, what in the world is there of which you are afraid to speak to me?" "It is of your undying soul, and I have acted like a coward about it." "Well, Frelinghuysen, *you* may speak to me on that subject, but not those who are inconsistent Christians."

A missionary of the Methodist Church, now laboring in China, who, when a mere child, had seemed to be converted, but afterward wandered very far from the true path, traces his recovery and present Christian hope to the Divine blessing upon frequent conversations Mr. Frelinghuysen held with him while visiting in the drug-store where the young man was acting as clerk.

Mr. Frelinghuysen seemed never to lose an opportunity. His heart was so burdened with concern for all out of Christ, that he has been known more than once, after passing unconverted persons in the street, to be constrained by his own painful emotions to turn back and speak with them on the state of their souls. Even his students, although so faithfully dealt with in his biblical instructions, and at other times when they were addressed as a body, were not neglected in private interviews, but then entreated with even more fervor to turn to God and give Him their hearts.

He was not discouraged by the fact that any whom he could address were intemperate, or otherwise very far estranged from the right path, but, on the contrary, seized every occasion to speak to them the fitting word; and, however such persons might object to appeals and remonstrances coming from others, they always listened to Mr. Frelinghuysen at least with outward attention and respect. His purity and consistency of character were so eminent and undeniable that those who were hardened in impenitence could not close their ears to what he said.

In November, 1859, a state convention of Sabbath-school teachers was held at Trenton, New Jersey. Mr.

Frelinghuysen, as president of the body, opened the sessions with an earnest and instructive address. When he sat down, the late John P. Jackson, Esq., of Newark, followed with these remarks:

"Mr. President, I came here to listen and to learn; but I am delighted to say, before this great assembly, that all my early principles, all the great foundations of learning which I esteem valuable for time and eternity, I have derived, sir, as a pupil of yours; and were it not for the opportunity of making this acknowledgement, I should not have arisen. And it is precisely in the mode which you have employed this afternoon in your plain and simple address that I have received that instruction. * * * And, sir, I have been prompted by your noble example to engage in the delightful work of Sabbath-school instruction; and now I come here with you to engage in council on its great interests, although some thirty-five years have passed since I studied law in your office, and received my early impressions of duty from your example and instructions."

There were few public men in New Jersey, or in Washington, or in New York, with whom Mr. Frelinghuysen was in the habit of meeting, to whom he did not at some time or in some way bring the subject of personal religion. He was judicious and unobtrusive in his methods of approach, and his delicacy of feeling and vivid sense of propriety rendered those whom he addressed more willing to open their hearts upon a theme of such deep personal interest. He certainly often found access where other persons had failed, and there are many still living who could bear a decided testimony to his Christian faithfulness. Mr. Frelinghuysen rarely spoke of these interviews; never, indeed, save in circumstances when a reference to them would be not only unobjectionable, but of useful tendency. He was quite content to do good in secret, and wait for recognition until the resurrection of the just. Many, therefore, who have long known his public reputation as a consistent Christian, will be surprised to learn that, perhaps, no layman in the land ever made so many private personal appeals on the matter of the soul's salvation as he habitually did during the last forty years of his life. It was not a fitful, occasional thing, pursued during some season of revival and then abandoned, but a fixed habit, followed at home and abroad with the undeviating constancy of a deep-seated principle. His catholic sympathies took in the worth of all souls as such, and there was no human being so low or degraded, so alien or hostile, that he did not feel for its spiritual welfare, and speak the proper word whenever an opportunity offered or could be made to occur. He was on the watch to seize favorable occasions, and his own walk with God was so close, and his own experience of divine things so rich and satisfying, that it was nothing unnatural or constrained for him, on any day of the week, or during any season of the year, to invite the unthinking and worldly to consider the things which belonged to their everlasting peace.

He was not always successful. Some to whom he had been faithful during a long term of years, and for whom he had prayed with very great fervor and constancy, at last went down to the grave giving small and dubious signs of being prepared for the great change. But he was not chilled, much less soured by the disappointment. His zeal was destitute of the least tincture of fanaticism. His sorrow was not for the failure of the means, but for the loss of the end; and the only result was to set him more diligently at work to do what he could for the salvation of such as remained still within the reach of human efforts. His entire life was an exemplification of the sentiment expressed in his letter to Mr. Lincoln: "I suppose that while, for the more solemn duties of the sanctuary and its worship, and for the governance and order of Christ's Church, the ministers are to be called and set apart, yet for exhortation, and prayer, and witnessing for the truth, and warning sinners, and encouraging the trembling believer, we are all to labor for Christ, and to have a heart and a tongue for His blessed service."

CHAPTER XI.

EXTRACTS FROM HIS CORRESPONDENCE.

Its general Character.—Fifteen Letters to a young Relative pursuing his Education.—Two to another young Relative.—Four to the Rev. Dr. J. A. H. Cornell.—A Letter of Condolence to the Rev. Dr. De Witt.

In the discourse pronounced by the Rev. Dr. Campbell on the occasion of Mr. Frelinghuysen's death, there occurs the following passage: "What a volume of letters his vast correspondence on behalf of good objects would furnish! Letters of condolence with those who were in trouble—letters sending pecuniary aid and kind words to the daughters and widows of old associates whom the reverses of life had overtaken—letters to the sons of old friends, who, prodigal-like, had wandered from the path of rectitude—letters in aid of the Bible, Tract, Missionary, Colonization, and Temperance causes, for all of which he labored, and gave, and prayed—letters to those upon whom he pressed the claims of Christ—what a volume of letters it would make! And I dare affirm that he who will read all that vast correspondence of the last forty-two years will not find one censorious remark, one bitter expression." There is no exaggeration in this statement. Mr. Frelinghuysen's correspondence was very large, and every letter bore the stamp of his own generous, manly, Christian character. In his later years writing became irksome to him, and his letters rarely exceeded a single page, but what was said answered the purpose. His reluctance to write disappeared whenever the prospect of usefulness to the souls of men presented itself, and a full heart quivered in every line of innumerable epistles. The range of his correspondence was very wide, and in no case where the circumstances would at all admit of an allusion to the chief concern, did he fail to make such allusion. The things of the kingdom held such full and habitual possession of his mind that it was easy to bring them forward, and his long training and social culture enabled him to do it without giving offense or occasioning an unwelcome surprise.

The most of his letters are irrecoverably lost or dispersed. Of those which have been recovered, many are so interwoven with private details and interests of persons yet living as to be unfit for publication. A score or more, composed mainly of such as were addressed to young friends, are here inserted, as showing under his own hand, in the most familiar and confidential utterances of his heart, what manner of man he was.

The following are extracts from a series of letters addressed from time to time to a young relative pursuing his studies away from home:

"My dear ——,—We received your second letter last evening, and regretted to learn that you had encountered so many difficulties in your going to W——. If I had thought that your way would have been so difficult, I should have waited for some friend with whom to send you. But I am thankful, my dear child, that the Lord has been your friend. He, I trust, has brought you safely to your residence. We miss you much from our dear little circle, but your improvement under the many advantages of the college consoles us. Now is the season for you to lay the foundation for your future usefulness, and let me entreat you to found it well in the fear of the Lord, in diligence to acquire solid learning, to store your mind with the instructions of wisdom. Your Maker claims your first, best thoughts. My dear ——, realize that you are a sinner, that you need a Savior, and that whatever else you may gain, if you do not secure an interest in the mercy of God through the blood of His dear Son, you will be an everlasting victim of His wrath.

"Read daily the Word of God, and when you read, pray over it that the Holy Spirit would open your understanding and heart to receive and love it.

"Be careful of your company. It is a truth written upon the grave of many a ruined youth that 'evil communications corrupt good manners.'

"Discipline yourself to spend half an hour each day in examining your condition and prospects. Dwell on such questions as these: What am I? Where will my present course end? What am I to do for God, who gave me my being, my friends, and my all? Could my dear father and mother speak to me from the eternal world, what would be their counsels to their child? Oh, my dear child, I feel my soul deeply anxious for your spiritual welfare. Let us so live that we may forever live together in the presence of our blessed God and Savior, with all the redeemed.

* * * * * * *

"Your affectionate uncle,

"THEO. FRELINGHUYSEN.

"Saturday evening, Jan. 3, 1829."

"DEAR ——,—We received your last letter, and are happy to learn of your health and welfare. That you should occasionally feel the depressing influence of a home-sick fever is natural, but you must take care that it does not master you; and the best remedy against it is steady employment for the mind in your studies. It is now the season in which you are to fit yourself for future usefulness. My dear ——, I hope your aims will be high. I mean not that you should cherish a vain ambition—far from this; but I mean that you should strive after that substantial usefulness which a well-educated mind, disciplined by study and self-denial, will generally attain.

"You say nothing of the state of your feelings on the most important of all subjects—how you stand affected toward your Creator, Preserver, and Benefactor. He has claims, my dear child, which can not be disregarded without great danger and guilt; and I should be wanting in faithfulness to your soul not thus affectionately to warn you that every day you put off repentance and submission to Christ you run an awful hazard of eternal wretchedness. God has given you His Word. He has at times brought you to the verge of eternity, and made you feel how dreadful it was to enter there with a heart unreconciled to Him. Now be persuaded to defer no longer. Suffer not the precious season of youth to pass away, only to furnish matter for bitter regrets. May the rich grace of the blessed Redeemer be shed down upon your soul, and do you earnestly pray for this daily. * * *

"Very affectionately, T. FRELINGHUYSEN.

"Newark, Feb. 5, 1829."

"DEAR ——,—I was much refreshed by your letter received last evening. I intended to write to you from Washington, but my stay there was short and hurried, and I arrived at home the evening before your letter came, happy to learn of your health and welfare.

"The scenes at Washington were to me quite novel, and, in some measure, interesting; but, my dear child, they all confirmed the dictate of sound reason and religious truth that 'man walketh in a vain show.' The strifes of ambition that engage the whole energies of many great men are unsatisfying, and more, they are perplexing and delusive. An immortal mind can not be filled with such vain satisfactions. God has formed us to enjoy Him, and when our powers are debased and perverted to inferior purposes, we do violence to the great end of our existence, and only furnish occasion for disappointment here, and, if left to our perverse choice, to everlasting confusion and wretchedness hereafter.

"I hope, from your remarks in your letter, that you sometimes feel that religion is the one thing needful; and if you realize, my dear ——, that it is your own unbelief that prevents your enjoying the favor of God, I beg you to be concerned at the condition in which you stand before Him. He is waiting to be gracious. He points you to the blood of His Son as your refuge. He calls, invites, and commands you to turn unto Him and live—to repent and believe, and be saved, or perish. Oh, will you resist all this, and go on in rebellion?

"Do you sometimes anxiously inquire, What shall I do? Fall down at the foot of the cross. There mourn over this dreadful unbelief. Cry to Him who is mighty to save that He would have mercy upon you, that He would take away the heart of stone and give a heart of flesh. Never raise up any other obstacle than a hard and perverse heart, and raise this as the ground of all your guilt and wretchedness, which, if not renewed by sovereign grace, will justly condemn you forever. Make it your plea for mercy, and not your apology for remaining in sin. I pray that the Lord will in rich grace lead your soul to Himself. Cherish every serious impression; endeavor to fix them upon your heart; remember it is not a light thing, but for your life. * * *

"Sincerely and affectionately yours,

"THEO. FRELINGHUYSEN.

"Newark, March 25, 1829."

"Washington, Jan. 27, 1832.

"DEAR ——,—I am happy to hear that you are again seated at your studies, and hope that no interruption will break in upon the diligent pursuit of your professional duties. I hope, my dear ——, that you feel the deep importance of a solid education. Lay the foundations of usefulness in a thorough knowledge of the whole range of medicine. But be not content here. Draw from the sources of history and biography, the springs of human action. Become familiar with the noble specimens of taste and genius in the English and Latin classics. Be, my son, an accomplished scholar. But I should fail in my duty, as you would in yours, if I did not urge, and you yield to it, that you should seek first the kingdom of God. My dear ——, let me entreat you to look at this momentous subject promptly; what shall we do when God takes away the soul for eternity? Eternity! oh, how full of meaning! How dreadful is that thought to a sinner who must be driven away! Pray over it, and may the Lord lead you to himself.

"Yours very truly."

"Washington, Feb. 27, 1832.

"DEAR ——,—We duly received your letter on Saturday, and are rejoiced to learn the interesting state of religion in Mr. H——'s church; and what increased our interest, and concern also, was to find that your mind felt at such a season the comparative unimportance of all other mere worldly pursuits.

"My dear ——, it is a deeply momentous crisis for you. When the Lord comes near to you by His Spirit, and when, as I trust, His motions are felt upon your heart, it makes the hour one of the most solemn on this side of eternity. Be persuaded by all the just claims which your Maker and Redeemer has to your affection and service—by all that is precious in the blood shed for your sins—by all that is valuable in the favor of God or terrible in his eternal powers, *now*, *to-day*, to surrender your heart to Him. Go mourning over your sins, over your past ingratitude and rebellion, and, with the temper of the prodigal, seek the reconciled face of your heavenly Father.

"How could the Lord make terms more easy? That He ever held out a hope on any terms is matter of wonder with angels; but that His own blessed Son should leave His glory to suffer and die that a way of deliverance should be opened for the guilty children of rebellious men, this, this is astonishing grace indeed. And shall we, shall you, my dear son, stand out against such love, refuse to repent of your sins, and reject this Savior? Has your heart ever anxiously inquired, What shall I do? Go to the throne of grace, and plead for mercy and guidance. Cast yourself upon God's sovereign pleasure. You can take nothing that deserves His favor, but you *can* take a broken heart for sin, and this is all He asks of you. I commend you, my dear ——, to this Infinite Grace, and pray for you that your heart may turn from every idle vanity and all other refuges to the strong-hold as a prisoner of hope.

"Very truly and affectionately yours."

"Newark, September 10, 1832.

"DEAR ——,—We received your letter from P——, and were glad to hear of your safe arrival, and that you seemed so far pleased with the situation. I hope that you may soon be comfortably lodged, and in good earnest improve the facilities offered for your improvement. It would have been very pleasant to have you with us until the time of our returning to Washington, but your welfare was of still greater importance than the comfort of your society. You must now settle it in your mind that the present session is to be a time of serious business, hard study, and laborious investigation. To be useful in your profession, you must enjoy the confidence of the public, and nothing will secure this but skill, intelligence, and virtue. No man ever became eminent in any service but through severe and constant industry. Genius, without this, is but a shining nothing, to dazzle and blaze a little, nd then to pass away with no memorial of solid usefulness. Remember, my dear child, that all your advantages are a trust, to be accounted for to your friends, to society, and, above all, to your Maker. These confer corresponding obligations. Days and months pass rapidly away, but every hour bears a record of our conduct, and, when the brief career of life is concluded, everlasting consequences follow in inevitable connection. My dear ——, you must meet these consequences. Oh, ponder deeply and prayerfully the solemn truth that you can never escape, evade, or repel them. You have entered on the pilgrimage for eternity, and must go forward to realize its retributions. The blessed God demands as His reasonable service your heart with all its affections and desires, and do you not feel that you justly owe all to Him? What kindness and mercy has He not strewed all along your path? Who provided for you all the blessings which so richly crown your life? Often, when disease has invaded and threatened to cut you down, who was it that rebuked the sickness, and healed, and bade you live? And what does the Lord require of you but that you repent of all your sins, and receive and rejoice in His dear Son? Be persuaded to bow before His throne of mercy, and render up your powers to the service of your generous and unwearied Benefactor. Then you will have a sure refuge in every season of trial, and a resting-place from a world of anxiety and trouble.

"May you enjoy the best of your heavenly Father's blessings, share in His love, and be kept by His Spirit.

"Yours very truly."

"Newark, September 6, 1833.

"My dear ——,—As I know that you will feel a little of the low spirits which occasionally come over us when separated from those who are dear to us, I concluded to drop you a few lines. I deeply feel the trial of parting from you, and am only reconciled to it by the persuasion that your welfare will be promoted by the change in your plans. It is an anxious purpose with us to have you qualified for solid usefulness in your profession, and we should forego the sincere pleasure of your society for the attainment of this important object.

"These separations, my dear son, are of merciful ordainment, with all their pains. They are designed to lead our souls up to the blessed God, the only satisfying portion; all below is transitory and vain. His favor is life eternal. By our sins we have forfeited this rich blessing; and yet He offers us restoration, on terms glorious to His mercy. He speaks to, nay, He pleads with you, 'My son, give me thine heart.' Come with ingenuous sorrow for sin, believe in the Lord Jesus Christ, and all will be well, your sins forgiven, and your precious soul accepted.

"I hope we shall often hear from you, and I commend you, my dear ——, to the grace and favor of a kind and gracious Father.

"Very sincerely and affectionately yours."

"Newark, October 28, 1833.

"Dear ——,—I received your acceptable letter on my return from Bergen Court on Friday evening last. It gave me sincere and great pleasure to learn of your welfare, and that your studies had become so agreeable to your taste. I hope, my dear son, that you will not relax your industrious exertions to master your useful profession in all its branches. It is knowledge here, as in all science, that will found safely and surely successful enterprise. Do not take a zest in the mere *physical* branches. Remember that the laws and operations of the mind are intimately connected with your profession, and this opens a wide and deeply interesting range for study and reflection. And, above all, my dear ——, remember with prayerful conviction that it is a mind in ruins, a spirit that has destroyed its moral beauty by rebellion against its blessed and glorious Author. Here I rejoice to know that your Bible is of daily perusal. Search its divine pages as for your life. Pray to be guided to the only Physician for this dreadful malady, even to the Lord Jesus Christ, who came into the world to save sinners.

" * * * I wish the best blessings of Heaven on your plans in prospect, and hope they may realize your hopes.

"Very truly and affectionately yours."

"Washington, Feb. 18, 1834.

"DEAR ——,—My public engagements have pressed very heavily upon me, or I should oftener have written to you through the winter. I have heard of you, by various ways, during your home visit. You must have greatly enjoyed the sight and society of your friends. But what gives me more pleasure than all besides is the report of your studious habits and correct deportment. Here my feelings are all ardently enlisted, and the best and sweetest return for all our anxious cares is your personal welfare and good conduct. I said the best; but, my dear son, I must make one exception, a vital and fundamental one. There is a dearer wish that I cherish for you: that you may turn away from the vain show of this perishing world, and place your affections on Him whose you are, and whom you are bound to love and serve. This, my dear ——, is the highest wisdom. 'Seek the Lord while He may be found.'

"Yours very truly."

"Washington, June 2, 1834.

"MY DEAR ——,—Your letter to Aunt C—— was duly received, and we are glad to find that you are well, studious, and *home-sick*. I long again to have you, with F——, by my side, riding the *roan* and buying the seabass. Home will be very sweet. I hope we shall get away by the 1st of July.

"I should think you had learned enough of the bones to set them when broken, and of the constitution to patch it somewhat when out of order; but this I leave with the doctors. How does it fare with the mind? There is a great salvation wrought out for us at infinite cost. It has been tendered to you, my son, in repeated offers, under many favorable circumstances. Your eternal destiny depends on your treatment of it, and where does it stand in your regard? Do not, I beg of you, hurry over this subject as one which you expect to have referred as a matter of course by me. It is a deep, personal, practical concern. Could we realize in any measure its vast importance, its connection with ages of interminable existence, our wonder would be that we could feel so little anxiety. May the good Spirit of God guide you into all truth, and to a happy choice, that when death shall summon you away (and, my dear ——, this may be soon, and can not, at the longest, be very far), you may be ready to meet your Maker and Judge in peace.

"Yours very truly."

"Newark, Nov. 13, 1834.

"DEAR ——,—I am happy to learn from your letters that you are at *hard* study. I know that it is wholesome. The brain needs action. It is like a flint—to have fire you must strike it. And this calls up another forcible illustration. Look at the hardy forgeman, with his brawny arm and vigorous sinew. What gave him all this but swinging the ponderous sledge that he holds. Once it made him pant to wield it;

now he can toss it as a plaything. So it is with the mind. If you wish to give it strength, and tone, and compass, you must put its powers to the trial, bring them out to stern, severe, and laborious exercise. There is but one way to eminence, and it is not a royal road. It is rough, thorny, up-hill, full of lions to the indolent and faint-hearted, but, with all its adversities, delightful to the earnest and enthusiastic. To them it repays, as they struggle up and over its difficulties.

"And thus too, my dear son, would you attain the far more exalted place, even a place and a name among the followers of the Lord of life and glory. You must *strive* to enter it; give all diligence; pray with all prayer and supplication; deny yourself, and renounce this vain world as a portion. You must come down as a humble penitent to the foot of the cross; there, where the blessed Son of God shed His own blood for the remission of sin—there confess all your transgressions, and look up in His name to a gracious God, if, peradventure, He will look upon you in mercy, and receive you to His everlasting favor. His promise is sure and large as the world: 'Him that cometh unto me I will in no wise cast out.' Believe this precious declaration, cast your soul upon it, and all will be well with you. * * *

"Very truly and affectionately yours."

"Washington, December 3, 1834.

"Dear ——,—Your favor was duly received, and we are glad to learn that your cold is better. I think you must enjoy the delights of study; no cares except the student's, so far as this world is concerned, and a regular and systematic course of study. The latter is invaluable to literary advancement. By-and-by the knock of the patient and the calls of business will interrupt all this order. Therefore, my son, improve the present occasion, and while anxious to learn how you may heal the maladies of the body, do not forget that sin has spread its poison over your soul, and look to the great Physician who alone can heal.

"I send you a copy of the Message. It has length and variety; a little too harsh upon France, and a great deal too severe against the Bank. It exhibits the tact of its authors. But enough of politics; I am very tired of them. It will be, my son, very pleasant to meet again at our own fireside, and there rejoice together in the goodness of our heavenly Father.

"Yours very truly."

"Washington, December 5, 1834.

"MY DEAR ——,—Your letter was received this morning and read with deep interest. I rejoice to learn that your mind has been so long impressed with the importance of religion and of making your peace with God, and the recent and unexpected breach upon our little circle should increase your anxiety. It does speak to us all in affecting language to be also ready when the summons comes. That a merciful God has restrained you by His grace from the commission of many sins is matter for unceasing thankfulness; that you can trace His kind hand in all this is encouragement for you to cast your soul upon His grace, and give yourself away to His service forever. Religion concerns the state of the heart toward God. By nature this is at enmity with Him. Can you require farther proof of this than your own past course? Have you not preferred the world or your own interest to Him? Do you not feel a proneness to get away from God, and to place your affections supremely on other objects than Him and His service? All this must be mourned and repented of. The way of salvation by the Lord Jesus Christ must be approved of and trusted in. Christ died for our sins, that we might be pardoned through faith in His blood. God will not accept our righteousness, but requires us to *believe* in His Son for righteousness. 'He that believeth shall be saved.' Is your heart willing to be saved in this way—a way that gives all the glory of your salvation to Christ, and humbles and strips the sinner of all merit? So far, my son, as pardon and justification are concerned, God has been graciously pleased to make this depend on our belief and acceptance. Christ offers us peace freely, without money and without price, and if we will, He is abundantly willing to save us. Read and pray over the third chapter of the Gospel of John. There our blessed Savior brings out the love of God, the condescension and grace of the Redeemer, and the only way of salvation.

"One of your dangers will or may arise from your heart being unwilling to go to Christ without some other reliance—on your prayers, or good resolutions, or breaking off the practice of sin. But God requires you to come, guilty and helpless as you are, and trust all to His infinite grace. Receive the Savior, and then you will love and strive to be holy. Faith works by love and purifies the heart.

"My dear ——, this is a most solemn crisis for your soul. Be in earnest, my son. Be constant in prayer for His divine teaching. Pray over His Word, especially the Gospels, and particularly the whole of John. And, in addition, I recommend to you Doddridge's 'Rise and Progress of Religion in the Soul.' It has been blessed to thousands. Oh, that it may be so to you! Be not ashamed of the religion of the Gospel. The adversary, the world, probably your own heart, may try you here. Believe not their false and wicked suggestions. Religion is the glory of our nature. Ashamed of the service of the Infinite God!—a worm of the dust guilty of such hateful pride—that service in which the purest and most exalted spirits around His throne delight to engage as the highest glory of their natures! No wonder our Savior denounces the awful malediction on all such, 'Whosoever shall be ashamed of me and of my words, of him also shall the

Son of Man be ashamed when He cometh in His glory.'

"If Mr. J—— be still in ——, I hope you will converse freely with him. He is a judicious, excellent counselor. He loves you as a friend, and loves your soul. My dear son, be sober, be vigilant. Watch unto prayer. Strive to enter in at the strait gate. And may the Lord in infinite mercy guide, and enlighten, and save you, is the fervent prayer of

"Yours very sincerely and affectionately."

"Washington, December 17, 1834.

"MY DEAR ——,—I have just read and been deeply interested in your letter. I am rejoiced to learn that you feel a measure of your own foulness as well as guilt. Be not too soon discouraged, my son. Bless the Lord that He has given you any sense of your character and condition, and led you to feel at all your need of a Savior. Pray for His Spirit to teach, and sanctify, and strengthen you. Cast your soul entirely upon the infinite grace of God in Jesus Christ. Stay not back for *worthiness;* the best preparation is to realize your unworthiness. I send you a precious little volume that I pray may be helpful to you. It is by one of the best men of England. It is rich in thought and scriptural directions. Let us hear soon again from you. I am vividly anxious for your eternal welfare.

"Yours very truly."

"Washington, January 13, 1835.

"MY DEAR ——,—Your very grateful and satisfactory letter was received yesterday morning, and I trust that my heart does in some feeble measure bless the Lord that He has led you by His Spirit, as I hope, out of nature's darkness and from the reigning power of sin to the love of His blessed and holy character, law, and service. I have never desired for you the great things of this world, but that you might have a portion among His own children. The matters of which you speak as depressing your spirits should not dishearten you.

"My dear son, this life is a trial of faith and patience, of conflict and endurance. Our joy is in the promise, 'My grace shall be sufficient for thee. My strength shall be made perfect in weakness.' Repair, then, constantly to the throne of grace. Strive to walk with God, to be daily and hourly in the exercise of believing prayer and humble confidence. *Love your closet and your Bible.* Keep near to these means of grace. The closet is a fountain of living influences. But, above all, look to the Author of all these means that He would make them effectual.

"I will write soon to our dear ——. I pray that her heart may be touched by the Holy Spirit and quickened into life, convinced of sin and recovered to the service of God. I hope you will write to ——, and be faithful to his soul.

"Very truly and affectionately yours."

The ensuing was addressed to another young relative on the choice of a profession:

"Newark, September 24, 1833.

"My dear Nephew,—I duly received your favor, and, in respect to the pursuit of your studies, I think it preferable to enter Mr. ——'s office. The advantage of his experience and counsels will far more than remunerate the expense. Perhaps it will be better to wait until after the fall election, for probably he may again fill the ——'s chair. So far as to advice upon a specific case stated.

"Now I must beg a moment's attention to the whole matter. You desire, I trust, to take that station which will most glorify your Redeemer by your labors in His cause. Now is it clear to your mind that such place is at the bar? The profession is crowded with lawyers—many more now in it than can be usefully employed. I know this is not a sufficient reason to debar one who will bring industry and piety to his aid; but still it is an item to be weighed. The call for laborers in the Lord's vineyard is louder and louder every day. Thousands are now needed to bear the message of life and salvation to a dying world; and will not the gracious returns be sweet and precious through eternal ages, of a life devoted in self-denying efforts to win souls to the Lord Jesus Christ? You have talents well fitted to the pulpit, and I commend the case to your careful consideration. *Weigh it well;* ponder it in all its relations; pray earnestly for Divine direction; and may the Spirit of all truth guide you in this important matter.

"Remember, my dear nephew, that to decide safely you must strive to regard the claim as single, and involved in the proper answer to the inquiry, How shall I best live to the glory of my Maker and the good of my fellow-men? Yours very truly."

To another he wrote thus:

"Newark, June 23, 1838.

"MY DEAR NEPHEW,—There has been a chasm in our correspondence that I intended to prevent by an earlier reply to your last letter; but my engagements have been unusually pressing the present season, and left me little time or leisure in my office. I was gratified by the general spirit of your remarks on the subject of religion, but, my dear ——, I wish you to regard this great subject with a more personal and practical consideration. One of my fears for you is delay —a postponement of the soul's eternal interests from one period to another, on a sort of indefinite assurance to your own mind, not very distinctly made, that it shall in the future receive its due reflection and concern.

"Now you have no hold upon the future. God has it all, with every breath of our nostrils, under His absolute control. He may grant many days; He may cut them off in a moment, long before the noon. He claims, my dear son, your best affections, your time, your whole heart. In His Gospel He meets you as a fallen sinner, not in His wrath, but in His mercy, and offers to pardon your sins and smile upon you with His favor if you will return in the exercise of a penitent heart, believing in His blessed Son as your Savior. Surely these terms are easy and reasonable. We may have eternal life if *we will choose it.* We may have an atoning Savior if we will accept of Him, and yield our hearts to His service. We may hope in the mercy of God if we will forsake our sins and return to His service.

"Life and death are thus set before you. All that is glorious in heaven and terrible in the world of despair press upon your attention to consider—now, while you are a prisoner of hope, while God waits to be gracious, that you would forsake your sins and fly to the Savior.

"Seek the light and strength of His blessed Spirit to enlighten your mind and to enable you to lay firm hold of the Gospel hope. That you may be thus guided and blessed is among the constant prayers of

"Yours affectionately."

The following characteristic letters were addressed to the Rev. James A. H. Cornell, D.D.:

"New Brunswick, March 4, 1854.

"My dear Nephew,—I am concerned to find that you are still so much of an invalid, but rejoice in the tokens of returning health. I suppose that your heart to labor was rather stronger than the frame-work in which it beats, and when this is the case it will strike against the sides, and thus vindicate the rights of the poor body.

"But I hope and must believe that you have enjoyed some sweet seasons in your suffering. There is a precious kind of logic in God's Word which does not need any syllogism to give it strength. 'Rejoice in tribulation; for tribulation worketh patience, and patience experience, and experience hope, and hope maketh not ashamed.' The fruits are so rich and comforting; and, when the pains are past, these remain to cheer and bless us here and forever.

"May you soon be enabled to show your dear people how faithful and true is the everlasting covenant. With best regards to your good wife.

"Very truly yours."

"New Brunswick, April 24, 1860.

"DEAR NEPHEW,—I am quite anxious to hear of your welfare. A severe influenza for a fortnight has detained me from New York, so that I am uninformed of your condition and plans. I concluded to provoke a letter by a letter. I hope that you are better, and will soon move again in your cherished labors in your blessed Master's vineyard.

"Since I saw you we have parted with Brother Judd. He died full of peace, in sweet and tranquil hope. It was very grateful to witness the affectionate respect to his memory at the funeral in Bloomfield. A committee of his Montgomery Church attended, and a very large concourse of his Bloomfield congregation and the surrounding churches of Newark, Caldwell, Orange, etc., etc. It was a beautiful illustration of the word of promise, 'The memory of the just is blessed.' It is a blessed Gospel which, as Robert Hall remarked, takes up its friends where the world forsakes its votaries. Bloomfield provided the burial lot, inclosed by a neat iron fence. Montgomery and Catskill have resolved to erect the monument to the memory of their beloved minister. * * *

"Very truly yours."

"New Brunswick, April 1, 1861.

"DEAR NEPHEW,—I learned with great concern from the papers that the state of your health had constrained you to resign your place in the Education Society.* I sympathize with you in this trial. I trust the needed relaxation will, by the blessing of Divine Providence, soon restore you, and that a large measure of usefulness in the Gospel ministry will yet remain for you.

"Your agency has been richly compensated in its abundant fruits—fruits that will be felt for generations to come in time, and that will flow over to the ages of eternity. Our Dutch Church owes you much for the enlargement of her borders and the increase of her ministry.

"When the weather softens, it will be a very good restorative for you to make us a visit with your good wife, and take a look on the ground of your labors, and see whether the plants you put in here have taken root, and how they grow. It will cheer me amid many perplexing cares of the college, and I hope will refresh you. * * *

"A few lines from you will also do good to me and to yourself. It is the next best to the sight of a friend. These trials of health and patience are part of the 'all things that work together for good to them that love God.' How sweet is the consolation to take the trial to the throne, and plead for and expect the benefit. The very recourse to God that it urges is itself a rich blessing, as is any cause which brings us near to our Savior and keeps us there.

"Very truly and affectionately yours."

"New Brunswick, Feb. 7, 1862.

"Dear Nephew,—It seems a long time since I have heard from you or of you. I have been meditating an assault in this mode for some days, and this not only to hear a word of your welfare, but also to assure you that you have the same warm place in my

* Dr. Cornell had been for some years the Secretary of the Board of Education of the Reformed Protestant Dutch Church.

remembrance that you have always held. And how is it with you? Is your health improved? Hath patience its perfect work? Do you feel thankful for its trials?

"How is your good wife? We often speak of you. We have had a winter of much ill health. My good wife was confined for four weeks by a serious cough, and I for ten days. But the Lord has kindly restored us. The students have suffered much; four are now recovering from fevers. * * *

"Very truly yours."

In the autumn of the year 1861, the Rev. Dr. De Witt was bereaved of his youngest daughter, a young lady of uncommon excellence. Soon afterward the following note was addressed by Mr. Frelinghuysen to his intimate friends, the mourning parents:

"New Brunswick, Nov. 7, 1861.

"MY DEAR AFFLICTED FRIENDS,—I deeply feel and mourn your severe bereavement. My heart bleeds with you and for you. There is no alleviation from earth, or I would earnestly seek it for you; but there is precious consolation in the thought that the Lord has done it—that it is a part of His counsels from everlasting—that every stage of it, with every pain, and sigh, and tear—not one more nor one less, formed the scheme of His dispensation. And, my dear friends, is it not a sweet comfort to remember that 'He knows your sorrows,' and His compassionate heart says to you, 'Call upon me in the day of trouble, and I will deliver thee?' May His gracious Spirit be with you, to sustain your afflicted hearts, and enrich you with the choicest fruits of sanctified tribulation! In all which my dear wife unites.

"Very truly your friend and brother in the best of bonds.

"The Rev. Dr. and Mrs. De Witt."

CHAPTER XII.

CONNECTION WITH BENEVOLENT INSTITUTIONS.

A. B. C. F. M.—American Bible Society.—American Tract Society. — American Colonization Society. — American Sunday-school Union.—American Temperance Union.

From an early period of his life Mr. Frelinghuysen was in the habit of advocating on the platform the claims of organized Christian benevolence. This habit was due not to any zeal for notoriety or any love for the excitements of popular speaking, but to his deep interest in philanthropic enterprises, and his earnest desire to do what he could for the welfare of his fellow-men. His name, and position, and character added attractiveness to his speech, and his efforts were received with general acceptance. Being thus brought into contact with those intrusted with the direction of the great benevolent associations of the age, and the benefits of his counsel and influence being perceived, he was gradually introduced into a closer connection with their interior working, and a more responsible position in their management. This extended so far that it may be truly said that no American layman was ever associated with so many great national organizations of religion and charity. He was or had been president of no less than four, while his name is found upon the list of officers of all the rest, with scarcely an exception.

FOREIGN MISSIONS.

The institution over which he presided for the longest term of years, and in which his interest was the most deeply cherished, was the AMERICAN BOARD OF COMMISSIONERS FOR FOREIGN MISSIONS, founded at Boston in 1810, well known throughout Christendom for the faith of its founders, the wisdom of its management, the wide extent of its operations, the zeal, ability, and piety of its laborers, and the large success which has attended its efforts. He was chosen one of its corporate members in 1826, and attended its annual meetings as often as circumstances permitted. His farther connection with the Board is well shown in the following extract from a communication made to the author by the Rev. Dr. Treat, one of the secretaries:

"Mr. Frelinghuysen was chosen President of the Board in 1841. No selection could have been more acceptable to our entire constituency. His career as a member of the United States Senate had secured for him a most enviable reputation. As a man of integrity and ability he had the respect of all. As a Christian and philanthropist he stood second to none. Much as Jerseymen loved and honored him, it admits of a serious question whether others were a whit behind them in this regard.

"During the sixteen years of his presidency, nothing occurred to lessen the esteem in which he was held. His deportment in the chair, always dignified and courteous—his annual address, always earnest and effective—made him a universal favorite. It was with the profoundest regret, therefore, that we saw him relinquish his position. We felt that we were parting from a dear and venerable friend who had long been the central figure in our pleasant convocations.

"The reason of his withdrawal is thus stated in a letter written by him to the nominating committee of the Board, dated Providence, September 10, 1857:

"'DEAR BRETHREN,—The recent action of the General Synod of the Reformed Protestant Dutch Church, of which I am an humble member, in deciding hereafter to conduct their foreign missions on their own distinct Church organization, renders it becoming and proper for me to decline, as I hereby do, a nomination and choice to the office of president of your Board. The generous Christian confidence that first elected, and has long continued me in that place of distinguished honor, will be among the precious recollections of my life. With deep personal regret I part with you.'

"The committee appointed to express the sense of the Board, in view of its bereavement, reported the following resolutions, which were cordially adopted:

"'*Resolved*, That in addition to the deep regret which this Board has experienced in the separation, not in feeling, but in action, from our brethren of the Reformed Dutch Church, we feel that our trial is rendered more severe, and our regret more deep, by the fact that, in consequence of the sundering of these ties, we have also been compelled to relinquish our beloved presiding officer.

"'*Resolved*, That this Board have received with deep emotion and unaffected grief the communication from our late president in which he declines to be a candidate for renomination or re-election.

"'*Resolved*, That we can not permit him to retire from an office which he has filled to such universal acceptance for a period of sixteen years without an expression, not simply of regret at parting, but also of our high appreciation of the valuable services which he has rendered during his period of office.

"'*Resolved*, That in THEODORE FRELINGHUYSEN we have found combined qualifications which singularly fitted him to preside over the deliberations of such a body; bringing to the discharge of his official duties ripe experience in parliamentary rules and forms, promptness, accuracy, and impartiality in the transaction of business, keen insight into character, tact and judgment in facilitating the dispatch of business, uniform courtesy in his intercourse with all the members of the Board—wisely and happily blending mildness, and even gentleness, with unhesitating firmness and energy; one of whom we can safely say we have not known his superior as a presiding officer; and combining with these peculiar qualifications for his station warm-hearted piety and fervid eloquence.

"'*Resolved*, That we tender to Hon. Theodore Frelinghuysen our cordial wishes that he may yet enjoy many years of usefulness and happiness in his new field of honorable duty.'

"These resolutions were prepared by one who has enjoyed a large acquaintance with deliberative assemblies, and who therefore knows whereof he affirms.

"For reasons which were perfectly satisfactory, Mr. Frelinghuysen refused to make a farewell address at Providence; but, a few days later, he sent a letter to 'the secretaries and presidential committee,' which I will transfer to these pages. It is as follows:

"'DEAR BRETHREN,—In our interesting interviews at Providence, I suggested that the matter of a farewell speech I could better arrange by letter; that the separation involved to me so much of feeling that I could not well intrust it to a public occasion. When our several Christian denominations, the Congregational, Old and New School Presbyterian, and the Reformed Protestant Dutch, all labored in love together on benighted and heathen fields, it struck me as a beautiful type of our blessed Master's religion in its aspects toward these lands of darkness. The heathen saw that, indeed, the followers of Christ were 'one;' one in profession, in principle, and in action; that they who thought alike could and did work together. But it seems that this good time is yet to wait. I believe that we shall hail this blessed temper in universal prevalence, when the salvation of our fellow-men shall so fill our anxieties and our prayers, so shape our plans and quicken all our endeavors, that Christians will have time only to rejoice that in so many things they agree, and will want time and heart to detect and expose the few unessential things in which they may differ. For this heavenly union let us, dear brethren, pray and labor.

"'In parting from you, I feel as a child parting from a venerated and beloved mother. Like a mother you have cherished us, when we were few and feeble. You took us under the wings of your care, and linked our interests together. We thank you for all your kindness. We thank God for the precious seasons of Christian privilege that we have enjoyed together. We have often gone up to the heights of Zion, and looked down upon this dark world, and traced the footsteps of our wonder-working God and Redeemer. And from these "heavenly places" we have together hailed the first streaks of the morning, the sure tokens of that coming glory which the Sun of Righteousness shall shed upon this benighted and sin-stricken world. These hallowed seasons will be for grateful thanksgiving in that blessed world where partings never grieve, and the past shall be recalled only to augment the pleasures of a sanctified memory.

"'As the American Board was the first Christian association to which, in my youth, I found it a privilege to give, so it shall continue to receive the yearly contributions of a very humble store, as God shall prosper me.

"'With affectionate regards, dear brethren, very sincerely your friend and brother in the best of bonds,

"'THEO. FRELINGHUYSEN.'

"To this communication, one of the secretaries, in behalf of the prudential committee and of his associates, replied, 'For yourself personally we shall ever cherish the highest regard and the warmest Christian affection. Your whole course in respect to the Board has been such that we could not wish it to have been otherwise, and we have no doubt that this is the universal sentiment among the members and friends of the Board. These delightful and hallowed seasons which we have spent together on earth will be remembered in heaven, increasing the richness and sweetness of that blessed communion of saints which will have no interruption and know no end.'

"Allow me to say that my own acquaintance with Mr. Frelinghuysen commenced in the spring of 1836, when I became pastor of the Third Presbyterian Church in Newark. I had formed a very high estimate of his character, but when I knew him personally my regard for him only increased. I have often said Mr. Frelinghuysen is one of the select few whose greatness does not contract upon a nearer approach.

"I am, dear sir, very respectfully and fraternally yours, S. B. TREAT, Sec. of A. B. C. F. M."

AMERICAN BIBLE SOCIETY.

The constancy and thoroughness of Mr. Frelinghuysen's devotional study of the Scriptures has already been mentioned. The rich experimental knowledge he thus attained of the value of the Sacred Volume naturally led him to take a deep interest in all proper schemes for increasing the circulation of it among all classes of men. He did much in this respect in a private way all his life, and at the same time cordially co-operated with the great national institution founded for the purpose in the year 1816. A succinct statement of his connection with the American Bible Society is given in the following letter, kindly furnished by one of the secretaries:

"Bible House, Astor Place, New York, March 3, 1863.

"REV. T. W. CHAMBERS, D.D.:

"DEAR BROTHER,—At your request I submit the following brief statement respecting the services of the late Hon. Theodore Frelinghuysen during the thirty-two years of his official relations to the American Bible Society.

"In 1830 he was elected a vice-president, in the room of that eminent Christian jurist, the Hon. Andrew Kirkpatrick, chief justice of the Supreme Court of New Jersey, who had deceased a short time before. In the year 1846 he was unanimously elected to the presidency of the institution, succeeding the Hon. John Cotton Smith, of Connecticut, who for fifteen years previous to his death, in a ripe old age, had occupied the high station. (The date of this election was April 2, 1846.) Mr. Frelinghuysen was not the least of the illustrious men who have filled the presidency of the American Bible Society, and his name will be cherished by all who can appreciate the memories of Elias Boudinot, John Jay, Richard Varick, and John Cotton Smith—men whose services were given to the state and the Church with the power of a noble Christian consecration. The following is his letter of acceptance of the office:

"'Newark, April, 17, 1846.

"'GENTLEMEN,—Your favor of the 3d inst., informing me of my appointment to the office of President of the American Bible Society, has been duly received.

I am deeply impressed with the honor done me by this mark of confidence on the part of the Board of Managers. And, in accepting the important station proffered, it shall be my earnest purpose, after my humble measure, to co-operate with the Board of Managers in giving increased circulation to that sacred Book, which reveals the best and only lasting hope for ourselves, our country, and the world.

"'With great esteem, gentlemen, your obedient servant, THEO. FRELINGHUYSEN.

"'Messrs. P. G. Stuyvesant,
J. C. Brigham,
Joseph Hyde,
} Com. of Board.'

"During his residence in this city as Chancellor of the University of New York, he frequently presided at the meetings of the Board of Managers, where his presence was ever welcomed and his counsels were valued. He adorned his place with peculiar dignity, grace, and administrative ability, while his courtesy, candor, and decision made him the model of a presiding officer in a body whose meetings have always been distinguished for an order and a spirit which befit the great cause they have advanced to its present proportions. He was not a member of the standing committees, although his advice was doubtless sought by all of them when needed. During the seventeen years of his presidency, Mr. Frelinghuysen was present at every anniversary of the society, and delivered the opening address on each of these great public religious assemblies. These productions were brief, pointed, classical in style, varied in matter, fragrant with the spirit of the Bible, full of unction and wisdom. They were delivered with that silver-tongued eloquence of which he was a master, and on certain occasions produced grand effects upon his audiences, while they were always welcomed with favor. Most of these addresses were printed in the reports of the society and other documents, and I am persuaded that a collection of them would add not a little to the treasures of an eloquence which should not be left to the traditional memories of a generation that is fast passing away.

"The greatest service which Mr. Frelinghuysen rendered to this institution was by the continual power of his name, character, and influence. He was the representative man of our American evangelical catholic Christianity, and as such it was fitting that his most eminent position during the last seventeen years of his life should have been—what he himself regarded as the highest honor conferred on him by men—the presidency of the American Bible Society.

"I append the testimony of the Board of Managers after his lamented death. The preamble and resolutions were prepared and presented by his successor in the office of president, the Hon. Luther Bradish.

"With warm personal recollections and high veneration of our noble friend, and praying that your memorial of him may, by the blessing of God, long perpetuate his good name, I am yours, very fraternally, WILLIAM J. R. TAYLOR,
Cor. Sec. Am. Bible Society.

"'*Whereas*, In the dispensations of Providence, the Honorable Theodore Frelinghuysen, long the beloved president of this society, has been removed from the scene of his activity and usefulness here to his final rest and reward; therefore

"'*Resolved*, That this society, while it bows in humble submission to this deeply afflictive dispensation, desires to place on record an expression of its high appreciation of the character and services of the deceased, and of its deep sense of the loss the society, the Church, and the community have sustained in his death.

"'*Resolved*, That the life of the distinguished deceased, whether passed in the councils of his country, in its higher educational or charitable institutions, or in his social and private relations, was a bright and beautiful illustration of the principles and teaching of that Bible he loved so well, and labored so zealously to extend to the benighted and the destitute. Those precious principles and that divine teaching were the constant subject of his earnest thoughts and deepest affections. They not only formed the standard of his faith, but were the uniform and governing rule of his daily life. By them he lived, and by them he died. They moulded his character here, and were the unfailing foundation of his hopes hereafter.

"'*Resolved*, That while the society mourns the loss of such a colaborer in the prosecution of its high and benevolent objects, it is deeply grateful for the example of such a character as that of its distinguished associate—a character whose influence is not confined to the narrow limits of the life or the circle in which it was manifested, but will be as extensive and enduring as the memory of what is highest and purest in the history of humanity.

"'*Resolved*, That while thus recording its own, the society desires to express its deep sympathy in the grief of the immediate family of the deceased, at the loss of one so endeared to them, and so exemplary in all the tender relations of domestic life.

"'*Resolved*, That the above preamble and resolutions be entered at large upon the journal of the society, and that a copy thereof, duly authenticated, be communicated to the family of the deceased.'"

AFRICAN COLONIZATION.

Mr. Frelinghuysen's interest in this important enterprise was intense and life-long. At the very beginning it came to him commended by the character of the founder of the American Colonization Society. This was the Rev. Dr. Finley, under whose instructions he had been prepared for college at the beginning of the century. But his attachment to the cause did not depend upon personal influences so much as upon its own intrinsic merits. Having been himself a slaveholder by inheritance, and personally familiar with the condition and character of the negro race, his benevolent sympathies were aroused by the prospect of restoring them, with their own consent, to the land of their forefathers, there to erect a free Christian commonwealth. His sober reflection confirmed the impulses of his heart, and he became a stanch advocate and supporter of the colonization scheme. He candidly considered the various objections which from time to time were raised against the enterprise, but his original convictions of its philanthropy and expediency never wavered. He contributed largely to its funds, gave his counsels to its officers, advocated its claims upon the platform, and devoted the only article he ever contributed to a quarterly review to a defense of its character and policy.

The following letter from the Rev. Dr. R. R. Gurley presents some interesting reminiscences of his early and prolonged attachment to this great scheme of enlightened philanthropy:

"Washington, Office of the Colonization Society,
July 1, 1862.

"MY DEAR SIR,—I am most happy to learn that you are preparing a memoir of my lamented and ever-to-be-honored friend, Mr. Frelinghuysen, whom it was a privilege for any one to know, and hardly less so to commemorate. He was so humble as not to seek for human praise, yet so disinterested that I believe he would take pleasure in knowing that others were moved to admiration and imitation of his illustrious example, although felt by him to be dim in the light and power of a *Greater*. It was his happiness to study, in all the relations of life, the character of that holy and just One, who did no sin, neither was guile found in his mouth. Few men have ever approached nearer to the perfection of the Author and Finisher of the Christian faith.

"It is about forty years ago since I first met Mr. Frelinghuysen, in his own house at Newark, in company with several gentlemen who were invited to confer together in regard to the application of a fund, in the hands of Mr. Jefferson, for the education of female colored children, and which a society in New Jersey hoped might be placed by the trustee, Mr. Lea (to whom it had been conveyed by Mr. Jefferson), at their disposal. The meeting was rendered exceedingly agreeable and instructive by the conversation of Mr. Frelinghuysen, and the earnestness and kindness with which he entered into the benevolent object for which it had been convened. The sudden decease of Mr. Lea, and the attempt of the heirs of Kosciusko to defeat the object of the testator, led the society to abandon their benevolent scheme. But from that time Mr. Frelinghuysen evinced an ardent and constant interest in the design of the American Colonization Society, and became one of its most generous and able friends. He subscribed liberally to the publication of the Life of Ashmun, subscribed one thousand dollars [to the purposes of the society], on the plan of Gerrit Smith (paying one hundred dollars a year for ten years), and gave generously to the cause to the closing years of his life.

"For many years he sustained the office of vice-president of the society; he ever stood ready to afford his best counsels to the directors, and he pleaded with the persuasiveness and power of his eloquence for Africa and her dispersed and afflicted children. As a statesman, his unblemished morality and eminent Christian character gave great weight to his opinions;

and his warm devotedness to all patriotic objects, as well as those embracing all mankind, attracted the attention and confidence of all philanthropic societies, and disposed them to ask the aid of his eloquence on many great occasions, and probably no man in the country exerted a more cheerful or more widespread influence for the public good and for the kingdom of Jesus Christ. In the hearts of the great and good, in the admiration of Christians of every name, in this and many lands, will his memory be cherished and honored forever. Africa will remember him forever as one of her truest and best friends.

"I have pleasure in supplying, in the publications herewith sent, many reminiscences of this admirable man, with copies of several of his speeches, persuasive both in thought and language.

"Most respectfully yours, R. R. GURLEY."

AMERICAN TRACT SOCIETY.

Mr. Frelinghuysen's interest in the work of this beneficent institution dates almost from its origin, and continued without interruption or abatement to the end of his life. He made one of the addresses at the third annual meeting, held in 1828, and at frequent intervals afterward. The senior secretary, the Rev. Dr. Hallock, in a letter to the author, dated July 24, 1862, bears distinct and cordial testimony to his services. After mentioning some documents and manuscripts sent with the letter, the writer proceeds:

"I can not express how precious, cheering, elevating, and ennobling was Mr. Frelinghuysen's influence during the whole of his six years' presidency, from 1842 to 1848. In his addresses, and in his whole life and intercourse, there was a deep, mellowed spirituality, drawn from the depths of God's Word and the teachings of his Spirit, blended with a high and chastened intellect, and urbanity, and heart-reaching kindness and Christian love, that I have never been conscious of meeting in any other man, nor do I expect ever to witness and enjoy it so fully again. His memory is embalmed in all our hearts, and will remain fragrant till death, and then go on, in a brighter sphere, I trust forever. It is a high privilege to prepare the memoir of such a one, and I gladly furnish you the rich material he has bequeathed to this society.

"With respect and esteem, your affectionate brother,
"WM. A. HALLOCK, Secretary."

From the "rich material" kindly furnished by the secretary, the following selections are made.

In May, 1842, when he was first appointed president of the American Tract Society, he used these terms in replying to the notice:

"To be associated with an institution of such distinguished usefulness, and with a board of officers of such public esteem and personal worth, is no common honor. And in accepting the place to which your indulgent kindness has chosen me, I cherish the hope that, through the grace of our blessed Redeemer, I may be in some humble measure made useful."

Four years afterward he deemed it his duty to retire from the station, and so expressed himself to the secretary, adding, at the same time, these words:

"In retiring at this time from the office, I hardly need to assure you that my decision arises from no diminution of confidence in the Tract Society or its management and aims. I regard it as a blessed agency for our country, full of promise, and rich in the testimonials of God's favor. It is my purpose, as it will be my privilege and duty, to co-operate with you in extending its influences widely as the ripening fields indicate the need of the reaper and the sickle."

He was, however, prevailed upon to retract his refusal to serve, and continued two years longer in the office. But in 1848, despite farther solicitation, he renewed and persisted in his determination to withdraw, as appears by the following letter:

"DEAR SIR,—I have farther considered the matter of the Tract presidency since I had the pleasure of your visit, and have concluded that the way is quite open for the appointment of another president. If you had encountered any serious difficulties in selecting a successor, I should have regarded the matter as of more difficult duty; but the choice is of one so deservedly high in the confidence of his country and in the affectionate esteem of the Church, that I am grateful that, while my own feelings are relieved of a painful position (in the *one* respect *only*), the cause and the society will have in such near connection a long-tried, judicious, and excellent friend. With my fervent wishes and prayers that God may continue to smile upon your labors of love in spreading far the principles of His blessed Gospel, and give you at last a place among those who have turned many to righteousness, I remain with sincere regard, your friend and brother,

"THEO. FRELINGHUYSEN."

Of the many addresses made by Mr. Frelinghuysen in behalf of the Tract cause, one is reproduced here, mainly because it expresses views and maxims upon which he himself habitually acted from the period of his first consecration to the Savior. It was delivered in the Broadway Tabernacle at the anniversary of the City Tract Society in December, 1836. The scope of the resolution in support of which the speaker arose was the importance of "prayerful personal efforts for the salvation of men." According to the report made at the time, Mr. Frelinghuysen said,

"The eye of God is upon those engaged in this cause with peculiar complacency, for their trials are peculiar. To give liberally is a privilege to the liberal soul. There is so much that is delightful in the promise of the great plans of public beneficence, that the trial of the service has passed away. Christian men would deem it a lost blessing if the occasion did not meet them for pouring into the treasure-house of God. So a public convention, where the pulse of Christian sympathy is warmed by fellowship, where the law of kindness reigns, where face answers to face, and prayer mingles with prayer, and heart with heart — why, instead of a cross, it is a jubilee. It is one of the heavenly places which gladdened the apostles' heart, and now rejoices every heart that loves Zion. But to go alone into the by-paths of sin; to approach the thoughtless in the world of fashion, and, with a face set as a flint in the stern discharge of duty, faithfully admonish, exhort, and plead the cause of God and the soul—to meet the scorn and taunts of ridicule, and take them meekly—to bow the head, and rejoice to suffer shame for Jesus—this is a service which no fortitude can endure but that which a deep conviction of the value and the danger of the soul inspires.

"But the rewards become the enterprise. A just sense of the momentous interests at hazard, an established faith in the retribution which awaits us, and a growing love for the souls of men, will sustain the mind amid all the tribulations which lie in the path. The tract missionary looks to the end, and there he casts his hopes. He knows that the hour will come when every anxious thought and every faithful warning will be indicated, not only by the joys of the redeemed, but also by the despair of the lost. He is assured that when the trump of God shall awaken the dead of all generations, whatever wailings of anguish may break from the opening tombs, there will then be no reproaches heard that he stood the fiery trial of cruel revilings, and met the world's laugh with the meek firmness of a steadfast heart.

"When we consider the constitution of the soul, as God has endowed it, with all its sympathies, we can not be surprised at the result of such means. True, He is sovereign in all this, but His sovereign pleasure is to act and save according to the laws of the mind and the dictates of the soundest philosophy. There is a chord in the bosom even of the vile that responds to kindness. Self-respect is soothed by the regard which personal faithfulness betokens. And although the thoughtless and profane may scorn the message and hate the counsel, they must and do defer to the concern you manifest. Conscience pleads for you, and, when face meets face—when the missionary of mercy enters the abode of the wretched, seeking the everlasting welfare of its inmates, they can not always stifle the conviction that such earnestness, so clear of all selfish motive, and so pure in its design, must be prompted by causes which the infidelity of the heart can neither change nor control.

"A case, not long since, in your own state, happily exhibits the power of this agency. An aged culprit in one of your prisons, who was suffering for his crimes, was one Sabbath morning approached by the missionary. He sat down by his side, and, with affectionate solicitude, inquired of him the state of his feelings. The unhappy man instantly burst into tears. So peculiar was his agitation that the man of God was struck with it, and sought the cause of such strong emotion. 'Sir,' said he, 'it is the first time in forty years that I have heard the language of kindness, and it overwhelms me.' He had passed through scenes of awful transgression, and had hardened his heart; he had met unmoved the rigors of imprisonment; he had gone through the trial and endured the penalty; he had heard iron bolts driven, and his eye never faltered nor a nerve gave way; but when the sound of Christian sympathy fell on his ear, it penetrated his heart, and brought down that proud spirit that never had quailed before.

"With such exalted motives to urge us, why shall not this effective instrumentality be greatly enlarged in its numbers and influence? With so much of distraction in business, so much of dangerous allurement in ambition, and pleasure, and fashion, to quench any serious feeling and desire, who does not rejoice that we may sometimes be met in the path of worldliness by him who dares to tell us the truth, and, at the price of our scorn or displeasure, to be faithful to our eternal interests? With all its trials, I doubt not, it brings a peace that passeth all understanding. It must be so; for it is that direction and application of talents which He who bestowed them designed.

"Think you, sir, that Harlan Page ever knew a regret because of his toils in this blessed service? It was the glory of his life, it was the joy of his dying hour; it will be his bright and imperishable crown forever. And when that blessed spirit shall meet the goodly number whom he turned to righteousness, as they strike their harps together in the new song of praise to the Lamb that was slain, then, and for endless ages thereafter, he will begin to learn of the heights and depths of the recompense that grace awards to those who have done good to souls. He has furnished a new chapter on Christian faithfulness. Every follower of Christ should study his life, should tread closely in his footsteps, should covet such blessed gifts of the Spirit. Sir, we are bound to engage in this work. Every dictate of duty and every sentiment of regard for our friends and fellow-men not only invite, but demand such consecration of personal influence.

"I am persuaded, sir, that we are prone to mystify religion and its high duties, and thus we are often appalled by terrors which our own fancies have created. We exaggerate difficulties often where the way is smooth, predict harsh repulses where we should meet with respectful attention. Sir, our irreligious friends expect us to be faithful to them. Their surprise is far more awakened, and oftener too, by our guilty silence, than by our affectionate and earnest solicitude. Let us bear our living testimony, in the face of our fellow-men, to the reality and the tremendous issues of eternal things. Granted that there are trials. It is just such discipline as is needed to test and develop the strength of Christian character—just such as is indispensable for the cultivation of a vigorous piety. How else shall we cherish the stern virtues of self-denial, holy fortitude, and triumphant faith? These conflicts lead us to the only refuge where we may gain grace to suffer and faith to prevail."

THE AMERICAN SUNDAY-SCHOOL UNION.

The active personal interest which Mr. Frelinghuysen took, from his first connection with the people of God, in the Sunday-school of the church which he attended, would naturally lead him to regard with favor the society which aimed to secure the establishment of such schools throughout the country. The author is indebted to Frederick A. Packard, Esq., the accomplished secretary of that society, for the following statement of Mr. Frelinghuysen's zeal and efforts in this behalf. Here, as elsewhere, the scale of the duty to be performed made no difference in the conscientious fidelity with which he discharged it. He was regular and faithful as the teacher of a single class, and at the same time ready efficiently to help the efforts made to diffuse the institution over the breadth of the continent.

"If any conviction had a deeper hold upon the mind of Theodore Frelinghuysen than another, it was *the absolute indispensableness of moral and religious as well as intellectual culture to the preservation and perpetuity of a popular government.* Throughout his public career this great subject seems to have been always present to his mind, and, as the system of instruction in SABBATH-SCHOOLS became more and more manifestly adapted to the need of the country, and especially the new and sparsely-settled parts of it, he entered with all the warmth of his benevolent heart into its support. What were his early local relations to the Sabbath-school is known to others; the present paper is concerned only with his more general and public sympathy with it, and, though our means are very imperfect, we can trace with no little interest the progress of his opinions and convictions on the subject. In June, 1826 (in acknowledging the notice of his election as a vice-president of the American Sunday-school Union), he says:

"'I have long regarded the Sabbath-school as among the most efficient means, under the Divine blessing, of advancing the Redeemer's kingdom, and as intimately connected with true national prosperity. Their blessed influence is beginning to be seen in this town (Newark, New Jersey), where upward of 1000 children are under their weekly instruction.'*

"In acknowledging a similar notice in June, 1828, he says:

"'To be in any way connected with the objects of this blessed charity I feel to be an honor and a privilege. I have long looked to this moral engine as, under the Divine blessing, identified with the best hopes of our country.'

* The number now in attendance is, of course, vastly increased.

"The rapidity with which the Valley of the Mississippi was filling up, and the inadequacy of existing means to supply the moral and religious as well as the intellectual wants of the people, had moved the heart of Christian benevolence, and, as the most hopeful field of effort was found among the children and youth, the friends of the *American Sunday-school Union* conceived the purpose of expanding its missionary work to embrace that vast region; and, without comprehending very definitely the extent and difficulties of the undertaking, they resolved (May 25, 1830), 'in reliance upon Divine aid, to establish a Sunday-school within two years in every destitute place, where it is practicable, throughout the Valley of the Mississippi.' In the following February, the late Rev. JOHN BRECKINRIDGE volunteered his valuable services to bring the subject, which he regarded as of great national importance, to the notice and appreciation of our leading public men, and to this end a meeting was appointed at Washington, February 16, 1831, at which the late Hon. FELIX GRUNDY, of Tennessee, presided; and such men as ELISHA WHITTLESEY, of Ohio; N. D. COLEMAN and CHARLES A. WICKLIFFE, of Kentucky; CHARLES E. HAYNES, of Georgia, and DANIEL WEBSTER, of Massachusetts, advocated, with eloquent earnestness, the great purpose which had been undertaken. At this meeting Mr. Frelinghuysen, then a member of the Senate from New Jersey, expressed his convictions with great force and freedom, and probably understood more perfectly than any of his coadjutors the comprehensive bearings of the subject. Mr. Frelinghuysen offered the following resolution:

"'*Resolved*, That the objects contemplated by the late resolution of the American Sunday-school Union, adopted in May last, commend themselves to the patronage and best wishes of every American statesman, patriot, and Christian.' And in support of it addressed the meeting as follows:

"'Mr. Chairman, I always rejoice in the occasion that enables me to raise my voice in behalf of the Sunday-school. I regard it, sir, as the most benignant enterprise of modern benevolence. It is the fountain-spring of good. In all its aspects it is full of promise. That season of existence which has been most neglected, in which the seeds of a future harvest are sown, and in which life and destiny are controlled — this eventful era is introduced to the direct influence of the purest moral and religious instruction. Heathen Rome, in the proudest day of her glory, never remitted her concern for the education of her youth. She felt that in her schools was to be achieved all that hope could expect or desire; and with a morality defective in its principles, by the aid of this great lever she rose to the summit of earthly fame. We enjoy the means of far more elevating instruction. We can draw motives from the pure treasury of the Word of God in all its exalted hopes, momentous sanctions, and eternal retributions; and we are encouraged to the faithful cultivation of these means by the promise of Him who gave them: "Train up a child in the way he should go, and when he is old he will not depart from it." This is as sure in philosophy as it is in Scripture. The proof of it is broadly spread out over the whole history of man. Although his native tendencies are depraved and degenerate, this *training*, sir —a most emphatic word to denote the nature of the process—this training is constantly counteracting these tendencies. It persuades from degrading pursuits to exalted aspirations. When the heart would seek some groveling, earth-born good, that perishes as we grasp it, this points the desires to a portion in the heavens, pure, and satisfying, and perpetual, and, with the Divine blessing, the self-love of the heart is enlisted on the side of virtue; the mind perceives its profit as well as pleasure in the ways of wisdom, and habit adds the confirmation of a second nature to the dictates of truth and duty.

" 'Wherefore, then, does the man illustrate the principles of virtue? Sir, he has been trained up in the way he should go. The lessons read to him in childhood were not only incentives to virtue, but his surest defenses against vice. They not only allured him to the right way, but effectually admonished him to shun the wrong way. I am fully aware that all this process would be fruitless without the blessing of God—that *He* is sovereign when He gives and when He withholds. But I also know, sir, that it is His sovereign good pleasure to bless the faithful labors of His people; that His faithfulness is pledged in the promise, "Them that honor me I will honor, and those that seek me early shall find me."

" 'Mr. Chairman, if farther proof were needed, we might find it in the history of all the profane. Take any convict of your penitentiary, and his brief and sad biography would form an appropriate history for the great majority of his fellows in crime. Ask him, sir, what it was that brought him to his wretched dwelling-place, and he must reply, "I was trained up for it. I early broke away from the restraints of conscience. I had no kind friend to instruct me, or I despised his counsels.

" ' "No mother's tender care
Shielded my infant innocence with prayer.

From a youth I have defied my Maker. I thought it manly to blaspheme His sacred name. I made a mock at sin, entered the broad way of transgression, and disregarded the beacon lights that warned me of my danger. Such has been my training, and here I reap its bitter fruits. I ought not to be disappointed; for from such a childhood and youth, who could expect other than such a doom?" Let us then, sir, assiduously cultivate these moral influences. Who that has the heart of a man can refuse them his best wishes? Sir, is it not of the last importance to have the sources of national prosperity pure, and the aims and pursuits of our people elevated? and where but in the Bible shall we find the record of sound principles? Permit me to say that the occasion was never more urgent for the friends of truth to send forth the healthful influence of the Gospel. Sir, in this day of benevolent action, the enemies of God and man are not idle. The disciples of infidelity are striving with sleepless effort to break down the defenses of religion and virtue. She has her ministers and her altars. Her votaries are assailing the citadel of truth with every weapon that promises the least infliction. They would blot out the Bible, and roll the wave of desolation over all that is dear to us as men and Christians. Then I would say to parents, as you love your children, and to statesmen, as you love your country, cherish this blessed enterprise. Who would not rejoice to behold the pure spirit of religion pervading the whole mass of our population—these sacred rules of life inculcated and circulated in every valley, reaching to every mountain-top, and tracking the course of every mighty river of the West? Who does not desire that the hopes of immortality might animate every heart and fill every bosom through the whole breadth of the land?

" 'Nothing besides can give stability to our institutions. Let us ponder with deep reflection, and cease not to repeat and reiterate the interesting truth that our boasted liberties will not long survive the wreck of our public morals. The destruction of the one will witness the passing away of the other. They will go down in melancholy companionship to the same grave. So the Father of his Country deemed, and with a paternal solicitude counseled us. Mr. Chairman, I heard with heartfelt approbation the sentiment already eloquently advanced and sustained, that the genius of our Constitution is propitious to the interests of the Sunday-school. It is true, sir. The pure spirit of republican liberty invokes its aid and cherishes its fellowship, and he is unfaithful to his country who would seek to impair its influence or check its progress.'

"It was not the value of the Sunday-school as an instrument of enlightening and elevating the popular mind that formed its chief attraction in the view of Mr. Frelinghuysen, though he by no means underrated its efficiency for this purpose. But the influence of such a host of voluntary religious teachers, inculcating from week to week the simple central truths of Divine revelation, combined with the personal incidental connection which the teacher's office gave him with the pupil's family, he regarded as of inestimable importance. 'I assure you,' he says, in a private letter, dated June 17, 1831, 'that it is grateful to me to be in any way connected with an institution which encourages so much hope for the welfare of our fellow-men for the world and for ETERNITY.'

"It is obvious, from many of the public declarations of his views, that Mr. Frelinghuysen had very grave apprehensions concerning the endurance of our political frame-work through the prevalence of ignorance and licentiousness. His spirits were oftentimes depressed and his hopes dimmed because of the apparent inadequacy of our moral forces to withstand the powers of darkness. His faith was steadfast in the Divine promise, that 'when the enemy should come in like a flood, the Spirit of the Lord would lift up a standard against him;' but in the terrible conflict, what would become of our institutions of civil and religious liberty?

"In such a mood, under date of August 1, 1832, he says: 'It is matter of frequent thankfulness to God, when there is so much of irreligion and licentiousness in our country to deplore, that we can turn to the Sabbath-schools and Bible-classes, and there cherish the reviving hope that with these blessed influences we shall yet see better and brighter days.' In November, 1833, Mr. Frelinghuysen advocated the cause of

Sunday-schools in a public meeting in New York, but no report of his speech was preserved.

"At the public meeting held at Philadelphia in connection with the eleventh anniversary of the American Sunday-school Union, Mr. Frelinghuysen made an address of a very remarkable character. The resolution in support of which the address was made was evidently framed with a view to urge the claims of Sunday-schools upon public attention, mainly, though by no means exclusively, because of their bearing on the *political and social welfare of the country;* and the tenor of his remarks coincides with this idea. It was in these words:

"'That Sunday-schools, by laying the foundation of public and private integrity and intelligence, provide the best preservative of our rights and liberties, and the best guarantee for the peace and good order of society; and that in this view they deserve the special patronage of the statesman and patriot.'

"In enforcing the resolution he said:

"'There are considerations connected with our country that present causes for melancholy apprehension. The spirit of freedom, with all its rich benefits, is not without its dangers. Every mind in any measure acquainted with its own operations knows that there are propensities within us which require control —that must be brought into subjection to wholesome regulations and discipline.

"'Now one startling danger lies in the very heart of our blessings. We are too proud of our liberties and of our country. Self-confidence is engendered, and a spirit of individual independence almost *too strong for law.* We are *our own rulers,* we boast. Politically, it is true. The fear is reasonable that we shall practically refuse or deny the authority even of *our own rulers.* There is a constant propensity to break away from all restraints. "Resistance," "liberty," "independence," "the rights of man," are so familiar—and so grateful too, I grant—that we are prone to forget not only Him whose unspeakable goodness has made us to differ, but to forget, also, that these animating terms, and the glow of patriotism, and the love of country, if not sustained and cherished by sound principles, will become the mere watchwords for licentiousness and all misrule.

"'I have not made this allusion, sir, for any purpose of severe censorship at this interesting season, when I would far rather mingle in the delightful sympathies that the occasion awakens; but, sir, I have given the hint, that we may perceive the benignant influence of the Sabbath-school on this *political tendency.* Yes, sir, every patriot should bless God for this agency that so admirably befits the service—that so wisely and seasonably meets the wants of our country.

"'*Opinion* is, under heaven, become the *arbiter of nations.* Power is despoiled of all its mystified incidents and prerogatives. The spell of long-established systems, of hereditary orders, is broken; and as the whole world is moving on from the quiet inaction of the one to the active, restless, and, I may add, feverish excitability of the other condition, what a public mercy was it that the Sunday-school should come up just as the elements began to quicken, and shed its healthful, purifying, forming influences over whole masses of mind, that were destined either to help forward, or with dreadful energy desolate the hopes of piety and human happiness.

"'I certainly shall not depreciate other blessed instrumentalities that adorn our age. I know that the *pulpit* stands at the head of all means to save our world. God has exalted it to that noble elevation, and there let it stand, the advocate of truth, and the faithful witness of God; the angel of His mercy, and the consolation of His people. But in its connections with the stability of our political institutions—in the preservation of the happiest and freest form of government in the world, the Sabbath-school falls not far behind the ministry. Indeed, it partakes much of its characteristics. It is itself a preacher of righteousness, and under most effective circumstances.

"'The faithful messenger of grace, as he ascends the pulpit and proclaims his Master's will, meets a promiscuous congregation, whose numbers encourage all unseen resistance to indiscriminate warnings and exhortations.

"'But mark the Sunday-school teacher as he pours the light of truth on the hearts of his little charge with affectionate and lively solicitude: he often feels that it must tell on their consciences; he almost reaches and touches the fountains of thought and sympathy. The seed may lie long buried, but herein is his hope: "Train up a child in the way he should go, and when he is old he will not depart from it."

"'He has another pledge. God has said, "My word shall not return to me void;" and no matter what impurity of motive may enter into the circulation of the truth, it shall accomplish all His gracious purposes.

"'The age on which this influence is exerted is the most *propitious*. Religion and the soundest philosophy of the mind alike assure us that the best mode of having the man as we wish is to train the child; to purify the fountain, go up to the spring-head if we expect a healthful stream.

"'The Sabbath-school approaches with its instructions just when they will sink the deepest and last the longest. It makes a sacred deposit of the soundest rules of life, of public duty, of private conduct; rules which form the faithful friend, the upright citizen, the godly man; rules that will found our hopes on "the Rock of ages;" that will raise a shield to guard our dearest earthly privileges, and train up a generation that we may hope will defend the cause of truth and civil liberty when those who train them shall have done with the duties and the toils of time.

" 'Sir, such an agency is beyond all human estimates of its value. I would most cheerfully trust even the cold calculations of philosophy for an approving award in behalf of a system that, from *Sabbath to Sabbath*, brings more than twenty-five thousand teachers,* imparting instruction from the very fountain of light and truth, and directing it upon more than one million of immortal minds, and this at the very *season* when impressions are more easily and deeply made. What madness of hard-hearted infidelity could doubt or oppose such an influence?

" 'We want no verdict of the schools of philosophy. Every heart feels to-day its value. Here, as we call up from the stores of memory the recollections and associations of childhood, a thought dropped on the heart twenty, thirty, or forty years ago, rises to the mind; and, as we perceive and feel how *clear*, and *strong*, and *vivid* it is—how fresh its impression, now hallowed by time—we all know by certain conclusive consciousness how unspeakably important are the lessons of childhood.

" 'Here it was a father's faithful counsels—there it was the silent eloquence of a mother's tears. They made a lodgment here that neither the follies nor the sins of after years could impair or remove. Lately I read of a pious youth, who, on examination for the ministry, in the history of his life, at that interesting period of it when he trusted that he felt the power of religion, in some such terms as these referred to the leading means of his recovery to God. Said he, "I trace the causes, under God, to a mother's faithfulness to my childhood. Yes," said he, "the taking of my little hand within hers (I can almost feel it still), as she led me to the closet, where she poured out her soul for my salvation; the sound of that dear voice as I would pass her chamber door as she wrestled with the God of Jacob for her child; these—these," said

* Now nearer 200,000.

he, "I mark as among the effective means by which the God of mercy led my soul to himself."

"'And the *Sabbath-school* is a kindred agency; it ranges by the side of parental instruction; and more than 50,000 witnesses of teachers and children converted to God from these nurseries of purity, demonstrate the blessed energy of this scheme of mercy.

"'Let every heart bid it God speed, and every hand be opened wide in its favor.'

"The salutary tendencies of the institution in repressing the inroads of vice and misrule were so obvious to his mind that, if no other advantage could be derived from it, this of itself would warrant all the labor and expense involved in sustaining it. He saw that even then (and much more in these latter days) there was a gigantic work of correction and repression to be done in our land, which can be accomplished only by moral forces; and not by them even, unless applied to the plastic minds and hearts of children and youth. The grand principle of subordination to lawful authority—to God as supreme, and to every ordinance of man for the Lord's sake—must rule from the cradle to the grave. It is the only safeguard under such a government as ours, and, to secure its supremacy, it must as surely begin at the cradle as it ends at the grave.

"In December, 1836, Mr. Frelinghuysen was urged to enter upon the exclusive service of the American Sunday-school Union at a salary of $3000. A deputation was appointed to wait upon him and express the views and wishes of the Board. He listened patiently for hours to the representations which were made; manifested a deep sense of the importance of the proposition and of the responsibilities involved, and desired time for reflection. In the interview, however, he intimated the conviction that the sphere of his influence, as a member of the bar, was quite as wide as he could wish and much wider than he could fill; and, after due consideration, he declined, on this ground, the proposed connection.

"It was unfortunate for the success of the attempt to secure Mr. Frelinghuysen's services that the place he was to occupy was not more accurately defined. To one of his methodical habits and child-like simplicity, it was important that any service required of him should be so clearly set forth that he could at once determine whether he had the needful qualifications for it, and whether the Providence of God called him to it. Of course, an invitation to fill a place without any specification of the duties to be performed or the responsibilities incurred was not accepted. That such a connection would have been agreeable to his feelings had the way been properly prepared for it, the deputation had no doubt; and that his greater professional influence and associations would have been no obstacle is apparent from the fact that in a few years thereafter he took the chancellorship of the New York University.

"In October, 1843, Mr. Frelinghuysen says, in a private letter, 'I love to cherish the Sabbath-school, and I continue my relations to it at this time as teacher of an interesting Bible-class. The number varies from ten to eighteen, composed of young men who have passed through the ordinary stages of Sunday-school instruction.'

"Seven years after this he was called to the presidency of Rutger's College; and in June of that year (1850) he thus expressed himself in response to a notice of his twenty-fourth election to the vice-presidency of the American Sunday-school Union:

"'I feel honored by such an association with a blessed agency of the Divine goodness for our whole race. I have long been connected with its labors of love. Some of my most favored hours have been in the Sunday-school; and my prayer is that God would enlarge its influence and extend its relations until every tribe and kindred shall be reached.'

"Meagre as are these memoranda of Mr. Frelinghuysen's interest and public labors in this department of Christian benevolence, they suffice to show that as a disciple of Christ, a citizen, a statesman, and a philanthropist, he embraced and held fast the Sunday-school as (in its proper sphere) one of the most efficient, wise, and economical agencies for the diffusion of religious knowledge, for the advancement of human happiness, and for the extension and prosperity of the Redeemer's kingdom, known to our age."

AMERICAN TEMPERANCE UNION.

Mr. Frelinghuysen at a very early period became connected with the movement made in this country for the discouragement of intemperance, and continued throughout life a steadfast friend of the cause. Ardent spirits, and afterward wine, were banished from his table and his house as a beverage, and he never failed, on any proper occasion, to counsel others to pursue the same course. His speeches in favor of total abstinence from all that can intoxicate were innumerable, and pronounced before assemblies of all kinds and numbers, from a Congressional meeting in the hall of the House of Representatives at Washington down to a neighborhood gathering in a country school-house.

His advocacy of this cause was marked by two features characteristic of the man. One was his deference to Scripture teaching. He gave no countenance to the impeachments of Divine truth and wisdom in which some overzealous speakers allowed themselves, but always planted his inculcation of the duty of abstinence upon the doctrine of Christian expediency as stated by the Apostle Paul. The other was the absence of harsh denunciation and invective. He spoke with meekness of wisdom. He knew that it is the soft word which breaketh the bone, and his intense earnestness was tempered and refined by Christian love. Hence even habitual drunkards were never alienated or embittered by the rebukes, in public or private, which his faithfulness led him to administer.

The following letter from the Rev. Dr. Marsh fitly indicates the scope and character of his public efforts on behalf of this great moral reform:

"Office of American Temperance Union,
July 30, 1862.

"REV. DR. CHAMBERS:

"DEAR SIR,—You ask from us at this office for some reminiscences of the Hon. Theodore Frelinghuysen, one of our late vice-presidents, and for a time chairman of our executive committee, but now numbered, we believe, with that glorious company of redeemed ones who stand before the throne of God and the Lamb. My acquaintance with Mr. Frelinghuysen commenced in the winter of 1831–2 at Washington, where I was deputed by the American Temperance Society to excite an interest for the temperance cause in gentlemen connected with the government. On propounding to him my views and objects, he at once gave me his friendship and support, introducing me to other gentlemen, and co-operating in a plan for a public Congressional temperance meeting in the Capitol. That meeting was held early in January. Governor Cass, then Secretary of War, presided; and the meeting was addressed by the Hon. Felix Grundy, United States senator from Tennessee; Mr. Frelinghuysen, senator from New Jersey; Hon. J. C. Bates, member of Congress from Massachusetts; Hon. James M. Wayne, from Georgia; and Hon. Daniel Webster, United States senator from Massachusetts. The assembly was large, and the meeting most impressive. The address of Mr. Frelinghuysen completely dissipated all the levity and hilarity with which such a meeting of the splendor and gayety of Washington was anticipated, and gave a tone of tenderness and solemnity in its portraiture of the personal and domestic evils of intemperance not easily forgotten. At subsequent Congressional meetings of a similar character, Mr. Frelinghuysen's voice was lifted up with great energy and power against the drinking usages of men in public stations, and when the Congressional Temperance Society was organized in 1833, he became chairman of the executive committee, and, in connection with his most intimate friends, Hon. A. Naudain, of Delaware, Hon. John Blair, of Tennessee, Hon. George N. Briggs, of Massachusetts, and Hon. Eleutheros Cook, of Ohio, he was instrumental of moulding a large portion of the Congress of that period to temperance principles.

"On his removal to this city in 1841, he at once gladly co-operated with us in our labors, and accepted the appointment of chairman of our executive committee, giving to us as much of his time and counsel as his situation allowed.

"Mr. Frelinghuysen was a thorough temperance man from principle. Devoting himself soul and body to the service of God, he kept his body under that it might be a fit temple of the Holy Ghost; but he held himself accountable for his influence upon others, and, seeing the awful ravages of intemperance, especially among men in the higher walks of life, in the legal profession, on the bench, and in Congress, he was resolved to set an example which all men might follow with safety; and in the stand he had taken from Christian principle, he found himself wondrously strengthened by his personal experience. In answer to a letter from Dr. Edwards, he said,

"'I have been favored with your circular requesting the results of my experience in the matter of entire abstinence from the use of intoxicating liquor, and especially as to its effects on health, on bodily and mental ability, and the feelings of the mind. I can, from personal experience, bear decided testimony to the happiest results, in all these particulars, arising from entire abstinence. For the last nine years I have wholly abstained from ardent spirits, and habitually from all fermented liquors. The last year, which has been the period in which I have relinquished even the occasional use of wine, I have enjoyed better health than in either of the nine. And it is an interesting and grateful fact to me that protracted and severe mental efforts can now be borne *without weariness*, bodily exercise and labor are refreshing, and the mind is far more cheerful, composed, and self-possessed than in the days of infatuation, when the spirits and wine cup met us on every sideboard, and assailed us at every table.'

"It will be remembered that in the early stages of the temperance reformation wine and fermented drinks were not excluded. Soon, however, as it was understood that this exclusion was essential to the perfection of the reformation, no man more heartily adopted it, and, as manifested in the above, with higher personal enjoyment. As a speaker in temperance meetings, no individual was more acceptable, whenever his services could be obtained, than Mr. Frelinghuysen. The seriousness and earnestness of his manner, the honesty and firmness of his soul, and the softness of his tones, can never be forgotten. He put men who indulged their appetite to their own ruin and the ruin of others to shame, and made the hosts of temperance rally around their standard with the greatest earnestness and confidence of triumph. In the extraordinary reformation of inebriates in 1840–41, he felt the deepest interest; and while he would use all moral influence to reclaim the victims of the cup, no man was more decided in bringing legislation to bear upon the traffic, the direct cause of almost all the drunkenness and crime of the land. His opinions on this subject were well matured, and were expressed with great strength, and do demand the attention of every legislator in our land. If you have room, I wish you would give them a place in your memoir. I could give you several expressions of them, but one embodies them all—a letter to Rev. Dr. Edwards, in 1834, relating to the Sixth Annual Report of the American Temperance Society, in which the system of license was ably discussed. In that letter he said,

"'I have read with great satisfaction the Sixth Annual Report of your society, and especially that portion of it between pages 44 and 69, on the immorality of authorizing by law the traffic in ardent spirit as a drink. It is almost unnecessary to say how fully and heartily I concur in the views and principles that are therein so ably sustained. If the use of ardent spirits be wrong, it seems to be a result of inevitable deduction that the traffic in it is at least equally so. And hence, while many have ridiculed, I have always honored the conduct of those persons who, under honest convictions of the evils of intemperance, have renounced all connection and terms with ardent spirits, *broken in the head of the cask*, and poured out the destructive poison on the ground. This was a noble tribute to principle that would not hesitate between the cold calculations of avarice, and the high claims of duty, and the peace of a pure conscience. How can a just mind engage in a commerce all the details of which are fruitful of evil?

"'The use of ardent spirit is attended by peculiar circumstances. It is not an ordinary and harmless beverage, as to which every man may be safely trusted with his own keeping, but it is an insidious and dangerous practice, that gradually forms an artificial and depraved appetite. It deranges and inflames the whole organic system of the body, aggravates instead of allaying thirst, and creates an inward craving that has, in some cases, seemed to me like the gnawings of despair.

"'And, worse still, this habit relaxes the hold of good principles by impairing the moral sense. A man's self-respect falls among its first victims. These sad results are confined to no class or condition. The strong men and the feeble are equally exposed to its ravages. The truth is (and every grave-yard proves it), the man who habitually drinks ardent spirit, no matter *how temperately*, has cause to tremble, for his danger is not only real, but imminent.

"'To a subject, therefore, of such peculiar and dreadful energy, reaching so far and assailing so many interests, we must apply peculiar remedies. It is mere tampering with temptation to come short of positive, decided, and uncompromising opposition. We must not only *resist*, we must *drive* it. To stand on the defensive merely is to aid in its triumph.

"'The second inquiry which you have proposed presents one of the most interesting questions of public duty. The ground taken in your report is, beyond all serious controversy, among the clearest and soundest conclusions of right reason: "That the laws which authorize the traffic in ardent spirit as a drink, by licensing men to pursue it, are morally wrong."

"'Law-makers are, of all men, bound to seek the public good. So broad is this duty, that they are under peculiar obligations to consecrate the influence of a pure and personal example to the promotion of the general welfare; but, first of all, should their *legislation be pure;* not only preventive of evil, but persuasive to good. No man fit to represent a free people will deny these propositions. Then what can we urge in excuse for the countenance given to the use of ardent spirit on almost every statute-book? On one page you will read of heavy penalties denounced against drunkenness, riots, and public disorders, and the next chapter authorizes the retail of the very poison which, all admit, brings on these outbreaking transgressions. Who can reconcile these glaring contradictions? It is time, every reflecting mind exclaims, it is high time to emancipate ourselves from these humiliating practices. The use of ardent spirit has introduced a course of reasoning and conduct that libels human nature. Who can dwell upon it without feelings of shame, that we should have gravely provided, by public law, that if men *will pay* for the mischievous faculty, they may set up a tavern, and sell as much rum as they please, short of drunkenness; may scatter firebrands and death all around them; beguile unwary youth, and poison the very fountains of moral purity, and inflict an amount of injury on the vital interests of the community that neither time nor law can repair.

" 'I rejoice, my dear sir, that you are endeavoring to bring this subject before the scrutiny of public men. You can not fail in a purpose so fraught with benefits. We owe it to our history, to our free institutions, and, above all, we owe it to Him whose benignant providence has so richly blessed us, that we purify our laws. And if men will engage in this destructive traffic—if they will stoop to degrade their reason and reap the wages of iniquity, let them no longer have the *law-book* as a pillow, nor quiet conscience by the opiate of a *court license.*

" 'I am persuaded that the course of past legislation has greatly increased the evil of which we complain. How could it be otherwise? Men can hardly avoid looking up to the halls of legislation for standards of duty; they expect to find models there that may be safely followed; and when these high places have deliberately sanctioned the use of ardent spirits when under *legal regulations*, the conclusion has been natural and prompt that, when it was clothed in these legal forms, it was not only excusable, but *lawful.* Men would not take time to question the moral power of a Legislature to make that right which God declares to be wrong. The lamented fact has been, they did not wish to believe in any defect of power; they loved to have it so, and accordingly reposed on the plausible authority of a positive statute.

"'I trust and pray that light will very soon become strong enough to expose all these delusions, and that, by your laudable efforts and the blessing of God, our public men, our state and national Legislatures, with the whole body of our people, will address to this subject the just and deep reflection that it deserves, and will, with heart and hand, by one combined and blessed effort, shake off forever the bondage under which our land has groaned.'

"On the adoption of the Prohibitory Law by Maine and other New England states in 1851, 1854, and 1855, he made an address before the New Jersey State Society at New Brunswick, endorsing the whole, and commending it most warmly to his fellow-citizens. The impression was most happy. But his most fervent prayer was that the ministry and the churches of our land might clear themselves from all participation of guilt in the existence and spread of intemperance, both for their own sake, and that the greatest hinderance to the conversion of sinners, the spread of the Gospel, and the evangelization of the world might speedily be removed.

"We all, sir, have reason to bless God that we have had a Frelinghuysen among us; that he has been associated with us; that he has taught us how to bear scoffings and revilings, how to breast opposition, how to persevere amid trials and disappointments, and how to cast all our care upon Him who careth for us, and will finally cause His people to triumph in every place to His own glory.

"Fearing I have written you too long a letter, yet having much more to say, I am yours respectfully,

"JOHN MARSH, Cor. Sec. A. T. U."

CHAPTER XIII.

THE CLOSING SCENE.

Origin of his Sickness.—Fear of Death.—Fear overcome.—Profound Humility.—Submission.—Temptations.—Remembrances.—Interview with Dr. Campbell.—Advice to a Youth.—Desire to Depart.—The peaceful End.

DURING the greater part of his life Mr. Frelinghuysen enjoyed good health. In the latter portion of it his constitution became impaired, and constant care was required to keep him in working condition. He felt especially the need of exercise in the open air, and this he was accustomed to take with great regularity. But the weather during the winter of 1861–62 was unfavorable for this purpose, especially to a man of his years. There were frequent falls of snow; and although no large quantity fell at any one time, yet there was enough to cover the ground, and when, after partially thawing, it froze, the roads and paths were coated with ice, and the walking became very unsafe. Mr. Frelinghuysen was thus cut off from his usual and necessary outdoor rambles, and, in consequence, the general tone of his system was lowered. About this time the proclamation of President Lincoln was issued, recommending the people to meet in their usual places of public assemblage on the anniversary of Washington's birthday, and attend the reading of the Farewell Address of the Father of his Country. The second Reformed Protestant Dutch Church in New Brunswick, the one in which Mr. Frelinghuysen regularly worshiped, was opened on that day, and he attended the services. But the day was a chilly one, and the house imperfectly warmed, so that he took a severe cold. He employed the remedies to which he had been accustomed, and enjoyed the benefit of skillful medical attendance; but, although the disease was subdued, his stomach began to fail, and he became unable to retain any nourishment. First one kind of food was rejected, and then another, until the whole list was exhausted, and he could take nothing but stimulants. At last even these were nauseated, and then, of course, the end drew rapidly on.

In the earlier period of his sickness he had no apprehension of a fatal issue, and even when the symptoms became more formidable he still cherished the hope that he should not die, but live, and labor still longer in the Master's vineyard. But at the commencement of the last fortnight the issue became very clear to his mind, and he looked death steadily in the face. Here occurred one of the most delightful surprises of his life.

During his whole previous career he had been, through fear of death, subject to bondage. It was not, as has been the case with many eminent Christians, that he dreaded dying, the physical act, the unknown pang which attends the article of dissolution. His apprehensions went deeper than this. It was death itself which alarmed him, the cessation of this earthly sojourn, where the means of grace are enjoyed, and there is time and room for securing the salvation of the soul. Death introduces man into the presence of his Judge and the retributions of eternity. He feared that when this occurred he would not be found prepared, but make shipwreck of his soul. No one else shared in the least in these apprehensions, and he himself could not justify them when calmly studying the case in view of the Savior's finished work and the Father's everlasting covenant. Still the fear remained, or, if for a time removed, it would recur again, and make death a hideous thing to his soul. Thus, just before the worst symptoms of his disease appeared, he had passed a tolerable night, and awoke in the morning refreshed and encouraged, when one of his nieces coming into the room, he said to her, "Ah! it is a solemn thing to be so near eternity." She replied, "We indeed feel that, but it should not seem so to you." To this his answer was, "Yes; but my shortcomings—my shortcomings!" The sense of his own sinfulness, the imperfections of his life, the vast distance between what he was and what he ought to be, ever pressed upon his mind, and overshadowed the fullness of that grace which alone can furnish a basis of hope to any enlightened mind. It was not because he expected to attain heaven by works and saw their insufficiency, but because he knew we must be born again in order to enter the kingdom of God, and it seemed to him as if his defects of obedience proved that he had not experienced the great change.

But, whatever be the precise origin or ground of his distressing apprehensions, they all disappeared at once and forever in the closing weeks of his life. For nearly half a century he had been carrying this grievous burden, which reason and faith seemed alike unable to throw off, but when the hour came, the burden, like Christian's at the wicket-gate, fell away of itself, and he saw it no more. He entered into the full assurance of faith and of hope. Not a cloud lingered in his sky. Faith performed its perfect work. Love was kindled into ecstasy. Beams from the heavenly glory played around his bedside, and his face was as if illumined by the *aureola* of the saints. This calm and sweet peace which diffused itself through his soul was not the dream of delirium, nor the excitement of fever, nor the rebound of tensely-strung nerves. It had no earthly or physical cause. It was the release which the Lord might be expected to bestow on his faithful servant, in anticipation of the unbounded liberty of the upper skies. Perhaps it had been needful, as part of the restraining discipline called for by the temptations of his life, that such a devoted Christian should walk so long in this bondage; but now, when the end was so near, when he had finished his course and concluded his warfare, it seemed good to the Lord to crown the holy and useful life with a happy and triumphant death. The dying man himself never grew weary of expatiating on the marvelous change, and praising the grace which had wrought it.

His profound and unaffected humility was often exhibited. He had nothing to say of his past life—that life so full of faith, love, charity, so pure, and simple, and stainless, so honorable to the Gospel, and so blessed to man. It had been, in the ordinary acceptation of the term, "a well-spent life;" one which, all things considered, has rarely been equaled in our own age or any other; yet no part of his peace, comfort, or hope was derived from looking back upon it, upon its years crowded with deeds of usefulness and continually advancing in holiness. His own oft-repeated words were, "I am nothing—nothing at all, only a poor sinner saved by grace." Not the thief who hung by the Savior's side—not the outcast saved so as by fire, depended more simply or more entirely upon the riches of free grace than did this honored Christian philanthropist, who was crowning a long life of active godliness with a death of serene triumph.

One of the greatest trials caused by death was the parting it involved from friends on earth. He was surrounded by a large circle of kindred and connections, in whom he took a deep interest, to whom he was always a faithful and unwearied friend, and by whom he was regarded with an affectionate reverence which it is not easy to describe. To these his house and his heart were always open, and it was one of his highest earthly pleasures to enjoy their society. But as the end drew on, the ties which bound here below were sensibly relaxed, and he looked forward with greater desire to the heavenly rest. This result was accelerated by his bodily sufferings, which were protracted and at times very severe. Once, on being told that he seemed to suffer much, he replied, "Yes; how glad I shall be to rest this weary head on my Savior's bosom, to tell Him how often I have grieved Him, and to speak of all His mercies to me."

The following more detailed account of what occurred in his sick-room has been kindly furnished by one who was present:

"MY DEAR SIR,—I take the first opportunity to give, as requested, some account of the closing scene of Mr. Frelinghuysen's life. To that I must confine myself, or I become his eulogist. I knew him as well as one man ever knew another, and I found in him less to condemn and more to admire than in any other man I ever knew. Nature had done much for him in his person, his voice, his mien, his genial, high-toned piety, in the easy play of his emotions, and in his gift of eloquence.

"Education, intellectual and social, did much for him. At school, in college, in his profession, in the councils of the nation, and as the head of literary institutions, he seems always to have been placed where the powers of a naturally strong and comprehensive mind could be advantageously developed; while at the home of his boyhood, as well as at his own family circle, he was always surrounded by those refining influences which do so much to purify taste and elevate sentiment. But it was to grace that he was the greatest debtor; its renewing and sanctifying influence was constantly observable in his life; and if I were asked what one thing did most to make him what he was, I would answer that it was his inflexible, undeviating habit of daily communion with his God. It was as his character assimilated to that of our Savior that he was most admirable.

"Pardon me, it was some account of his death-scene you desired. You are aware that Mr. Frelinghuysen had always been much afraid of death. Not that he was a coward; for what he did not dare to do, which was right to be done, no man would ever dare to do. His dread of death arose from his appreciating better than many others the fearful responsibilities of the change from time to eternity, and from the fact that while grace to live by had been freely given him, he had not yet received to his satisfaction dying grace.

"I had visited him several times after he was taken

sick, and when he was still able to move about in his room. About ten days before his death he made the first allusion to any impression that this might be his last sickness. He then said, 'I feel that matters are coming to a close with me. I can not bear this disease much longer.' On being told that there was a prospect of his recovery, he said, 'Perhaps so;' and then exclaimed, 'How gracious God in Christ is! and I feel happy in hearing Him say, Come up, come up.' On being prayed with, he expressed the pleasure which extemporaneous prayers, coming from the heart, gave him.

"In conversation I said to him, 'You were always much afraid of death, but seem now to contemplate its approach calmly.' He said that that fear had been removed, and that, some weeks before, God had placed in his way some beautiful lines [by a living English writer, Mrs. A. L. Waring], the spirit of which he fully felt. He then repeated them to me:

I love to think that God appoints
  My portion day by day;
Events of life are in His hand,
  And I would only say,
"Appoint them in thine own good time,
  And in thine own best way.

"All things shall mingle for my good,
I would not change them if I could,
  Nor alter Thy decree.
Thou art above and I below,
Thy will be done, and even so,
  For so it pleaseth Thee."

"The last week of his life I was constantly with him. He was always cheerful, sometimes indulging in pleasantry, in alluding to old anecdotes and scenes, and he never for a moment doubted his entire safety in the Redeemer. His interest in the affairs of time continued, and he frequently spoke about the condition of the country; but his views on that subject, as he had retired from the political world, I will withhold.

"It was an interesting feature of his last days that he had almost constantly, night and day, by his bedside, four persons, the heads of families, two gentlemen and two ladies, whom he had befriended in their orphanage; not alone by pecuniary aid—no, that is the least worthy of note. He had been to them a true father, loving, counseling, caring for them, continuing his interest through life, looking upon their children as his, to them all giving his dying benedictions and prayers. One of these, an accomplished and most interesting Christian lady, on one occasion when he was restless, leaned over the bed, took his hand, and with a voice full of melody, quietly repeated to him the twenty-third Psalm, 'The Lord is my Shepherd,' etc. 'May God bless you!' was the response of the aged saint. It was a beautiful scene. I thought, while standing there, with what exquisite tenderness God makes return to the benevolent man for each generous act.

"Another of the four persons alluded to was a skillful physician, who by night and day, with unremitting attention, nursed and cared for his benefactor. He kissed him farewell. He performed the last offices of friendship, and then stood unmanned beside the remains of him who took care of him when an orphan boy.

"I had frequent conversations with him. At one time when he was restless, and the family were sent for, the last twelve verses of the eighth chapter of the Epistle to the Romans were read to him. After prayer, he called me to the head of his bed, for he was very weak, and said that Satan was tempting him to doubt the divinity of the Savior; suggesting that the disciples performed miracles, and therefore the fact that Christ performed them was no evidence that he was God. He said that he met the suggestion by saying to the tempter that the disciples could not have possessed the power to work miracles, because Christ never gave it to them; that power He held in His own hands. They performed miracles in the name of Jesus of Nazareth, but Christ by His own power. 'Oh,' said he, 'it is a precious Gospel. It is the value of my soul. It is now my stay. Study it, my ——, study it, day and night. It is solemn for me, on the verge of eternity, to be thus urging you. I should like to talk more, but am too weak.' On being told that it would be strange if, in his weak state, he met with no temptations, he said, 'When I am tempted, I go to the promises from Genesis to Revelation, and from Revelation to Genesis. I seem to know them all.'

"To another gentleman of mature years, whom Mr. Frelinghuysen had cared for and educated, he said, 'This is a trying hour, but the Lord has sustained me. He promised that He would, and He always will do it.' Then bidding him farewell, he expressed the hope that they would all meet in heaven.

"One of the leading members of the New Jersey bar called to ask after his health, and told me that it was to Mr. Frelinghuysen's conversations with him, as they walked in the morning together when attending court at Trenton, that he attributed his first religious impressions. When this was repeated to Mr. Frelinghuysen, he replied, 'Those are precious remembrances.'

"One day, as we were leaving his room to go to dinner, some one pleasantly said, 'Uncle, we wish you could take dinner with us.' 'Ah! my son,' he replied, 'I am going to eat of the bread and drink of the wine of everlasting life.'

"A day or two before he died, the Rev. Dr. W. H. Campbell, who afterward became his successor as president of Rutger's College, called on him. I was not present during the whole interview, and, as I came into the room, I beheld what was to me a striking scene. Dr. Campbell held the almost dying man by the hand, and, the tears coursing rapidly down his face, said, with a cheerful, manly voice, 'Farewell, Mr. Frelinghuysen, farewell. I expect soon to join you. I shall not remain long here. Farewell, sir.' 'Farewell, my friend,' was the reply; 'but you must stay here. God has a work for you, and you will yet accomplish great good.' Then, as the reverend gentleman left the room, he said to one standing by his bed, 'You do not know that man; he is an honest, manly Christian.'

"Afterward, a youth of about seventeen years, the son of a friend, called, at Mr. Frelinghuysen's request, to see him. 'I have sent for you, my son,' said he. 'I want you to see how a Christian can die. I have been all my life in fear of that hour, and yet for seven weeks I have seen death day by day approaching, and never was calmer. Did you ever see me more calm?' Receiving no answer, he repeated the question, and then receiving a reply in the negative, continued, 'Now, my son, do not despise parents' prayers, mothers' tears, and sisters' supplications, but turn unto God. Now is the accepted time, now is the day of salvation. Seek the Lord, and you will find Him; despise Him, and He is a consuming fire. He has not come away from heaven and died upon earth to be lightly rejected. I have here a little keepsake for you; it is the Bible from Genesis to Revelation, published by the American Bible Society. I don't want to exact from you a rigorous promise, but I do want you to say that, by God's grace, you will try to do what I have done. For fifty—no, forty-five years, I have made it a rule, at noon, or as near to it as I could—perhaps there would not be an opportunity before tea-time—to read a chapter in the Bible, and spend fifteen minutes in private devotion. My son, farewell. Go now, and seek God's grace.'

"On one occasion, when he seemed to suffer, I asked what it was that troubled him. He replied, 'When I was a boy, I went to see Grandma Hardenberg when she was sick, and asked her how she did, and she said to me, "Schilde, I want to go home, and they won't let me."' With that anecdote, he seemed to consider that my inquiry as to what troubled him was answered.

"At another time, one present said to him that he had been enabled to do much good in life, and that should be a comfort to him now. And then was read to him that part of the twenty-fifth chapter of Matthew's Gospel, in which the King is represented as saying to those on his right hand, 'Come, ye blessed of my Father, inherit the kingdom prepared for you from the foundation of the world. For I was an hungered, and ye gave me meat; I was thirsty, and ye gave me drink,' etc., etc. But he said that his only plea was, 'God be merciful to me a sinner.' When reminded that those on the right hand used the same language, saying, 'When saw we Thee an hungered, and fed Thee? or thirsty, and gave Thee drink?' etc., he made no reply, but shook his head. He took much pleasure in listening to the parable of the Prodigal Son, recorded in the fifteenth chapter of Luke.

"The attending physician came into the room at a time when he was very low, and he said, 'This, I think, doctor, is my last struggle; and it is all peace—Christ is precious.' The doctor replied that we could do nothing without Christ. 'Yes,' said Mr. Frelinghuysen, 'I often said that, but did not realize it. Now I feel it. Christ has opened to me the truth. If there had been no sin, we should not have known how gracious God is.'

"He had, during the last week of his life, many interesting interviews which I have not referred to. He suffered but little. His mind was perfectly unclouded. He made every arrangement for his departure. He spent hours in endeavoring to reconcile his true wife to their separation. He frequently through the day asked that a short prayer might be offered. His faith was firm and confident.

"On the morning of the 12th of April it was manifest that he was sinking, and I, who had so often endeavored to cheer him when he was desponding, said, without fear of alarming him, 'You can live but a little while longer. You are almost gone. You may possibly live two or three hours, but probably not so long.' He asked if that was the opinion of the physicians. I told him that it was. He then took leave of the family and friends. The physician to whom I have referred as benefited when an orphan by him, and myself, kissed him farewell. I then asked him, 'Is it peace with you now?' He answered, 'All peace, more than ever before.' Shortly afterward he expired. 'Mark the perfect man, and behold the upright, for the end of that man is peace.'"

CHAPTER XIV.

CONCLUSION.

The Gift of God.—Mr. Frelinghuysen's Completeness of Character.—General Recognition of it.—Proven by Trial.—Theme of Gratitude to God.—Encouragement to others.—A Proof of Christianity.—An Example of cheerful Piety.—Its fundamental and characteristic Element.

At a large meeting held in 1844 to ratify the Whig nominations for national offices, Governor Lumpkin, of Georgia, pleasantly played upon Mr. Frelinghuysen's Christian name, Theodore, which, according to its origin, means *gift of God*, saying that this eminent Christian statesman was God's gift to the nation for the office of Vice-president. The result showed that this was an error, the fond anticipation of a political and personal friend, who thought that one who combined so many excellencies of character could not be defeated if fairly brought before the popular eye. Still the playful suggestion had an element of truth, although in a different application from that which the eminent civilian who made it intended. Theodore Frelinghuysen was the gift of God to the American people; not for the temporary occupation of any office, however dignified or important, nor for the accomplishment of any civil or secular aims, however lofty, but for a bright and shining example of the thorough and consistent Christian in all the walks of life, public and private.

There are many blameless believers on earth of whom the world is not worthy, but they are usually found either in the ministry or in private life; but here was a man whose necessary avocations led him into the whirl of business and politics, who was thrown into contact with all classes of society, who passed through prolonged scenes of the highest excitement, who took his full share of the duties devolving upon educated and professional men under the popular institutions of our country, and yet never once abated from the strictness of a holy life, never once gave occasion for unfriendly observers to bring a charge of inconsistency. Not that he was, or claimed to be, perfect; he had infirmities, as he himself was painfully conscious, both while he lived and when he came to die; but all who knew him would, with one voice, declare that they never saw the man who had so few.

His life was long, extending several years beyond the ordinary limit. It was, for the most part, a very active one, spent in arduous and engrossing employments. It was varied, leading him into many different circumstances and associations; yet throughout it was the life of "a good man and a just." He was not excellent at one time or in one relation only, but at all times and in every relation. Intimate friends, casual acquaintances, and those who knew him only by observation, all had but one opinion respecting him. His prominent connection with great enterprises in which Christians at large took a deep interest, rendered his name familiar to all the people of God in this land, and multitudes who never saw his face in the flesh looked up to him with affectionate reverence as a tried and chosen leader of the sacramental host. They mourned his death as a public calamity, and felt the stroke as keenly as if it were a personal bereavement. The keenness of their regret was not owing to their lack of full information on the subject; he for whose removal they sorrowed was one who did not loom largest when seen at a distance, but was more highly appreciated the longer and better he was known. Lofty as the figure seemed when seen through the mists of current reports, it lost none of its stately proportions when viewed standing in the clear sunlight of close personal knowledge. Perhaps there were no more hearty admirers of his character than the friends of his boyhood, residing in his native county, who had watched his career from the beginning to the end. One of these was present at his funeral, and heard the just and touching eulogy pronounced over the remains of the deceased by the Rev. Dr. De Witt; but, after the services were over, he exclaimed, with tears in his eyes, "All that the speaker said was true, but oh! he did not tell the half; it is only we who have seen that man at home in his everyday life who know his real worth."

That worth was not a mere negative excellence; it was not simply the absence of common faults, but the possession of rare virtues exercised for a great length of time, and amid manifold and searching temptations. The more the gold was tried, the purer it was found. He passed through the furnace of political life at the national capital, and came out without even the smell of fire upon him. Boy and man, advocate and senator, chancellor and president, church member and church officer, citizen and Christian, he bore his faculties so meekly, and discharged his duties so faithfully, that even the breath of slander never tarnished his escutcheon. There is nothing in his course or character which needs excuse or even explanation. The entire career speaks for itself. Men might differ from him in political opinions, in religious belief, or in minor questions, but none ever doubted the solid integrity of his principles, or the perfect conscientiousness of his life.

Many men have been quite as distinguished as he in professional and political life; many, too, have been just as eminent for Christian consistency, but very few, if any, have ever united the two kinds of distinction so thoroughly and successfully. As a civilian, statesman, and patriot, he did his full duty on the earth, yet held perpetual communion with God in heaven. He commanded respect by his intellectual gifts and attainments, yet won universal love and confidence by his meekness of wisdom. True to his clients, to his party, and to his country, he was also true to the Gospel and the Cross in every situation. He was not a different man at different times, combining, as it were, by mechanical cohesion, two opposite spheres of character and conduct—in one company or place the zealous Christian, in another the busy politician or lawyer; but his religious faith interpenetrated his whole life, and gave to it its characteristic tone. He was just as much a Christian in the court-room, or on the floor of the Senate, or at the hustings, as in his closet, or the Sunday-school, or a prayer-meeting. While never parading, he never cloaked his convictions. Instead of being held loosely, they were a part of himself, and could not be hid. Wherever he went, whatever he did, an exquisite combination of justice and goodness, of intelligence and meekness, of wisdom and love,

> Rose like a steam of rich distilled perfumes,
> And stole upon the air.

Such a life as the preceding pages have imperfectly unfolded calls for profound gratitude to Him who has been pleased in our generation to erect such a precious memorial of the ennobling and sanctifying power of His heavenly grace. An eminently good man, in any relation of life, is a great gift of God to those who behold the rays of the burning and shining light; but especially is this the case when the good man lives long, has wide influence, is extensively known, passes through trial and temptation, is uniformly consistent, is destitute of eccentricities, is actively useful as well as passively blameless, mingles in public and prominent scenes, avoids even the appearance of evil, and perseveres to the very end—that end fitly crowning the work. Such was Theodore Frelinghuysen; and what he was God made him. Providence did much for him in bestowing his fine bodily presence, his plaintive but melodious voice, his penetration and sagacity, his dignified station, his winning personal address; but grace wrought far more in moulding such an elevated Christian character, so spiritual, humble, and uniform, so sweetly blending the virtues of contemplation and of action, so full of love to God and love to man, so prominent in the features which are distinctively evangelical, so complete and harmonious in outline and detail.

Such a life is full of encouragement and stimulus to all the children of God. It presents an exalted picture of human excellence, yet one exactly proportioned to the means and agencies employed. Although far exceeding the ordinary standard of believers, it does not transcend what they are taught to aim at and expect. Given in any case the same habits of faith, conscientiousness, and prayer, the same result might be looked for, modified only by the differences of temperament and situation. All Mr. Frelinghuysen's natural advantages in constitution, birth, training, and position, would have amounted to but little but for the grace which was given him. It was this rich grace, so perseveringly sought, so largely received, and so carefully cherished, which made him what he was. This was his own life-long profession, sealed and confirmed over and over as he lay upon his deathbed. That grace has not exhausted its stores; there is enough yet to advance the whole Church permanently to the high position held by him, who, when he died, left behind him no equal in the completeness of his Christian character. If any fall short, it is not because they are straitened in God, but because of their own remissness.

To unbelievers in the Christian religion, Mr. Frelinghuysen's life presents an insoluble problem. His lofty and stainless integrity was, as has been said, acknowledged universally. There is literally no dissenting voice. No public man has ever lived in this country respecting whom so many persons would unite in saying that they never knew any one who so nearly approached perfection in all the relations of life as he; yet this man habitually ascribed whatever excellence he was enabled to exhibit to the Gospel of the grace of God. Nor was this mere prejudice, or the force of education, or the result of fanatical excitement, but the conviction of a mind eminently cool, cautious, and collected, accustomed to weighing evidence, wont to take comprehensive views of things, and always swayed by what appeared to be the truth. If, then, he made no mistake in the matter—and mistake is hardly possible in the circumstances—his life was a genuine product of Christianity, and the fruit, according to an invariable law, testifies to the character of the tree which bears it. A baseless system could not have produced such an illustrious example of public and private virtue. Whether Christianity be deemed a delusion, or an imposture, or a gradual hardening of mythical elements into a fixed belief, it must have lacked the power to shape a character so pure, complete, and rounded. The guiding principle would have betrayed its own defects by corresponding defects marked and manifest somewhere in the product; but none such are to be seen. Mr. Frelinghuysen's infirmities were either constitutional, and, as such, held under a control which was only not constant and habitual, or they were an excess of those Christian virtues which are most difficult of attainment. The question therefore remains, How could a system of faith and practice, cordially and intelligently embraced, lead to such a spotless life and character amid every variety of temptation, unless it were from God?

To those who identify godliness and gloom—who

confound Christian seriousness with austerity and melancholy, the life described in this volume administers a pointed rebuke. Here was a man whose conscientiousness was unequaled in any generation of believers—whose abstinence from the pleasures of sin was complete and life-long—whose religious convictions were so intense and pervading as to shape his whole life, and yet no one of his contemporaries enjoyed so much happiness as he. Nor is reference had here simply to the joy of communion with God, or to that which springs directly from spiritual duties and privileges—although, in his case, both of these were great—but to the ordinary kinds and sources of pleasure in common life. In all domestic and social scenes, Mr. Frelinghuysen was happy himself, and the source of happiness to every one around him. In consequence of his sensitive organization, and of occasional attacks of a depressing disease, there were times when his face was clouded. But these were exceptions. In the general, he entered with a keen zest into every form and scene of rational enjoyment.

Even his habitual dread of death, and the constant apprehension of unfitness for the judgment which he unfortunately and mistakenly cherished, could not break the spring of his character or chill the warm current of his social impulses. His manly sense rejected asceticism in every form. He believed that godliness had the promise of the life that now is as well as of that which is to come, and he showed his faith by his works. Cheerfulness without levity, wit without coarseness, familiarity without rudeness, gave an additional charm to his generous table, and made his society a coveted possession to persons of all ages and classes. His piety, instead of quenching his natural tendency to mirth, only purified and increased it.

It remains only to add a few words respecting what was the fundamental element in this remarkable career.* There is no possibility of mistake upon this point. It was so constantly avowed, on proper occasions, by Mr. Frelinghuysen—it shone out so clearly in his speeches, letters, conversations, and prayers—it did so much toward the shaping of his outward course—it entered so deeply and pervadingly into his religious experience, that all other influences must be deemed subordinate or auxiliary. This was his simple and absolute faith in the Lord Jesus Christ as the Lamb of God that taketh away the sins of the world. With this he began his career in the morning of life, and with this he ended it amid the gathering shades of the dark valley. He never seemed for a moment to rest upon his virtues, services, or honors, upon any thing which grace had enabled him to be or to do, but always and only upon the finished work of the one atoning Savior who had loved him and given Himself for him. The revelation which Scripture makes of the incarnate Son of God, as living, dying, rising, and reigning for the salvation of His people, fully satisfied his reason, his heart, and his conscience. He rested here with a conviction which nothing could shake. Whatever excursions he might make in the wide range of religious inquiry—whatever attention he bestowed upon the Christian evidences, he always came back to the one common foundation of all just and certain hope for the fallen children of men. He was a sinner and Christ was a Savior, and with his whole heart he believed in Him as such.

This faith made him what he was. It was the great granite foundation underlying all else that was true, and just, and pure, and lovely, and of good report in his whole development. It gave the tone to his thoughts and aspirations, to his domestic and social life, to his private charities and public usefulness, to his constant shrinking from self-assertion, and yet equally constant endeavor to win others to his own happy experience of Christ's preciousness, to his immovable adherence to principle, and yet graceful and easy concession in things indifferent. Believing as he did in all Scripture truth, his faith fastened itself with a peculiar intensity upon Him who is its sum and substance—upon Him who, as a personal Savior, by His great act of condescension and love, sheds a new sanctity upon every duty, and invests every privilege with a fresh attractiveness. To his mind Christ was first, last, and midst, in all theology, in all experience, in all hope. To Him his mind, as it were, instinctively turned from every pursuit, in every temptation, sorrow, or perplexity. The "Blood Theology," which to some is so repulsive, to him was the perfection of reason, the glory of the Scriptures, the last result of God's manifold wisdom and grace. His faith in it never wavered. To the end it was Christ and Him crucified to whom he looked for pardon, peace, holiness, and life everlasting. This faith controlled him while he lived and sustained him when he died. Nor did it cease its operation until the happy period when, having passed the dark river, to use his own sweet words, he laid his aching head upon the Savior's breast, and thanked Him for all His mercies.

APPENDIX.

THE following sketches of the two brothers of Mr. Frelinghuysen, and of his oldest sister, are appended here chiefly because of the influence which all of them exerted upon his character, and also because not a few of the persons into whose hands this book is likely to fall will be gratified with even a rapid outline of those whose memory, on various accounts, is precious to them.

> "Oh! bless'd are they who live and die like these,
> Loved with such love, and with such sorrow mourned!"

I. JOHN FRELINGHUYSEN, ESQ.

JOHN, the eldest son of General Frederick Frelinghuysen, was born March 21, 1776, near Millstone, N. J. His infancy was spent amid the clash of arms on the battle-field of the Revolution, and his youth under the languor which pervaded the whole country upon the conclusion of peace and until the national government was firmly established. He was, however, enabled to receive sufficient instruction to fit him for entering Queen's College, New Brunswick, then under the direction of its first president, the Rev. Dr. Hardenbergh. He was graduated in the year 1792, and immediately entered upon the study of law. He was admitted to the bar in 1797, and in the same year was married to Louisa, daughter of Archibald Mercer, Esq., then residing at what is now called Blackwell's Mills. In 1801 he purchased the estate which is still in the possession of his family; but a few years later, owing to the death of his father, he returned to Millstone, where he took the charge of his father's family, and superintended the studies of his two younger brothers. Here he was bereaved of his wife, who died, after a short illness, in March, 1809. She had been a great blessing to him, especially in the formation of his religious character.

In 1810 he returned to his own property near the county seat, and the next year was married to Elizabeth Mercereau, the eldest daughter of Michael Van Veghten, Esq.

Owing to an unconquerable aversion to public speaking, he figured but little in pleading before the courts, but in the quieter branches of the profession pursued a large and profitable practice. For a number of years in succession he represented his native county as member of the State Council, and afterward was appointed surrogate of the county for three consecutive terms of five years each. His capacity and integrity caused him very often to be made the executor of the estates of deceased persons, and these trusts were always administered by him with the strictest care, probity, and honor. When he lay upon his dying-bed, he said to his wife, "This property will remain in your and the children's possession, for none of it has ever been taken from the widow and the orphan—these I have never wronged—but all is the fruit of my own honest toil."

He inherited from his father a taste and a fitness for military life. At the time of the second war with Great Britain, he was for several months encamped with a regiment of the New Jersey militia, which he commanded, at Sandy Hook, with the view of preventing the enemy's vessels from passing up the bay to attack New York. No such attempt was seriously made; but the soldiers on service at the Hook were considered to have been instrumental in deterring the hostile squadron from any near approach. After the war, Mr. Frelinghuysen was made a brigadier general, by which title he was usually known and addressed. He was naturally adapted to be a successful military leader, for he had a quick eye, a clear head, a rapid decision, a sound judgment, a strong will, and invincible courage. He seemed to be quite insensible to fear. At one time there was, in the county of Somerset, a resident who, having become heavily involved in pecuniary embarrassments, and being threatened with legal process, shut himself up in his house with loaded arms, and declared that he would shoot any person who attempted to serve a warrant on him. As the man was known to be of very determined character, it was difficult to find any one willing to approach the house. General Frelinghuysen, on being informed of the fact, took the paper and declared that he would serve it. As he came near the dwelling, its occupant called out to him to return, or he would fire. "No you won't," was the reply, as the courageous man coolly continued his course until he reached the door, when he made legal service of the paper.

His first serious convictions on religious matters seem to have been produced by the conversion of his first wife. After a considerable struggle with himself, he was led to make a public profession of his faith while yet residing at Millstone. Being naturally of a somewhat imperious disposition, it was not easy for him to cultivate the peculiarly Christian graces of lowliness, meekness, and patience, yet

he did so with wonderful success. He feared God above many. If ever he fell through infirmity, his penitence and self-abasement were deep and earnest, and he sought anew pardon and peace from the ever-flowing fountain of the Savior's blood. He was a bold and decided Christian. The courage which was a part of his natural constitution gave tone to his religious life. In every relation, and among every class of persons, he acted up to his professed principles, sometimes pushing his consistency to an unusual degree. For example, he felt that every believer should not only himself sanctify the Lord's day, but labor for its observance by others. He was known frequently to arrest travelers on the post-road, in front of his dwelling, who violated the law of the land by journeying on the Lord's day. If they declared their inability to bear the expense of lying by until Monday, he would assume that expense himself. While on service at Sandy Hook, he frequently conducted public service at the head of his regiment, and used every opportunity to enforce the claims of personal religion upon the men. After the war, many letters were received by him from persons desiring to acknowledge the benefit they derived from these appeals, and to express their thanks to him.

He was a man of large heart, and devised liberal things. Pleasant, affable, social, he was far from being an anchorite, but enjoyed life abundantly. Yet he thought continually for others. Hand and heart were open to the poor or afflicted; and it was his constant study not only to provide for temporal wants, but equally to provide the means of grace for the destitute, and, so far as lay in his power, to secure the due improvement of those means.

In the midst of his usefulness, he was cut off by a bilious fever on the 10th of April, 1833.

A gentleman, who was for many years a leading member of the bar of Somerset County, has kindly furnished the author with the following notice of General Frelinghuysen:

"My acquaintance with the late General John Frelinghuysen commenced in 1814, and ended only with his death. We were neighbors, members of the same Church, and often associated in business transactions. These opportunities of knowing the man only made me esteem him the more highly in every relation of life. I know of no good quality, as a man or a Christian, which he did not possess in an eminent degree.

"He was a man of great business tact, a skillful and accurate accountant, prompt in the discharge of duty, systematic in his arrangements, and punctual to every engagement. Being very popular in the community, and enjoying the confidence of every one, he became extensively occupied in public affairs, and held, in turn or together, nearly every county office. As executor, administrator, guardian, or trustee, he handled more money than any other five men in the county, and never was there even a whisper of complaint as to his management of these trusts.

"He inherited from his revolutionary father a strong love for his country and its republican institutions. When called to serve in the field during the war of 1812, he took a very high position for courage, capacity, and self-sacrificing patriotism. His care of his regiment was unequaled. The sick soldier was sheltered in his tent and ate at his table; and when, by the neglect of others, the supplies of food for the regiment were inadequate in quantity or quality, he freely used his own means to relieve their wants, even going so far as to embarrass his estate for this purpose.

"He was a man of profound and ardent piety. This shone out on all occasions. Without any seeming effort on his part to produce such an impression, no one could be in his company, even for a short time, without feeling that he was a sincere and earnest Christian; yet he was humble and unostentatious. In the Church he was esteemed as a pillar. He was active in every good work, a devout attendant upon ordinances, a constant friend and liberal supporter of the minister, fond of the social prayer-meeting—which he usually conducted, and where his prayers seemed to be offered in the very presence of God and eternity—ever ready to contribute to benevolent associations, prompt to rebuke open sin, to warn impenitent persons, or soothe and comfort the afflicted. In the councils of the Church, his opinions were always looked for with interest and received with respect. The poor of every class looked upon him as their counselor and friend, and he spared no pains to administer promptly and efficiently to their relief in things spiritual and temporal.

"Indeed, considering General Frelinghuysen's activity, consistency, and uniform excellence in so many varied relations, it may with truth be said that he was a public benefactor. The place made vacant in the county of Somerset by his death has never been filled, and will not be for a century."

II. MARIA FRELINGHUYSEN,

WIFE OF THE REV. JOHN CORNELL.

Maria, the first daughter and second child of General Frederick Frelinghuysen, was born in March, 1778. When about twenty years of age she was married to the Rev. John Cornell, a young clergyman, who, after studying for a time in the famous Log College at Neshaminy, Penn., entered Queen's College at New Brunswick, where he completed his course in the year 1795. He then pursued the study of theology under Dr. Livingston, at Flatbush, L. I., and was licensed to preach about the year 1798. After performing missionary service for a year or two, he was called to the charge of the Presbyterian Church in Allentown, N. J. Here he remained for twenty years, a laborious, faithful, and successful pastor. Afterward he for seven years conducted the Classical Academy at Somerville, and then (in 1828), induced by the state of his health, retired to the homestead of his wife's family near Millstone, at that time in the possession of her brother Theodore. Here Mrs. Cornell ended her days on earth, in March, 1832.

Mrs. Cornell was a remarkable woman for vigor of mind, intelligent piety, persistent charity, and practical usefulness. She united thought, reading, and conversational gifts with the diligent discharge of every domestic duty, in this latter respect resembling more than is common in our day the picture of the virtuous woman drawn in the closing chapter of the Book of Proverbs. She was an admirable helpmeet to her husband in his pastoral office; and, wherever she resided, secured the unbounded respect and affection of the community. Her deep interest in the cause of temperance is worthy of especial note. Long before there was any public or general agitation of the subject, and while the decanter was invariably to be found on every hospitable sideboard, ardent spirits were banished from her house, and her whole influence thrown on the side of total abstinence. There is still in existence the "Constitution Book," as it is called, of an association established at Allentown in the year 1805, under the name of the "Sober Society," with fifty-eight signatures attached, in which the signers pledge themselves to abstain from all use of ardent spirits as a beverage. There is no doubt that the animating spring, if not the originator, of this first temperance society in America was Mrs. Maria Cornell.

Being nine years older than her brother Theodore, she naturally exerted a considerable influence over him, both in person, while he was still under the paternal roof, and afterward by letter, when he was pursuing his education, collegiate and professional. He has frequently been known to acknowledge his obligations to her intelligent, judicious, sisterly affection, and in a letter to the Rev. Dr. Hay, written in 1832, he thus expressed himself on the subject: "I have sustained a sore bereavement in the death of my sister. She stood in the early relation of a mother to me. I was deprived of my mother at six years of age, and this dearly-cherished sister, by a kind Providence, was ordained to fill her place, which she did most tenderly and faithfully. I bless God that He has been pleased to spare her to us so long, and has now afforded such precious assurances in her life that He has taken her to His own holy habitation."

After her death, which occurred March 13th, 1832, there appeared in the columns of the *Christian Intelligencer* a very touching obituary notice from the pen of the Hon. Peter D. Vroom. Governor Vroom bears high testimony to Mrs. Cornell's fidelity as a wife and mother, to her unusual excellencies of mind and heart, to her boundless charity, to her assiduous ministrations among all the children of sorrow, to her intelligent piety, to her humble, holy, exemplary life, and her calm, peaceful death.

From some of the statements made in this notice, it would appear that, notwithstanding her consistent walk, she was exposed to seasons of religious darkness, when a deep sense of unworthiness clouded every prospect. On one such occasion she thus expressed herself to an intimate friend: "I am sometimes ready to conclude all past experience delusive. And what then? Shall I remain satisfied, and give the enemy cause to triumph and the world to reproach? Oh no; I will not, can not give over the pursuit. If I perish, it must be by the way of the Cross. There, and there only, hang all my expectations, all my desires." In mere secular sorrows and trials her faith was triumphant; in the worst of them her language was, "If God in Christ is the portion of my soul, surely I may rejoice even in this valley of tears; and although billow after billow may be commissioned to roll over me, still will I rejoice. He can, and will say, 'Peace, be still,' whenever the design of His providence is effected."

III. FREDERICK FRELINGHUYSEN, ESQ.

Frederick, the fourth child and youngest son of General Frederick Frelinghuysen, was born at the family homestead at Millstone on the 8th of November, 1788.

He received the rudimentary elements of his education at New Brunswick, in company with Theodore, and afterward followed him, at the interval of two years, in the academy of Basking Ridge, in the College of New Jersey, and in the law office of Richard Stockton. He was graduated at Nassau Hall in the year 1806, and four years subsequently was admitted to the bar. He commenced practice in Somerset County, fixing his residence at Millstone. In the year 1812 he was married to Jane, the eldest daughter of Peter B. Dumont, Esq., an old and influential citizen of the county. Mr. Frelinghuysen soon secured an extensive and lucrative practice, which a few years afterward was greatly enlarged by his appointment as prosecutor of the pleas for the counties of Somerset, Middlesex, and Hunterdon—an appointment which he continued to hold up to the time of his death. During this time he formed many intimate acquaintances at the bar and in social life, but none which ever eclipsed or interfered with the close ties which bound him to his brother Theodore. "The love which these brothers had for each other was, in its depth and warmth, almost romantic. Their greatest pleasure was to be together, and the lively sallies of the younger brother never failed to dispel the depression of spirits to which Theodore was sometimes subject. The period of twelve years, extending from 1808 to 1820, was spent by them in professional life, but they were all the while framing pleasant excuses and urgent reasons why Theodore should go to Millstone or Frederick come to Newark. Were they to go to court, one must go by the house of the other, to enjoy as quickly, and continue as long as possible, the brother communion." Frederick was perhaps more of a natural orator than either of his brothers. His imagination was fervid, his temperament buoyant, and his sensibility very lively. Persons yet living, who in their youth heard him plead in jury trials, speak enthusiastically of his power and success.

On two occasions he delivered public orations which excited great interest at the time, and led the community to form high expectations of him, which, however, were blasted by his early death. One of these was before the Washington Benevolent Association at New Brunswick in 1812, the other before the Somerset County Bible Society at Somerville in 1820. Both of these were committed to the press, and a few copies are still extant.

A month or two after pronouncing the address before the Bible Society he was attacked with what proved to be a mortal disease. His religious views at first were clouded, but soon he was enabled to rest upon the Savior in simple faith, and thenceforward to the close of his five weeks' illness all was peace. The world was dismissed from his thoughts; he had no solicitude for his recovery; in weakness and suffering Patience wrought her perfect work. His sole anxiety was for those who were still out of Christ, and his communion with his Lord was such as to outweigh "ten thousand times ten thousand worlds." After bearing an ample and most intelligent testimony to evangelical piety, he fell asleep November 10th, 1820.

On the 14th of November, a meeting of the members of the bar of New Jersey was held at the State-house in Trenton, when Richard Stockton was called to the chair, and Joseph C. Hornblower appointed secretary. "The meeting being organized, L. H. Stockton, Esq., in an appropriate manner, announced the recent and solemn dispensation of Providence in the death of Frederick Frelinghuysen, Esq., a counselor of the Supreme Court of this state. Whereupon, the members of the meeting being deeply impressed with the irreparable loss sustained by society in this event, it was unanimously resolved,

"1. That we do most sincerely, cordially, and affectionately sympathize with the bereaved widow, the orphan children, and the other near relatives of our deceased brother on this afflicting dispensation of Divine Providence, which has deprived the bar of the society of an honest and honorable man, peculiarly endeared to his country by the characteristic traits that distinguished him, not only as an able and eloquent advocate, but as a Christian, a scholar, and a gentleman.

"2. That, in testimony of our attachment to his memory, and respect to his public and private character, we will wear the usual badge of mourning thirty days.

"3. That these resolutions be published in the several newspapers of this state, and that they be communicated to John Frelinghuysen and Theodore Frelinghuysen, Esqs., the brothers, and also to the widow of our deceased friend.

"By order of the meeting. RICHARD STOCKTON, Pres.

"JOSEPH C. HORNBLOWER, Sec."

INDEX.

N

It is a work of real historical value, the result of accurate criticism, written in a liberal spirit, and from first to last deeply interesting.—*Athenæum.*

The style is excellent, clear, vivid, eloquent; and the industry with which original sources have been investigated, and through which new light has been shed over perplexed incidents and characters, entitles Mr. Motley to a high rank in the literature of an age peculiarly rich in history.—*North British Review.*

It abounds in new information, and, as a first work, commands a very cordial recognition, not merely of the promise it gives, but of the extent and importance of the labor actually performed on it.—*London Examiner.*

Mr. Motley's "History" is a work of which any country might be proud.—*Press* (London).

Mr. Motley's History will be a standard book of reference in historical literature.—*London Literary Gazette.*

Mr. Motley has searched the whole range of historical documents necessary to the composition of his work.—*London Leader.*

This is really a great work. It belongs to the class of books in which we range our Grotes, Milmans, Merivales, and Macaulays, as the glories of English literature in the department of history. * * * Mr. Motley's gifts as a historical writer are among the highest and rarest.—*Nonconformist* (London).

Mr. Motley's volumes will well repay perusal. * * * For his learning, his liberal tone, and his generous enthusiasm, we heartily commend him, and bid him good speed for the remainer of his interesting and heroic narrative.—*Saturday Review.*

The story is a noble one, and is worthily treated. * * * Mr. Motley has had the patience to unravel, with unfailing perseverance, the thousand intricate plots of the adversaries of the Prince of Orange; but the details and the literal extracts which he has derived from original documents, and transferred to his pages, give a truthful color and a picturesque effect, which are especially charming.—*London Daily News.*

M. Lothrop Motley dans son magnifique tableau de la formation de notre République.—G. Groen Van Prinsterer.

Our accomplished countryman, Mr. J. Lothrop Motley, who, during the last five years, for the better prosecution of his labors, has established his residence in the neighborhood of the scenes of his narrative. No one acquainted with the fine powers of mind possessed by this scholar, and the earnestness with which he has devoted himself to the task, can doubt that he will do full justice to his important but difficult subject.—W. H. Prescott.

The production of such a work as this astonishes, while it gratifies the pride of the American reader.—*N. Y. Observer.*

The "Rise of the Dutch Republic" at once, and by acclamation, takes its place by the "Decline and Fall of the Roman Empire," as a work which, whether for research, substance, or style, will never be superseded.—*N. Y. Albion.*

A work upon which all who read the English language may congratulate themselves.—*New Yorker Handels Zeitung.*

Mr. Motley's place is now (alluding to this book) with Hallam and Lord Mahon, Alison and Macaulay in the Old Country, and with Washington Irving, Prescott, and Bancroft in this.—*N. Y. Times.*

The authority, in the English tongue, for the history of the period and people to which it refers.—*N. Y. Courier and Enquirer.*

This work at once places the author on the list of American historians which has been so signally illustrated by the names of Irving, Prescott, Bancroft, and Hildreth.—*Boston Times.*

The work is a noble one, and a most desirable acquisition to our historical literature.—*Mobile Advertiser.*

Such a work is an honor to its author, to his country, and to the age in which it was written.—*Ohio Farmer.*

HISTORY

OF THE

UNITED STATES OF AMERICA.

BY RICHARD HILDRETH.

FIRST SERIES.—From the First Settlement of the Country to the Adoption of the Federal Constitution. 3 vols. 8vo, Muslin, $7 50.

SECOND SERIES.—From the Adoption of the Federal Constitution to the End of the Sixteenth Congress. 3 vols. 8vo, Muslin, $7 50.

The first attempt at a complete history of the United States. The reader who desires to inform himself in all the particulars, military or political, of the American Revolution, will find that they have been scrupulously collected for him by Mr. Hildreth.—*London Athenæum.*

It has condensed into consecutive narrative the substance of hundreds of volumes.—*London Literary Gazette.*

The history of the Revolution is clearly and succinctly told.—*N. A. Review.*

Mr. Hildreth's sources of information have evidently been ample and various, and intelligently examined, his materials arranged with a just idea of their importance in the story, while his judgments are well considered, unbiassed, and reliable. His style is clear, forcible, and sententious.—*Christian Register.*

Mr. Hildreth is a very concise, vigorous, and impartial writer. His entire history is very accurate and interesting, and well worthy a place in every American library.—*Louisville Journal.*

He is laborious, conscientious, and accurate. As a methodical and very full narrative, its value is undoubted.—*New Orleans Bee.*

The calmness and ability with which he has presented his narrative will give his work rank among the standard histories of the country.—*Watchman and Observer.*

* * We have, therefore, read his book with distrust. But we are bound in candor to say that it seems to us valuable and very fair. Mr. Hildreth has confined himself to, as far as possible, a dispassionate collection of facts from the documents he has consulted and copied, and his work fills a void that has sensibly been felt in private libraries. As a documentary history of the United States, we are free to commend it.—*N. Y. Freeman's Journal.*

Mr. Hildreth has rendered an essential and permanent service.—*Providence Daily Journal.*

The volumes will be regarded as indispensable—it will take its place as a standard work. The author's style is dignified, perspicuous, and vivacious.—*Church Review.*

The work is very complete. The marginal dates, the two indexes, and running heads at the tops of the pages, render it very convenient for reference, points which scholars will find all important for utility.—*Newark Sentinel of Freedom.*

We should like to know what other book upon American history, or even upon any limited portion of it, presents any thing like the same distinctness of view, or can at all compete with it in that "lucid order" which is one of the first merits of every historical work.—*Boston Atlas.*

His work fills a want, and is therefore most welcome. Its positive merits, in addition to those we have before mentioned, are impartiality, steadiness of view, clear appreciation of character, and, in point of style, a terseness and conciseness not unlike Tacitus, with not a little, too, of Tacitean vigor of thought, stern sense of justice, sharp irony, and profound wisdom.—*Methodist Quarterly Review.*

It occupies a space which has not yet been filled, and exhibits characteristics both of design and of composition, which entitle it to a distinguished place among the most important productions of American genius and scholarship. We welcome it as a simple, faithful, lucid, and elegant narrative of the great events of American history. It is not written in illustration of any favorite theory, it is not the expression of any ideal system, but an honest endeavor to present the facts in question in the pure, uncolored light of truth and reality. The impartiality, good judgment, penetration, and diligent research of the author are conspicuous in its composition.—*N. Y. Tribune.*

In our judgment, this is the ablest, best, and most judicious popular history of the United States that has yet appeared. It will be a standard book on American history, and will not fail to secure a high reputation as a writer to its modest and unpretending author.—*Washington Union.*

This work is a valuable addition to our historical literature. It is the fruit of wide research and hard labor. It has those features of severe simplicity and truthfulness which will render it an enduring legacy to the future.—*Christian Watchman.*

Mr. Hildreth's work will be a standard of reference for the student of American history, and will become a favorite in proportion as it is known.—*Nat. Era.*

His narrative is lucid and succinct, his facts carefully ascertained and skillfully grouped, and his conclusions on all mooted questions are ably sustained and impartially weighed.—*New Orleans Bee.*

The most valuable work of the kind yet issued. It presents, in a clear, graceful, and forcible style, a full and faithful picture of the country from its first settlement down to the end of the Sixteenth Congress. It is marked no less by its completeness than its accuracy and the beauty of its narrative.—*Troy Daily Whig.*

In a most graphic, terse, and elegant style, it gives the history of each state, with its institutions, progress, and enterprise, civil, commercial, and agricultural, which makes the book a valuable addendum to the historical literatnre of the great republic.—*St. John's Morning News.*

No better chronicle of the more recent periods of our history has been given.—*Albany Evening Journal.*

The prevailing characteristic of Hildreth's history is its stern and inflexible impartiality.—*Boston Journal.*

The author has shown a most commendable industry.—*Baltimore Patriot.*

The chief merits of Mr. Hildreth's work are fidelity and candor of spirit, and perspicuity and terseness of style.—*Southern Literary Gazette.*

It is a plain, dignified, impartial, and fearless exhibition of facts.—*Genesee Evangelist.*

The author's grouping of men and events is skillful, and renders his rapid narrative pleasant reading.—*N. Y. Evening Post.*

These handsome volumes should be on the table of every American who desires the most thorough and clear report of our nation's history yet published.—*Rochester Democrat.*

The history is a reliable, and, in all respects, an admirable one.—*Ontario Repository.*

The author makes every thing plain and clear which he touches.—*Southern Christian Advocate.*

A history of the United States that could be regarded by all men as a standard of authority, as well as a model of impartial labor.—*Worcester Palladium.*

A work which should be in every American's hands.—*Springfield Republican.*

His style is clear and forcible, and his work is very valuable on account of the political information it contains.—*Savannah Republican.*

HILDRETH'S HISTORY OF THE UNITED STATES.

Written with candor, brevity, fidelity to facts, and simplicity of style and manner, and forms a welcome addition to the library of the nation.—*Prot. Churchman.*

Mr. Hildreth is a bold and copious writer. His work is valuable for the immense amount of material it embodies.—*De Bow's Review of the Southern and Western States.*

We may safely commend Mr. Hildreth's work as written in an excellent style, and containing a vast amount of valuable information.—*Albany Argus.*

His style is vigorously simple. It has the virtue of perspicuity. — *Zion's Herald.*

We value it on account of its impartiality. We have found nothing to indicate the least desire on the part of the author to exalt or debase any man or any party. His very patriotism, though high-principled and sincere, is sober and discriminate, and appears to be held in strong check by the controlling recollection that he is writing for posterity, and that if the facts which he publishes will not honor his country and his countrymen, fulsome adulation will not add to their glory.—*N. Y. Commercial Advertiser.*

We are confident that when the merits of this history come to be known and appreciated, it will be extensively regarded as decidedly superior to any thing that before existed on American history, and as a valuable contribution to American authorship. These stately volumes will be an ornament to any library, and no intelligent American can afford to be without the work. We have nobly patronized the great English history of the age, let us not fail to appreciate and patronize an American history so respectable and valuable as this certainly is.—*Biblical Repository (Bibliotheca Sacra).*

This work professes only to deal in *facts;* it is a book of *records;* it puts together clearly, consecutively, and, we believe, with strict impartiality, the events of American history. The work indicates patient, honest, and careful research, systematic arrangement, and lucid exposition.—*Home Journal.*

To exhibit the progress of the country from infancy to maturity; to show the actual state of the people, the real character of their laws and institutions, and the true designs of their leading men, at different periods, and to relate a sound, unvarnished tale of our early history, has been his design; and we are free to acknowledge that it has been executed with marked ability and triumphant success. Every lover of impartial history will accord to Mr. Hildreth his due meed of praise for the able and honest manner in which he has given the true history of the United States.—*Pennsylvanian.*

This work is full of detail, bears marks of care and research, and is written under the guidance of clear sight and good judgment rather than of theory, philosophical or historical, or of prejudice of any sort whatever. We trust that it will be widely read.—*N. Y. Courier and Enquirer.*

We pronounce it unsurpassed as a full, clear, and truthful history of our country so far. We rejoice that a work so important to our nation has been so ably performed.—*Literary American.*

Interesting, valuable, and very attractive. It is written in a style eminently clear and attractive, and presents the remarkable history which it records in a form of great simplicity and with graphic force. There is in it no attempt to palliate what is wrong, or to conceal what is true. It is a life-like and reliable history of the most remarkable series of events in the annals of the world.—*N. Y. Journal of Commerce.*

It is a valuable acquisition to American literature.—*Baltimore American.*

The history of our country with a scrupulous regard to truth.—*Buffalo Courier.*

We believe this to be a truthful, judicious, and valuable history, worthy of general acceptation.—*Philadelphia North American.*

The first complete history of our country.—*Chronotype.*

Published by HARPER & BROTHERS,
Franklin Square, New York.

*** Harper & Brothers will send the above Work by Mail, postage paid (for any distance in the United States under 3000 miles), on receipt of the Money.

CENTRAL AFRICA.

THE LAKE REGIONS OF CENTRAL AFRICA. A Picture of Exploration. By RICHARD F. BURTON, Captain H.M.I. Army; Fellow and Gold Medalist of the Royal Geographical Society. With Maps and Engravings on Wood. 8vo, Cloth, $3 75; Half Calf, $5 00.

NORTH AND CENTRAL AFRICA.

TRAVELS AND DISCOVERIES IN NORTH AND CENTRAL AFRICA. Being a Journal of an Expedition undertaken under the Auspices of H.B.M.'s Government, in the Years 1849–1855. By HENRY BARTH, Ph.D., D.C.L. Profusely and elegantly Illustrated. Complete in 3 vols. 8vo, Cloth, $9 00; Sheep, $9 75; Half Calf, $12 75.

SOUTHWESTERN AFRICA.

LAKE NGAMI; or, Explorations and Discoveries during Four Years' Wanderings in the Wilds of Southwestern Africa. By CHARLES JOHN ANDERSSON. With numerous Illustrations, representing Sporting Adventures, Subjects of Natural History, Devices for Destroying Wild Animals, &c. New Edition. 12mo, Cloth, $1 00; Half Calf, $2 00.

SOUTH AFRICA.

FIVE YEARS OF A HUNTER'S LIFE IN THE INTERIOR OF SOUTH AFRICA. With Notices of the Native Tribes, and Anecdotes of the Chase of the Lion, Elephant, Hippopotamus, Giraffe, Rhinoceros, &c. By GORDON CUMMING. With Illustrations. 2 vols. 12mo, Cloth, $2 00; Half Calf, $4 00.

WESTERN AFRICA.

WESTERN AFRICA: Its History, Condition, and Prospects. By Rev. J. LEIGHTON WILSON, Eighteen Years a Missionary in Africa. With numerous Engravings. 12mo, Cloth, $1 25; Half Calf, $2 25.

MADAGASCAR.

THE LAST TRAVELS OF IDA PFEIFFER: inclusive of a Visit to Madagascar. With an Autobiographical Memoir of the Author. Translated by H. W. DULCKEN. Steel Portrait. 12mo, Cloth, $1 50; Half Calf, $2 50. (Uniform with Ida Pfeiffer's "Second Journey Round the World.")

MADAGASCAR.

THREE VISITS TO MADAGASCAR, during the Years 1853–1854–1856. Including a Journey to the Capital, with Notices of the Natural History of the Country and of the Present Civilization of the People. By the Rev. WILLIAM ELLIS, F.H.S., Author of "Polynesian Researches." Illustrated by a Map and Wood-cuts from Photographs, &c. 8vo, Cloth, $3 00; Half Calf, $4 25.

www.ingramcontent.com/pod-product-compliance
Lightning Source LLC
LaVergne TN
LVHW020242110826
845151LV00003B/1010

* 9 7 8 1 4 2 5 5 2 8 9 4 2 *